NEGOTIATING the SPECIAL EDUCATION MAZE

A Guide for Parents and Teachers

WOODBINE HOUSE • 1990

Woodbine House
6510 Bells Mill Road
Bethesda, MD 20817
800–843–7323/301–897–3570

Copyright © 1990 Winifred Anderson, Stephen Chitwood, Deidre Hayden.
Second Edition

Library of Congress Cataloging-in-Publication Data

Anderson, Winifred
    Negotiating the special education maze: a guide for parents and teachers /
Winifred Anderson, Stephen Chitwood, Deidre Hayden. —2nd. ed.
      p. cm.
    Includes bibliographical references.
    ISBN 0-933149-30-1 (pbk.) : $12.95
    1. Handicapped children—Education—United States. 2. Handicapped children—
Civil rights—United States. 3. Home and school—United States. I. Chitwood,
Stephen. II. Hayden, Deidre. III. Title.
LC4031.A66   1990
371.9'0973—dc20
                                            88-40220
                                                CIP

Manufactured in the United States of America

5 6 7 8 9 10

To Danny Chitwood

Table of Contents

Acknowledgements

From experiences as trainers of parent advocates, as educational and legal advocates, as educators and as parents, we have endeavored to write a practical guide based on methods proven effective in obtaining appropriate special education services for children. This book represents the results of many people working together—the group brain—as we like to call it. In particular we express thanks to: Margaret Gajda, for her editing skills, her commitment to understandable English, her fresh eyes when others were tired, and for the hours of research developing the comprehensive glossary and appendices; Jamie Ruppmann for her careful and detailed preparation of the charts; Jean Durgin for mastery of the computer program to perfect the forms and charts, and her meticulous work on each page of the book to ensure its consistency; Carolyn Beckett, who contributed her professional and personal knowledge of career development for young adults with disabilities; Nona Flynn for her steadfast encouragement (relentless prodding!) to update and revise the original *Maze* book; Melinda Goss, Virginia Houston, Beatrice Ortez, and Nancy Hitz, whose expertise as educational advocates for their children gives reality to the case studies included in the book; Virginia Maloney for the checklist on "Assessing a Learning Environment"; Michael Woodard who developed "Action Steps for Evaluation"; and to Daniel Reed Chitwood whose life inspired us all.

In addition, we express admiration and appreciation to those parents and professionals who have formed teams to teach the process of educational advocacy to other parents in communities throughout Virginia, West Virginia, Maryland, and other states. These team members used this book to inform and guide their work with parent groups and have provided us with valuable comment. To the hundreds of parents who participated in our training courses in educational advocacy, we say thank you for teaching us as you shared common and unique experiences with us.

Winifred Anderson
Stephen Chitwood
Deidre Hayden

Parent Educational Advocacy Training Center
228 South Pitt Street, Suite 300
Alexandria, Virginia 22314

Foreword

After reading the new edition of *Negotiating the Special Education Maze*, I had intended to begin writing this Foreword. Instead, I found myself giving my copy of the manuscript to a good friend and fellow parent of a child with a disability. My friend, Katherine, has a fifteen-year-old son with a brain tumor. His declining health has recently resulted in a much more pervasive physical disability and hearing loss, and for the first time she is needing to learn to negotiate the special education maze to gain greater accessibility of the school building and greater adaptation of classroom instruction.

This book is exactly what Katherine and her family need at this time—it's comprehensive, yet manageable in length; assertive, but not abrasive; action-oriented, but not overwhelming. Katherine really does not know what lies ahead of her in working through the maze, but Win Anderson, Steve Chitwood, and Deidre Hayden have a very good idea. Although it is highly unlikely that Katherine and these three authors will ever meet, in a sense they will all four negotiate the special education maze together because of the personal and professional expertise and empathy that is shared in this important book. Katherine is grateful, and so am I. She is grateful because the information will make the difference in the success of her sojourn in the maze, and I am grateful because sharing the book enables me to offer real help to my friend.

I urge you to do as I did and share this book with your friends even before you finish reading it. You and your friends may be at the very beginning of your journey through the special education maze or you may be at some intermediate point. Wherever you are, there is information here that can help you. *Negotiating the Special Education Maze: A Guide for Parents and Teachers* is as relevant to novices as it is to veterans—there is valuable information for all of us who face the challenge of the special education maze.

As you will note, this book is the second edition and offers some major expansion and refinement over the first edition, which in itself was a very successful contribution. This edition has two new chapters—Chapter 7, The IEP Meeting, and Chapter 8, Transition: Pathways to the Future. Both of these chapters offer substantive help to families, who are critical contributors to programming decisions both for the current school year and for the future. Chapter 8 on Transition contains all new material and emphasizes planning early so that there can be career awareness, career exploration, and career placement as the student goes along through school. There are a couple of working documents, Personal Profile and Career Education Planning Chart, that will help you in making transition plans to accomplish future goals. Another new feature in this edition is information on a recent Public Law—P.L. 99–457—which mandates services for infants, toddlers, and preschoolers with disabilities.

Throughout this book, the clear emphasis is on the parent as the expert on his or her child. This philosophy is consistent with state-of-art programming, and it can be the catalyst for forming a collaborative parent-professional relationship that is in the best interest of children.

In closing, I want to reiterate how much I have learned from this book, how I plan to continue to use it both as a parent and professional, and how eagerly I share it with friends, knowing that it can be an invaluable guide through the inevitable special education maze.

Ann P. Turnbull
Bureau of Child Research
University of Kansas
Lawrence, Kansas

Introduction

Throughout the nation, parents of children with disabilities are perplexed. Those who have just learned that their infant or toddler has developmental problems may have heard of new laws that ensure their babies will get early education. Yet they wonder how to begin the educational process. Whom should they contact? Are educational services really necessary for a very young child?

Parents whose older children are already in the school system may well be aware of the Education for All Handicapped Children Act, a strong federal law which provides for special education for all children with disabilities. Yet they, too, have many questions. For example, when talking with school professionals, a father might wonder what educational jargon such as "scaled scores," "least restrictive environment," and "projective tests," has to do with his lively, lovable child. A mother comments, "For years I have heard school people say, 'If only we could get the parents involved...'—yet when I try to speak out for my son, I feel they want me to accept only what they think is best for him."

Parents of young people who are nearing graduation from school and from special education have other concerns. They ask, "Will our daughter have a job when she graduates?" "Are there laws that guarantee her services and benefits as an adult?"

These and many other common concerns of parents of children with disabilities are addressed in seven federal special education statutes known collectively as the Education of the Handicapped Act or EHA. The following chapters discuss those statutes which are most relevant for you to know as you make your way through the maze of special education rules and procedures. This book gives primary attention to the third statute of the EHA—Public Law 94–142, the Education for All Handicapped Children Act of 1975. Public Law 94–142 laid the foundation for all later federal special education legislation and legitimized parent involvement in the education of children with disabilities. Specifically, this law mandated the role of parents* as equal partners in making educa-

---

* The term "parents" in this book means anyone who is in charge of the care and well-being of a child. Included are single parents, guardians, grandparents, foster parents, or surrogate parents.

tional decisions for their children.

A mandate for parent involvement is a worthy goal. Yet, you may be wondering how such involvement is brought about. The answer lies in *educational advocacy*. An advocate is one who speaks in behalf of another person or group of persons in order to bring about change. There are consumer advocates, working to influence regulatory agencies to bring about change in the quality of products we purchase. Political advocates seek to bring about social and economic change through state and national legislatures. Legal advocates use the court system to bring about change in the interpretation of laws that affect our lives.

The Education for All Handicapped Children Act empowers parents to become *educational advocates* for their children. An educational advocate is one who speaks knowledgeably for the educational needs of another person. You, the parents, are the ones who know your child best. It is you who can speak most effectively in your child's behalf in order to secure her* educational rights under the law. This book was written to assist you in your role as educational advocate—to help you gain the knowledge required to be an effective educational planner for your child, to assist you in presenting your child in the best possible way, to suggest how to cope with your feelings, and to guide you through the often complex maze of special education.

To be an effective educational advocate for your infant, child, or young adult, you are well advised to understand the major provisions of The Education for All Handicapped Children Act, P.L. 94–142. The law requires that all school-aged children with disabilities be provided a full educational opportunity. Specifically covered are those children with mental retardation, hearing impairments, deafness, visual impairments, speech or language impairments, serious emotional disturbances, orthopedic handicaps, other health impairments (e.g., autism, serious heart conditions) or learning disabilities.

Special education is defined in P.L. 94–142 as "specially designed instruction designed to meet the unique needs of a child with disabilities." This is in contrast to most general education classrooms, where children are taught in groups—with educational

---

* To avoid sexist use of pronouns, the masculine gender is used in odd numbered chapters and the feminine gender, in even numbered chapters.

plans made for groups of children. Also in contrast to general education, instruction is provided by special educators, who are trained in the teaching techniques that best meet the learning needs of children with disabilities. These techniques, coupled with the individualization of instruction, promise that each child will be given the opportunity to travel successfully down her developmental pathways.

The following brief explanation of the six major provisions of P.L. 94–142 will provide a background for you as you read and work your way through this book and through the education system as your child's advocate. Each of these provisions is discussed in detail in later chapters.

1. *All children will be served.* The law is titled "The Education for All Handicapped Children Act." Congress intended that no child in need of special education will be excluded from receiving services—even those children with the most severe disabilities. Prior to P.L. 94–142, many parents remember being told by the school administrators, "We are sorry, we just don't have a program for her. She is too severely disabled." Then parents had no recourse. Now, *all* children with disabilities between the ages of six and eighteen are entitled to educational services. As of 1990, all states will provide services for children ages three through eighteen, and most states will provide them for children ages birth through twenty-one.

2. *Children will be tested fairly to determine if they will receive special education services.* Before children can be declared eligible for special education or placed in a special education program, they must be evaluated by a team of professionals. The law requires that schools and other agencies give tests to children that show both their strengths and their weaknesses. This is called non-discriminatory testing. All tests must be given to children in their own language and in such a way that their abilities and their disabilities are accurately displayed. Children will be placed in special education based upon several tests, not upon one single test or test score. Non-discriminatory testing ensures that children who

do not need special education will not be placed there, and that children who need special school services will get them.

3. *Schools have a duty to provide individually designed, appropriate programs for every child at no cost to their parents.* P.L. 94–142 provides a *free, appropriate public education* to all children who have been identified as needing special education. The state and local school systems bear the responsibility to pay for the education even if it is provided in a private or residential school outside of the local public school system. In addition, each child is guaranteed an *appropriate* education. The appropriateness is determined by a group of people, including parents and educators, who work together to design a program that addresses the child's individual educational problems. This program is called an Individualized Education Program (IEP). Your child has a right to a full range of educational services that may include such related services as special transportation, speech/language therapy, counseling, occupational or physical therapy, or other services necessary to enable her to benefit from special education. A description of the process for determining an appropriate education by writing an IEP is found in this book in Chapters 6 and 7.

If your child is younger than two, you will find that the process for receiving services differs somewhat from that of school-aged children. Services for very young children are covered by an amendment to P.L. 94–142 called P.L. 99–457. You, as a parent, will be working with professionals who are not necessarily employees of the school system, but are specialists in infant development. In some states these professionals will be school employees; but in other states they will be employees of agencies such as the Health Department or the Department of Mental Health and Developmental Disabilities. You will be partners with these infant specialists in writing an Individualized Family Service Plan (IFSP) for your baby. The IFSP is a written plan detailing the early intervention services a family requires to enhance their child's development. Early intervention services include family training and counseling as well as direct services to the infant or toddler. The skills and knowledge you will gain from this book are valuable no matter what the age of your child as you work with professionals to write an IEP or an IFSP. The emphasis on these plans is to individualize—to write a unique program for the education of your unique child.

4. *Children with disabilities will be educated with children who are not disabled.* Before P.L. 94–142, our schools almost always segregated children with disabilities from children without disabilities. Now, however, our nation has legal requirements that all students have equal access to education. As a result, increasing numbers of children with disabilities are being "mainstreamed," or integrated into their community's regular schools. Under P.L. 94–142, students with disabilities are guaranteed services in the *least restrictive environment.* That is, when the Individualized Education Program (IEP) is written, a determination is made regarding the amount of time each student with disabilities will spend with non-disabled peers both in classroom and all other school activities. Students are to be educated in a separate classroom or school only when the nature and the severity of their disabilities makes it impossible to meet their educational needs in a less restrictive environment.

5. *The decisions of the school system can be challenged by parents.* Prior to the passage of the Education for All Handicapped Children Act, parents had little or no recourse if they disagreed with the decisions made by the school authorities. Under P.L. 94–142, parents and students have a right to *due process.* Under these due process rights, provisions are made for the settlement of disputes by an impartial third party. Parents have the right to challenge decisions made about their children in the areas of inclusion or exclusion from special services, testing in a nondiscriminatory manner, the appropriateness of the education as written in the IEP, the placement of their child in the least restrictive educational environment, and other related areas.

In addition to the guarantee of the right to challenge, P.L. 94–142 provides parents with the right to notice. When any change is to be made with regard to testing, entrance to or exit from services, the IEP, or the amount of time the child will be with non-disabled children, the parents must first be notified. In many situations, the consent of parents is also required before school personnel can make changes.

6. *Parents of children with disabilities participate in the planning and decision making for their child's special education.* The basic premise of this book is that parents are their child's first and best advocates. Who else can possibly know your child in the ways that you do? Your love and caring were seen by the Congress of the United States to be a vital contribution to educational planning for your child. Therefore, P.L. 94–142 mandated the partnership between parents and school personnel. You, as parents, will be working with school and other professionals to see that a free, appropriate public education in the least restrictive environment is provided for your child. That is your child's right. And the school system has a duty to provide it. At each step along the way, the partnership will ideally ensure that your hopes, visions, and expertise will be combined with the caring and the specialized training of professionals to educate your child.

Each of the six major provisions of P.L. 94–142 involves you, the parents. The continuing importance of your involvement in the special education process has been reflected in numerous Congressional actions and court decisions. Since the passage of P.L. 94–142 in 1975, Congress has made several amendments to the law strengthening the rights of parents and their children. Likewise, court decisions have clarified various legal terms such as appropriate education, support services, and parent involvement so parents can now understand more precisely the breadth and limitations of their rights. Still, the complexity of this legislation and the way it is implemented by state and local education agencies often causes parents to feel overwhelmed.

Because of the law's complexity, many school systems and interest groups have written manuals to assist parents and teachers to understand and to fulfill their roles under P.L. 94–142. Most of these books or pamphlets describe the legal requirements for special education, the procedures of the school system, characteristics of handicapping conditions, and regulations prescribed by the state and local school systems. They are limited in that they all stress what the school system knows—its rules and regulations—and seem to overlook the parent and the child.

Negotiating the Special Education Maze is different. It begins with what you know better than anyone—*your own child*. This is a practical step-by-step guide based upon the experience of thousands of families as they have worked to secure special education services for their children. These parents have increased their knowledge of school systems' procedures, learned skills in organizing and presenting observations of their children, and become more assertive and effective in their role as educational advocates for their children. The understanding these parents have gained of the value of active participation in educational planning is shared with you; indeed, their experience is the basis for *Negotiating the Special Education Maze*.

If you follow the instructions well, this book alone should provide you sufficient training to become an influential educational advocate. You can also build on this text to start an advocacy course for parents in your community. This involves organizing a group of parents and locating someone to be a leader of the course. Parents can then work through these steps with help from others, enabling them not only to communicate about their child more meaningfully but also to learn from others' experiences in working with school systems. This book points the way toward additional sources of assistance—books, resource groups, and other training courses.

Whether you study alone or with a group, this book was written with you, the parents, in mind. Some of you have already spent many years working to get appropriate school services for your children. Others of you are just embarking on the road through the special education maze. Whatever the stage of your journey, the authors hope this road map will assist you in making a productive journey where your own personal resources are used and appreciated. At the end you should find your child making progress, because you and school personnel are partners in her well-being.

After this book was published, the Education of the Handicapped Act was amended by Public Law 101–476 on October 30, 1990. The following changes are particularly significant:

1. The name of the Education of the Handicapped Act (EHA) was changed to the Individuals with Disabilities Education Act (IDEA).

2. Two groups of children often requiring special education services were added to the definition of "children with disabilities." These two groups include "children with autism" and "children with traumatic brain injury."

3. Transition services are now defined by the new law to mean "a coordinated set of activities for a student, designed within an outcome oriented process, which promotes movement from school to post-school activities, including post-secondary education, vocational training, integrated employment (including supported employment), continuing and adult education, adult services, independent living or community participation. The coordinated set of activities shall be based upon the individual student's needs, taking into account the student's preferences and interests, and shall include instruction, community experiences, the development of employment and other post-school adult living objectives, and when appropriate, acquisition of daily living skills and functional vocational evaluation."

4. An individualized transition plan must be developed when a student reaches the age of 16, or if determined appropriate, at the age of 14.

ONE

= ✦ ✦ ✦ =

People and Procedures
Charting Your Course

As you prepare to explore the special education maze, you will need to know how the process of special education works. Your knowledge of the school system's procedures and your skills in communicating information about your child are essential to becoming an effective educational advocate. The introduction to this book explained the basic design and layout of the special education system. This chapter will get you started down the corridors of the maze. It will help you learn the terminology used in special education, introduce the important people with whom you will be working, and review the various decision points and meetings required as you advocate for your child.

Thinking back on times you have worked with various teachers and other professionals, you may find that you, like many other parents, experienced feelings similar to those listed below:

✓ inadequate	✓ hopeful	✓ exhausted
✓ fearful	✓ intimidated	✓ confused
✓ tentative	✓ challenged	✓ worried
✓ anxious	✓ overwhelmed	✓ troubled
✓ angry	✓ frustrated	

Although these feelings are shared by many parents, they usually make it difficult to communicate your hopes, plans, and expectations for your child's school life. Why might you be experiencing these feelings?

As parents going into school meetings, you are moving into a situation where the people you meet use a language and a body of knowledge you may not understand completely. They are familiar with routines and regulations you know little or nothing about. Then, too, everyone carries some remnants of their own school experience—good and not so good—into school buildings. Your perceptions of school professionals and your own school experiences may cause you to question your ability to say the right thing at the right time and to convey your cares, hopes, and opinions about your child's best interests and needs.

What helps you overcome your feelings of anxiety and confusion? To begin with, you can learn about the educational planning process and the people who participate in that process. This will help you be more comfortable in your role as advocate for your child. As you gain skills in presenting your view of your child to the school officials, your negative feelings will diminish, allowing you to be a more effective partner in the educational planning process. This book will help you gain the knowledge and skills you need.

The Special Education Planning Cycle

Almost as important as understanding *how* schools make decisions about your child is understanding *when* they make those decisions. Often, one of the first sources of conflict between parents and schools is the sequence and timing of the major decisions in the special education process. As the following case study shows, differences in how and when the parents make plans for their child can lead to problems and frustrations on both sides.

Susie Martin: A Case Study

During Susie Martin's year in kindergarten, her parents became concerned when they noticed that Susie could not use pencil and paper as well as the other children.

Susie's crayon pictures were mainly scribbles, and even toward the end of the school year, she was still unable to copy the letters in her name. Susie was also restless. During group and story time she often jumped up and moved about the room, playing with objects on other children's desks or in the storage cabinets. She didn't listen to the story. When her teacher called her back to the group, she would roll around the floor, twisting her hair, apparently off in her own world.

For the first months of the school year, the teacher said Susie would soon learn what was expected of her in the classroom and that her skills and behavior would improve. Mr. and Mrs. Martin continued to worry, but listened to the teacher's suggestions. Finally, late in the year, the kindergarten teacher recommended that Susie be tested by the school's psychologist. This testing would help to determine whether or not she needed special education during the coming school year. Mr. and Mrs. Martin readily consented to the testing. They felt relieved that something was finally being done to see if Susie had a learning problem.

Since most of the school psychologists were away during the summer, Susie's testing had to be postponed until early in September. Reluctantly, the Martins waited. When September came, the testing began. But in the meantime, Susie was having an even harder time in the first grade. She noticed that other children could easily do many things she couldn't, and her behavior both at school and at home was often unacceptable. The Martins were angry that the school system was not giving Susie the special help they were now sure she needed. The school administrators, on the other hand, defended themselves by citing the regulations they were required to follow before declaring a child eligible for special education. Everyone was frustrated and angry.

What can ease a situation like this? Parents and school systems each have their own planning cycle for children with special needs. Understanding the two cycles and how they should work together can often help you resolve the disagreements. The parents' cycle looks like this:

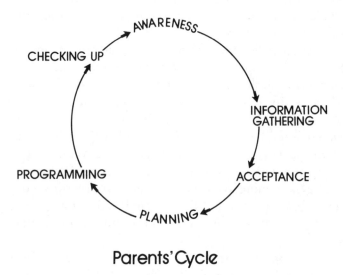

Parents' Cycle

The Parents' Cycle

The Martins' *awareness* of problems in Susie's school life came early in her kindergarten year. They began to *gather information* that might help them to understand and to help Susie. They talked with their pediatrician, observed other children Susie's age, read books on child development and learning problems, and talked frequently with the kindergarten teacher. On the basis of their observations of Susie and the knowledge they gained through other sources, the Martins gradually came to an *acceptance* of their original hunch that Susie did indeed have some problems needing special education at school. At this point, they talked again with the school principal and kindergarten teacher, hoping that *planning* for Susie's special needs would begin. They were ready early in the school year for Susie to have special education *programming*.

The School System's Cycle

The school system, on the other hand, was reluctant to refer Susie for special services so early in her school life. The kindergarten teacher at first adopted a "wait and see" attitude. Toward the end of the school year, though, the teacher activated the school system's planning cycle. She made a *referral* to the school principal, requesting that Susie be considered for special education testing.

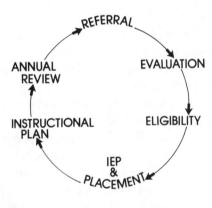

School System's Cycle

The principal convened the local screening committee, sometimes called the child study committee, to discuss Susie's problems. The committee determined her problems were severe enough to warrant a full evaluation. This set in motion the *evaluation* process of psychological, educational, and other testing. A teacher, the school psychologist, the school health nurse, and a social worker comprised the multidisciplinary team that worked to understand Susie and her educational problems. This evaluation process, interrupted by summer vacation, was completed in the fall. The results of the series of tests were presented to a committee of school professionals who determined that Susie needed special services; they recommended Susie's *eligibility* for special education. The Martins were invited to participate in this meeting, which summarized the findings of the evaluation and made the determination of her eligibility for special education.

Following the eligibility decision, the Martins and the school personnel, including a special education teacher, met together to plan an *Individualized Education Program* (IEP) for Susie. The IEP included long-range educational goals based on Susie's needs as well as the special services she would require to help her reach her goals. After the IEP was developed, the placement decision was made identifying the appropriate school program which would provide the services needed to meet Susie's educational goals. Only at this time did the parents' planning cycle and the school system's planning cycle come together.

Finally, some of the tension and frustration was alleviated. The Martins had been ready for Susie to receive special education *instruction* several months before the school system had completed the required cycle of referral, evaluation, eligibility, Individualized Education Program, and placement. Once the two cycles meshed, cooperative planning for Susie's well-being became possible. Subsequently, Susie began to have a more successful time in school.

Susie Martin's case illustrates only one type of conflict that can arise when parents' and school systems' planning cycles differ. Not all parents realize as early as the Martins did that their child needs special services. Sometimes school personnel recommend a formal evaluation of a child whose parents feel certain that there is no problem. Often the parents believe that their child will outgrow any difficulties in school, and are therefore unwilling to give the required permission for the school evaluation to proceed. When this happens, the school is ahead of the parents in the cycle. Whereas the parents are barely, if at all, in the first stage of their planning cycle—the awareness phase—the school system is ready for the second step in its cycle—evaluation. This means that before the school and parents can work together as a team, school personnel must first convince the parents of their child's educational needs.

These planning cycles, both for parents and for school systems, repeat themselves. The IEP must be reviewed at least once a year at a meeting in which the parents, teacher, and school administrator discuss the child's progress. During this *checking-up* and *annual review*, a need for change is sometimes apparent. Further, any time there is a change or a change proposed in the IEP by parents or school people, the team meets to determine the steps that need to be taken to revise the special education program. In addition, every three years, there is a new evaluation and eligibility decision, called the *triennial review*, for each child in special education. During this review, a multidisciplinary team determines whether the child's educational placement is still the appropriate one for him, and recommends a new one if it is not.

For you, the parents of a child who may need special education, a better understanding of the school system's cycle can help to clarify your participation as educational advocates. The school system's cycle is described in the rules and regulations published by the school system in your community. These rules and regulations must comply with the minimum requirements set forth in P.L. 94–142, the Education for All Handicapped Children Act. A brief description of the major provisions of P.L. 94–142 is found in the Introduction to this book. The following two activities will help you understand how your school's special education process works. The understanding you gain will help to change any feelings of inadequacy and uncertainty you may have into ones of competency.

Activity #1: Rules of the Road

Every school system in the country has a set of regulations governing special education. The complexity of these regulations varies, however, from locality to locality. Some large school systems have documents of a hundred or more pages outlining their procedures. Other school systems have no more than a page or two of printed regulations. The first part of Activity #1 is to contact your school superintendent, director of special education, or special education advisory committee and ask for a copy of your local school system's procedures and regulations for special education. These are available to all citizens. Having a copy of your school system's regulations will help you gain confidence in your ability to be an advocate for your child—you, as well as the school people, will know the procedures!

When your local school system wrote its procedural guidelines, it had to follow the regulations of your state division of special education. So a second part of Activity #1 is to write your state director of special education at the address listed in Appendix B, and ask for a copy of the state regulations governing special education. This step is especially important if your school system's regulations are not highly structured and developed. Your school system, like many local school systems, may simply follow what the state has written with no elaboration. While you are requesting a copy of your state regulations, ask about the availability of handbooks describing the special education process in your state or locality. Again, because you are a citizen and because special education regulations are public documents, you should have easy access to this information. At the very least, these documents should be available in either your public library or a public school library. If you have trouble locating the regulations, contact the office of your state legislator for assistance.

Once you have the regulations as developed by your local school system and your state department of education, you are ready for Activity #2.

Activity #2: Key People

Key individuals are involved in every phase of the educational planning process. Among others, these include people such as the principal of the school who chairs the committee which decides whether your child should have special testing, the school psychologist who conducts some of the testing, and a teacher who knows your child particularly well. By making your own personal directory of school personnel, including names, addresses, and telephone numbers, you will better understand the roles of certain individuals in the educational planning process, and you will save time in identifying them when you need their assistance. On the next page you will find an example of a Key People Chart.

As you read the parent handbook or regulations from your locality, you may find that terminology and titles of key positions differ from those in the example. Generally, however, titles will be similar. Using your parent handbook and state and local regulations as a guide, you will want to complete the Key People Chart, as found on pages 12 and 13, to reflect the process in your school system.

This chapter has introduced you to the cycle of referral, evaluation, eligibility, IEP, and placement that your school system must complete before your child can begin special education. You have also obtained the rules and regulations describing and guiding the special education process in your school system. Along the way, you have identified the key people who can help you secure appropriate services for your child. Now you are ready to begin developing the picture and the understanding of your child you wish to convey in school meetings.

Key People Chart

School
Jurisdiction _Middletown, USA_

Director of
Special Education _DR. Harold Brown, Central Admin Bldg. 691-9220 EXT 46_

Name	Address	Telephone

I.   Referral/Child Study Committee

Louise Fischer   _Westbriar Elem. School_   _691-4261_
Principal or designee
(chairperson)

Eileen Collins   _Westbriar Elem. School_   _691-4261_
Referring person

Anna Chase   _Westbriar Elem. School_   _691-4261_
Teacher(s)/Specialist(s)
(as appropriate)

II.   Evaluation Team/Multidisciplinary Team

Kathy Lothian, psych.   _N. Central Admin. Bldg._   _691-9220 x34_
Evaluation Team Coordinator

Kathy Lothian   _"_   _"_
Case Manager

Anna Chase   _Westbriar Elem._   _691-4261_
Teacher(s)/Specialist(s)
(with knowledge of
suspected disability)

DR. Roger Hackett   _7 Oleander Road_   _263-2651_
Independent Evaluator
(when appropriate)

Alina Stone   _Westbriar Elem._   _691-4261_
Classroom Teacher

1

III.   **Eligibility Committee**

DR. Martin Robinson   N. Central Admin. Bldg.   691-9220 X34
Administrator of Special
Education Program or
designee

Kathy Lothian   N. Central Admin. Bldg.   691-9220 X34
Evaluation Team Member(s)
(presents evaluation
findings)

DR. Joanne Wilson   N. Central Admin. Bldg.   691-9220 X48
Appropriate Special
Education Administrators

Nancy Henderson   ''   '' X52
Other professional staff

IV.   **Individualized Education Program/Placement Meeting**

Louise Fischer, principal, Westbriar Elem.   691-4261
School division representative
qualified to provide or supervise
special education services

Anna Chase   ''   691-4261
Teacher

Others, at your or school's request.

V.   **Individualized Education Program Annual Review**

Same team as in the IEP Meeting.

2

Key People Chart

School
Jurisdiction_____

Director of
Special Education_____

Name	Address	Telephone

I.   Referral/Child Study Committee

Principal or designee
(chairperson)

Referring person

Teacher(s)/Specialist(s)
(as appropriate)

II.   Evaluation Team/Multidisciplinary Team

Evaluation Team Coordinator

Case Manager

Teacher(s)/Specialist(s)
(with knowledge of
suspected disability)

Independent Evaluator
(when appropriate)

Classroom Teacher

1

III.   **Eligibility Committee**

Administrator of Special
Education Program or
designee

Evaluation Team Member(s)
(presents evaluation
findings)

Appropriate Special
Education Administrators

Other professional staff

IV.   **Individualized Education Program/Placement Meeting**

School division representative
qualified to provide or supervise
special education services

Teacher

Others, at your or school's request.

V.   **Individualized Education Program Annual Review**

Same team as in the IEP Meeting.

2

TWO

=== ❖ ❖ ❖ ===

You and Your Child

Strengthening Exercises for the Journey

You, as parents, have valuable information that can be extremely helpful in identifying the special education needs of your child. This chapter assists you to identify the unique knowledge you have of your child, to understand the importance of that knowledge for educational planning, and to learn ways to develop and provide that critical information to professionals working with your child.

Preparing for the Journey through the Maze

How do you prepare for your journey through the maze? You begin by looking at the central figure in the whole planning process—your child. This book suggests a number of activities, or "strengthening" exercises, you can do to help clarify and organize what you know about your child. These exercises are useful at any stage of the planning process, whether you are preparing for your baby's first infant assessment, your school-age child's first formal evaluation, or your child's IEP meeting. You can wend your way through the maze without completing the "Strengthening Exercises," but they will make your trip more productive—you will be less likely to go up blind alleys in the maze. The exercises build upon each other; each prepares you for the next.

To assist you in focusing on your child, a Learning Style Questionnaire, Strengthening Exercise #1, follows. Take some time right now to write your responses to the five questions. Examples of Strengthening Exercise #1 completed for Sara and Tony by their parents can be found on pages 30 and 31.

Save this questionnaire. As you will see later in the chapter, your responses will help you to pinpoint specific information about your child and to discover keys that make it easier for her to learn.

Observing Your Child in a Systematic Way

Sometimes parents have trouble answering the questions in Strengthening Exercise #1. You know a lot about your child, but your knowledge is often felt in a general sense rather than in the specific terms needed to answer these questions. Yet while you are absorbed in the routine of everyday living, you are constantly and automatically gathering information about your child. Perhaps you do not realize how much you do know!

Since planning an appropriate program for your child requires specific, documented facts rather than generalized impressions and concerns, you will need to collect your own facts. To convey a personal knowledge of your child to school personnel—people accustomed to dealing with test scores, specific behaviors, goals, and objectives—written, concrete facts will be most influential.

One way to collect these facts is to observe your child in a formal way. "Observe!" you say. "When? How?" You think of the days you barely have enough time and energy to brush your teeth before turning in for the night. But observations can be made. Gathering and organizing information is a vital part of becoming an effective educational advocate for your child.

For example, family uproar occurred almost every morning in Sara's house because of her slowness in getting dressed. Sara's mom wondered if the main reason for Sara's being late was her difficulty in using her hands to fasten buttons and zippers, or if it was her indecision about what to wear. As a result, Sara's mother decided to observe her getting ready for school one morning.

Another family was troubled because their son Tony made such a mess at the table at each meal. Tony's parents decided to observe their son carefully during mealtime. The family was hopeful that his behavior could be changed so that mealtime would be more pleasant for everyone. The next section offers suggestions to help you develop and sharpen your observation skills.

One Step Backward—Three Steps Forward

STEP BACK. Suspend for a brief time (three to five minutes) your normal role in family life. Step back from your family situation to put some distance between you and your child. By not intervening where you normally would, you may see your child's abilities and problems in a new light. For example, when Sara's mother wanted to understand better why Sara was so slow getting ready for school, she decided not to push and prod her as she usually did. She asked her husband to prepare breakfast that morning so that she would be free to observe Sara.

START FRESH. Current eyewitness reports supply better data than do events of the past. Although the past is important in describing your child's development, school personnel are interested in up-to-date information on what she can do now. Start fresh, also, in how you view your own child. Try to be open to new aspects of behavior you may have overlooked before. For example, rather than becoming irritated as Tony ate with his fingers, his father decided to watch carefully when Tony tried to use his spoon. In this way he noticed new things about Tony's difficulties in the precise use of his hands.

Be alert yourself, as the observer. A preoccupied observer cannot record what is happening as accurately as one who can concentrate.

GET FOCUSED. Decide upon a specific behavior or skill to observe by thinking about areas of your child's behavior that puzzle you. Sara's mother, for example, wondered if the main reason her daughter was late was because she had trouble getting into her clothes properly, or if she had difficulty deciding upon and assembling what she wanted to wear.

How, you ask, should you decide upon a certain skill or behavior to observe? The best rule is to look at those areas that trouble you or your child. You may want to examine one of the problem behaviors you have listed in Strengthening Exercise #1, or you may want to ask a doctor or other professional to suggest behaviors to observe. For example, your pediatrician might suggest you watch your baby to see how she rolls from her stomach to her back. You can plan your observation to include various factors: who will be with your child, as well as where and when you will observe her. Concentrate on the skill you have chosen, ignoring as best you can other aspects of behavior.

GO WITH THE FLOW. As you watch your child's activities, record what you see actually happening, not your interpretations of your child's actions. You should become a "candid camera," waiting until later to reflect upon what you see. For example, Tony's dad observed that Tony held his spoon upside down and that he missed his mouth when he raised the spoon from his bowl. Tony's dad wrote down both of these observations, waiting until later to interpret what seemed to cause these problems.

Recording detailed, factual information is easier if a short time is spent observing—perhaps five minutes or less. Observing your child frequently for short periods will help you in your task of recording facts—exactly what happens. You can go back later, review your collection of observations, and interpret the data. On pages 19 and 20 you will find examples of people, places, and activities you might include as you plan to observe your child.

When parents observe their children carefully and systematically, they are able to offer specific information to teachers and other professionals to assist in educational planning. One mother noticed that her daughter's friends used complete sentences when they talked. She was concerned because her child's language seemed less advanced. She wrote down exact words and phrases her daughter used as she played with a friend. These specific examples were very useful when it came time to talk with her child's teacher.

In another family the pediatrician suggested the parents watch their baby to see if her eyes followed an object as it moved in front of her face. On several occasions during the week they observed their daughter's eye movements. When they met next with an infant specialist, they were able to share their careful, repeated observations and to learn ways to help their baby.

Guidelines for Planning an Observation

Before you begin to observe your child, here are some guidelines to assist you:

A. *What* will you be looking at in the observation? Here is a sample of information you can seek and obtain through observation:

1. How your child solves disagreements or problems.
2. How your child moves her arms and legs when crawling.
3. What distracts your child; what holds her attention.
4. How your child dresses or feeds herself.
5. Which toys or games your child prefers.

B. *Who*, if anybody, will be interacting with your child?

1. parent
2. relative(s)
3. brothers or sisters
4. unfamiliar person(s)
5. best friend
6. tutor
7. several friends
8. teacher(s)
9. unfamiliar children
10. professional(s)

C. *Where* will you observe your child—in what setting?

1. HOME
   a. your child's room
   b. TV room
   c. dining room
   d. backyard
   e. homework space

2. NEIGHBORHOOD
   a. neighbor's house
   b. friend's house
   c. playground
   d. park

3. FAMILY EVENTS
   a. picnics
   b. car trips
   c. birthdays
   d. visits to relatives

4. LARGE AND SMALL GROUPS
   a. eating out
   b. shopping
   c. museums
   d. riding the bus
   e. ball games
   f. parties
   g. zoo

5. SCHOOL
   a. classroom
   b. therapy session
   c. field trip
   d. playground
   e. evaluations
   f. vocational classroom

D. *When* will you observe your child?

1. at meals
2. at bedtime
3. at work or homework
4. during leisure time
5. under stress
6. when sick

Now! Actually observe your child, with a specific behavior or skill in mind. Children behave differently, with different people, in different places and at different times. In order to understand more fully your child's strengths and problems, you will want to have several examples of behaviors and skills you have observed.

The information you gather by observing will add to the specific data necessary in planning an educational program to meet your child's unique needs. Strengthening Exercise #2, Parents' Observation Record, provides you with a sample form to assist you in keeping a log of your observations. Examples of the Parents' Observation Record completed for Sara and Tony can be found on pages 33 and 34.

Organizing Your Observations

After you collect several observation records, you can compare and contrast them, looking for trends, consistencies, or inconsistencies in your child's behavior. Organizing your observations is a vital step in preparing yourself to meet with school personnel.

Here are some examples of behaviors parents recorded in their observations in Strengthening Exercises #1 and #2:

- Jason does homework best in a quiet, uncrowded place.
- Fred can recite the alphabet.
- May Lin can put two words together to speak in phrases.
- Virginia has learned to catch herself with her arms as she falls.
- Barbara can roll from her stomach to her back.
- Orin catches and throws a large ball.
- Enrico can write a short paragraph with the ideas in proper sequence.
- Jamie puts on her shoes and socks by herself.
- Henry can pull himself to a standing position in his crib.
- Tyrone shares his toys with Sandra.
- Dee eats with a spoon.
- Carl makes his own lunch to take to school.
- Steve writes capital and lower-case letters in cursive.
- Shantell learns best when she is with one or two good friends.
- Denise can copy a pattern of colored beads strung together.
- Carolyn shows off her school work with pride and excitement.
- Margaret understands thirty-two words in sign language.
- Susie identifies the right bus to ride to her after-school job.

- Sylvia does her homework subjects in the same order each day.
- Alexander can put together a three piece puzzle.

To use the observations you make to your child's best advantage, you need to organize your information so that you can discuss it effectively with everyone involved in planning your child's educational program. In particular, you can group your bits and pieces of observed behavior into the developmental categories like those used by school personnel. Organizing your observation records into general areas of child development will help you think about and discuss your child in language similar to that used by educators.

The preceding list of behaviors parents have observed can be organized into six broad developmental areas:

1. Movement;
2. Communications;
3. Social relationships;
4. Self-concept/independence;
5. Senses/perception;
6. Thinking skills.

Definitions

Here is what these terms mean:

MOVEMENT. The ability to use muscles to move the body and to control small and detailed movements such as walking, jumping, writing, holding objects, rolling, chewing, and balancing.

COMMUNICATION. The ability to understand and respond to spoken language, gestures, or written symbols, and to express oneself clearly and with meaning.

SOCIAL RELATIONSHIPS. The ability to relate to others—for example, to play with other children or to develop attachments to family members.

SELF-CONCEPT/INDEPENDENCE. The ability to distinguish oneself from others and to care for one's own needs.

SENSES/PERCEPTION. The ability to use eyes, ears, and the senses of touch, smell, and taste to learn about the environment.

THINKING SKILLS. Often called cognitive skills, they include the ability to reason and solve problems, to classify, to make associations, to understand similarities and differences, and to comprehend cause-and-effect relationships. School skills such as reading, arithmetic and spelling can be placed in this category.

Now, you ask, are these the categories child development specialists or schoolteachers use? In fact, other common terminology might include such terms as cognition, self-help skills, gross or fine motor skills, expressive language, receptive language, auditory or visual perception—and on and on. There are many classification systems, but basically they accomplish the same purpose. They serve to structure observations about human growth and development. Some people suggest parents should learn the terminology of physicians, educators, therapists, and other specialists. This guidebook assumes the viewpoint that your language about your child is the best language. So, for purposes of educational advocacy in this book, very generalized developmental categories are suggested. They should fit with very little squeezing, translation, or interpretation into the categories used by teachers and specialists working with your child.

Your Child's Learning Style

In addition to having different abilities in the various developmental areas, every child has a particular learning style. A learning style is the combination of unique personal characteristics which determine the way in which a person learns best. For instance, some people learn best through reading and writing; others, through listening and talking. Often a talent in one area—drawing, music, or athletics, for example—can influence how a person learns. Characteristics such as neatness, sensitivity to noise, accuracy, and distractibility will also affect learning. Think for a minute about the way you learn best, your learning style. For example:

- You may learn best by reading information.
- Perhaps you understand things better when you have participated in group discussions.
- You may need to work in a neat environment, or you may feel more comfortable having a messy desk.
- You might need absolute quiet when you concentrate, or you might prefer music as background to your thinking.
- You may need to draw pictures, diagrams, or charts to help you analyze a problem.
- You may take frequent, short breaks while working, or you may concentrate until the task is finished.

Thinking about your own learning style can help you become aware of your child's special ways of learning. Remember, there are no right or wrong ways, only different ones. In addition, most people learn using different aspects of their learning style in various situations. Sharing information about your child's individual ways of learning with those who are teaching her can help to create the best setting to meet her needs. Good teachers make adaptations to the classroom and to their teaching methods in order to accommodate children's various learning styles.

Analyzing Your Observations

The following section shows how to analyze your observations from Strengthening Exercises #1 and #2 so that you can communicate effectively with school personnel. The recorded observations parents have made of their children, found on pages 33 and 34, can be placed within these areas of development and learning style:

MOVEMENT:

- Virginia has learned to catch herself when she falls.
- Orin catches and throws a large ball.
- Steve writes capital and lower-case letters in cursive.
- Barbara can roll from her stomach to her back.
- Henry can pull himself to a standing position in his crib.

COMMUNICATIONS:

- May Lin can put two words together to speak in phrases.
- Margaret understands thirty-two words in sign language.

SOCIAL RELATIONSHIPS:

- Tyrone shares his toys with Sandra.

INDEPENDENCE/SELF CONCEPT:

- Jamie puts on her shoes and socks by herself.
- Dee eats with a spoon.
- Carl makes his own lunch to take to school.
- Carolyn shows off her school work with pride and excitement.

SENSES/PERCEPTION:

- Denise can copy a pattern of colored beads strung together.
- Susie recognizes the right bus to ride to her after-school job.

THINKING SKILLS:

- Fred can recite the alphabet.
- Enrico can write a short paragraph with the ideas in proper sequence.
- Alexander can put together a three piece puzzle.

LEARNING STYLE:

- Jason does homework best in a quiet, uncrowded place.
- Shantell learns best when she is with one or two good friends.
- Sylvia does her homework subjects in the same order each day.

Perhaps you are puzzled by the way some of these behaviors have been organized into developmental categories. For example, you might think that Jamie's ability to put on her shoes and socks independently fits into the areas of *movement* and *thinking skills*, as well as *independence*. No single behavior falls exclusively into one category or another. Jamie's movement skills are not a problem. Physically she is able to put on her shoes and socks. The emphasis she needs is in developing her independence. Therefore, her parents place "putting on shoes and socks" under *Independence/Self-Concept*. Think about the developmental areas you believe are particularly important to your child's growth now, and put your observations of her accomplishments into that category. Remember, there need not be only one "right" category.

To organize your observations about your child's development and learning style, transfer the work you have done in the first two Strengthening Exercises into a Developmental Achievement Chart like the ones completed for Sara and Tony on pages 36 and 37. Notice that Question #1 on the Learning Style Questionnaire provides information for the column *Can Do*. Question #3 on the Learning Style Questionnaire coincides with the second column, *Working On*. Question #5 corresponds with the column *To Accomplish in 6 Months*. Questions #2 and #4 give information about your child's *learning style*. These observations can be recorded in the bottom row of the chart.

If your observations have not given you a complete picture of your child's development, repeat Strengthening Exercise #2, targeting the specific developmental areas in which you need more information. For example, if you are satisfied with what you know about your child's movement skills, but want to know more about her social skills, you can arrange to observe that area of her development.

Other Sources of Information

Often people outside of your immediate family can offer fresh perceptions of your child and new insights into her growth and development. Bear in mind, too, that when your child participates in activities outside of the home, opportunities may arise to observe skills and behavior she does not demonstrate at home.

Family documents and projects can also provide you with a wealth of information as you build a complete picture of your child. One family brought pictures of their son to show in a meeting with school officials; another mother made tape recordings of her child's language while they were riding in the car. Your imagination will tell you many ways to use your daily routines to increase your observations of your child.

There are many times, places, and ways of collecting information about your child's growth and development. Here are some sources other parents have found useful—add your own to the lists:

PEOPLE

Grandparents
Brothers, sisters
Scout Leaders
Coaches
Neighbors

Playmates
Bus drivers
Teachers
Doctors
Employers

PLACES

Fast food restaurants
Family camping
Doctor's office
Car pools

Church
Grocery store
Scout troop
Swimming pool

FAMILY DOCUMENTS & PROJECTS

Photo albums
Examples of school work
Preparing for holidays
Home movies

Art projects
Tape recordings
Gardening
School and hospital
 records

Conclusion

Throughout your child's infant, preschool, and school years you will need to make new observations of her growth and development. Fresh observations collected prior to meetings with teachers and other professionals working with you and your child can assist in providing specific recommendations for her special education program. By completing the two Strengthening Exercises and the Developmental Achievement Chart, you gain a better understanding of your child's unique strengths and needs. By having this valuable information at your fingertips, you will feel confident as you participate in the special education planning process.

Strengthening Exercise #1

Learning Style Questionnaire

I. List three things your child has recently learned or accomplished.

   1.

   2.

   3.

2. Choose one of the items in question #I. What about your child helped him learn this?

3. Think of three things your child is working to learn now.

   1.

   2.

   3.

4. Choose one of the items in question #3 that your child is having trouble learning. What is causing him trouble?

5. What one thing would you like your child to learn within the next six months?

Learning Style Questionnaire

I.   List three things your child has recently learned or accomplished.

1. Sara can ride her bike without the training wheels.

2. She can make her bed and takes her dishes to the kitchen.

3. She answers the telephone correctly

2.   Choose one of the items in question #I. What about your child helped him learn this?

Sara marked a home chores chart daily which pictured the different activities she was learning to do. She received an reward if she completed her chores at least five times during the week. Sara could see (and count) how she was doing. Sara also likes to have her room neat.

3.   Think of three things your child is working to learn now.

1. Sara is learning to write her name and address.

2. She is learning to set the table

3. She is working on getting ready for school without constant reminders from Mom.

4.   Choose one of the items in question #3 that your child is having trouble learning. What is causing him trouble?

Sara has difficulty choosing what to wear, difficulty remembering all needed items to go in her school bag. Sara dresses very slowly.

5.   What one thing would you like your child to learn within the next six months?

I would like Sara to be ready for school — dressed appropriately, school bag packed — in time for the bus, without Mom's help or reminding.

Learning Style Questionnaire

I. List three things your child has recently learned or accomplished.

1. Tony hangs his coat on the hook by the back door.

2. He can sit for a few minutes and listen to a story.

3. He pats Gretchen (the dog) gently instead of hitting her.

2. Choose one of the items in question #1. What about your child helped him learn this?

The classroom aide sat next to Tony with her arm around him when he became restless during story time -- he responds well to people.

3. Think of three things your child is working to learn now.

1. To wipe his face with handkerchief when he drools.

2. To learn the sign for "thank you."

3. To climb stairs without help.

4. Choose one of the items in question #3 that your child is having trouble learning. What is causing him trouble?

Lack of fine motor control.

5. What one thing would you like your child to learn within the next six months?

To eat a meal without smearing food on his face, in his hair and on his clothes.

Strengthening Exercise #2

Parents' Observation Record

Observer_____Date of Observation_____

Beginning Time of Observation_____Ending Time_____

Who Was Observed?_____

Where?_____When?_____

What was the focus of the observation?_____

_____

Why was this focus chosen?_____

_____

What occurred during observation?	Reflections on the observation

Parents' Observation Record

Observer ___Gina___ Date of Observation ___October 29, 1989___

Beginning Time of Observation ___7:15 am___ Ending Time ___7:20 am___

Who Was Observed? ___Sara___

Where? ___Sara's bedroom___ When? ___Getting dressed for school___

What was the focus of the observation? ___To watch and understand Sara's morning routine.___

Why was this focus chosen? ___Parent's frustration over Sara's difficulty in getting ready for school, causing family chaos.___

What occurred during observation?	Reflections on the observation
Opens closet, stares at clothes. Takes out skirt and lays it on bed. Takes out blouse, lays it on bed by skirt. Looks at blouse and skirt. Put clothes away, gets out another blouse and skirt. Repeats this action once more. Takes out and examines several pairs of socks and tights. Chooses one, folds and replaces others in drawer	Sara has trouble making choices when there are alot of alternatives. Sara is more concerned about being neat than being on time.

Parents' Observation Record

Observer ___Ralph___ Date of Observation ___November 7___

Beginning Time of Observation ___5:00 p.m.___ Ending Time ___5:05 p.m.___

Who Was Observed? ___Tony___

Where? ___At the kitchen table___ When? ___During dinner___

What was the focus of the observation? ___Tony's eating skills___

Why was this focus chosen? ___So we could enjoy dinner as a family - at home and in restaurants___

What occurred during observation?	Reflections on the observation
Picks up spoon with right hand - digs into spaghetti	
Takes a bite of spaghetti.	
Digs into spaghetti again - holds spoon upside down.	
Drops spoon onto table.	Tony has trouble holding onto the spoon, especially with his left hand!
Picks up spoon with left hand - takes another bite.	
Drops spoon onto floor. Uses both hands to pick up spaghetti, smearing onto face and hair.	He uses his hands when the spoon is not within reach.

Developmental Achievement Chart

	Can Do	Working On	To Accomplish within 6 Months
MOVEMENT			
COMMUNICATIONS			
SOCIAL RELATIONSHIPS			
SELF-CONCEPT/ INDEPENDENCE			
SENSES/PERCEPTION			
THINKING SKILLS			
LEARNING STYLE			

Developmental Achievement Chart

Sara

	Can Do	Working On	To Accomplish within 6 Months
MOVEMENT	Rides a bike, walks a balance beam. Prints, does not use cursive writing. Throws a ball.	Pedalling faster and pumping-up hills on her bike. Smaller and neater printing. Catching a large ball.	To keep up with a group when bike riding. Printing on wide-ruled paper. Catch and throw a with more accuracy.
COMMUNICATIONS	Responds to simple directions. Answers the telephone clearly. Can respond appropriately to caller.	Following instructions without getting mixed up.	Understand and follow through on more complex directions.
SOCIAL RELATIONSHIPS	Goes to Brownie Troop meetings. Sits with a small group of girls on the bus. Plays with younger neighborhood children.	Learning to make her way into a group of girls without her mom's help. Establishing close friendship with girl her own age	Participate in small group activity without adult hovering over. Have a friend come to play and have dinner regularly.
SELF-CONCEPT/ INDEPENDENCE	Gets dressed in the morning if clothes are laid out and if Mom helps. Walks from bus stop alone. Expects mom to be waiting at home.	Getting dressed and ready for school in the morning without Mom's help. Learning what to do if Mom is late coming home.	Dress completely without help or reminders. Know what to do if Mom is not at home.
SENSES/PERCEPTION	Takes care of matching clothing, coordinating colors. Sings along with songs on the radio.	Learning names of shades of colors. Learning words to songs in music class at school.	Name over two shades of each primary color (i.e. "pink," "turquoise,") Be able to sing two songs from memory.
THINKING SKILLS	Knows how to count accurately to 50 by ones. Recognize at least half of the lower case alphabet letters.	Knows name, address and phone number. Count to 20 by ones. Knows upper case alphabet letters.	Learn to count to 100 by ones. Learning to count to 100 by ones. Learning to recognize lower case alphabet letters.
LEARNING STYLE	Very neat and orderly. Needs visual aids to see progress.	Works for rewards (prizes, candy), praise from adults. Daydreams and is distractible.	

Developmental Achievement Chart

Tony

	Can Do	Working On	To Accomplish within 6 Months
MOVEMENT	Holds spoon in either hand. Climb stairs while holding someone's hand.	Using his right hand to hold the spoon. Climbing stairs without help.	To use a spoon to eat his meal. Climb the 4 front porch stairs by himself holding the rail.
COMMUNICATIONS	Understands signs for hungry, thirsty, thank you. Can say "yes-no" in a way that family understands.	Signing "hungry," "thirsty," "thank you," so he can be understood. Saying "yes-no" more clearly.	Will be able to sign "hungry," "thirsty," "thank you" clearly. To say "yes-no" so most people understand him.
SOCIAL RELATIONSHIPS	Watches a group of friends playing a game. Says "no" to classmate who pushes him, then pushes him back.	Playing the game with his friends. Ignoring pushy classmate, rather than pushing back.	Be able to play a game with a group of friends. Say "no" to pushy classmate "ask someone for help.
SELF-CONCEPT/ INDEPENDENCE	Can turn bathroom faucets on and off. Hangs up coat on hook by the back door.	Identifying hot and cold. Unzipping coat by himself.	Wash hands with little or no supervision. Take off coat with some help.
SENSES/PERCEPTION	Looks at person calling his name.	Keeping eye contact when spoken to.	Always looking at familiar people when being spoken to.
THINKING SKILLS	Can follow a simple one-step direction with help. For example, "pick up the spoon."	Follow a simple two-step direction with help.	Following a one-step direction without help.
LEARNING STYLE	Tony is cautious about trying new things, and learns best by watching an activity before trying it. He is persistent when allowed to try new tasks on his own.		

THREE

=== ✣ ✣ ✣ ===

Referral and Evaluation
Ready? Go!

You have collected important information describing your child's educational and developmental achievements and learning style. By systematically observing your child in a variety of situations, you have developed a picture of his present strengths and needs, and have also begun to set goals for his future accomplishments. But where does all this fit within the school system's special education planning process? How, and at what point, can you get school personnel to discuss with you your concerns and findings regarding your child's educational needs? How do you obtain a thorough evaluation from the school system? What information is contained in these evaluations and other school records which may be used to obtain appropriate educational programs and services?

Chapter 1 briefly described the phases of the planning cycle used by school systems to provide educational services for special-needs children. This chapter examines in detail two of these phases: *referral* and *evaluation*. Each phase is described in terms of its purposes, activities, and participants. More important, suggestions are made as to how you, as parents, can actively participate in these phases.

Identifying Special-Needs Children: The Referral Phase

Every school system is required by P.L. 94–142 to conduct a public awareness campaign, often called "Child Find," to inform the public of the rights of children with disabilities to an education that meets the child's individual needs and is provided at no cost to the parents. School systems must also tell parents in the community about the availability of special education programs. Additionally, each school division, as part of the Child Find process, must identify, locate, and evaluate everyone from birth through twenty-one in need of special education services.

Efforts to identify and to provide services for very young children with disabilities increased greatly in 1986 when Congress passed P.L. 99–457. This new law brought about significant changes for young children with disabilities. One part of P.L. 99–457 benefits preschoolers who have developmental delays. The law extends the rights and protections of P.L. 94–142 to all disabled children ages three through five. Schools are required to provide educational services to these preschool children by school year 1990–1991 in order to continue receiving federal funds for preschool programs.

A second part of P.L. 99–457 benefits developmentally delayed infants and toddlers ages birth through two. This law authorizes federal grants to the states to develop and provide comprehensive services to these very young children. Comprehensive services include special education, speech, occupational and physical therapies, health and medical services, and family support such as training, counselling, and support groups. Additionally, families are entitled to a case manager who serves as a coordinator to assist them in locating and receiving other services they need. These services, called "early intervention services," are based on a family's and child's needs as identified in and provided through a personalized written plan called an Individualized Family Service

Plan (IFSP). By 1988 all states had accepted federal funds under P.L. 99–457 and had begun planning their programs for infants and toddlers.

While state education agencies must conduct "Child Find," the governor of each state designates an agency, which may be different from the department of education, to plan and implement the early intervention program. For example, early intervention services in your state might be provided by the Department of Health, while in a neighboring state the Office for Children and Youth is responsible. As a result, eligibility requirements and program procedures for obtaining early intervention services differ from state to state and from those used to obtain educational services under The Education for All Handicapped Children Act. Nevertheless, the ideas and techniques this book describes to assist parents of older children in working effectively with school professionals should also help you in advocating for services for your very young child. If your child is two or younger and you feel he may be developmentally delayed, you should contact the agency responsible for early intervention programs in your state. The director of special education in your local public schools will be able to direct you to the right person, or you can refer to the Resource Guide at the back of this book.

If your child is school-aged, the referral process is somewhat different from the referral process for very young children. Once a school-aged child has been identified as possibly having disabilities, the rules and regulations of both your local school system and your state division of special education specify how to make a referral for special education services. Generally, however, the first action is a written referral to the principal of the school the child is attending or would attend if he were in a public school. If a child is just beginning school and parents or others believe that special education is needed, they may request that the child be considered for such assistance immediately. If you think your child needs special services, you can obtain a referral form from the principal, or you can write a letter to the principal requesting your child be referred for special education. Or if teachers and counselors notice your child is having problems in school, they, too, may make a referral.

No matter who makes a special education referral, the next step is for the principal to convene a committee to consider the referral. Committee members most often include: (1) the principal or someone designated by the principal; (2) the person who referred the child, if that person is from the school system; and (3) teachers or other specialists who have particular knowledge of the problems the child seems to be experiencing.

In many school jurisdictions this initial committee is called the "local school screening committee." Other terms for the same committee might be the "child study committee," the "school-based committee," and the "educational management team." The committee's major purpose is to determine whether a child's learning and developmental problems are severe enough to require a formal evaluation by the school psychologist and other specialists. To reach a decision, the committee discusses the child's problems, considers adaptations to the current school program to address those problems, and suggests strategies to the classroom teacher that might help the child. If the committee members believe a full evaluation is required, they send the necessary recommendation to the school's special education administrator. The committee's decision must be made in writing and include the information leading to the committee's conclusions. The number of days in which the committee must act should be set forth in your school's rules and regulations.

In some instances parents may be unaware that their child has even been referred to the local school screening committee, unless they themselves have made the referral. School systems treat the initial stages of the referral process in a variety of ways. Some are very careful to notify parents of any meetings held to consider or to make decisions about a child's needs for special education. Others are more informal about their approach and will notify you of the meeting only if they want to obtain your consent for a formal evaluation.

When you have referred your child for initial screening, or are otherwise aware of the screening, you should request that the chairperson of the local screening committee notify you as to when they will meet and allow you to participate in that meeting. The regulations of some school systems require parents to participate in this stage of the process; others do not. In any case schools usually are agreeable to parent participation when asked. In preparation for this meeting, you should observe your child as described in Chapter 2 and develop a presentation of information you believe would help the local screening committee reach its decision.

As previously discussed, the purpose of this screening committee meeting is both to review your child's records and other relevant material and to decide whether to recommend further evaluation. If you attend the screening meeting, you should ask to take part in the discussion leading to that decision. Once again, the regulations will probably not require the committee to allow your participation in their final discussion and decision- making. At your request, however, they often will let you remain for the discussion and decision. So go ahead and ask.

If the screening committee does not recommend that your child be referred to the special education director for formal evaluation, you can dispute the decision through a formal procedure called a *due process hearing.* Chapter 9 describes the due process procedures you may follow in appealing this and other decisions made by school officials.

If you have not been part of the screening committee's activities, you may first learn that your child is being considered for special educational services upon receipt of a letter from the school requesting permission to evaluate your child. Under federal and state laws, the school system must notify you of its wish to evaluate your child for purposes of receiving special education services. It must explain to you what tests will be done and the reasons your child is being evaluated. Further, in the instance of a first-time evaluation, your consent must be granted before the testing begins. If you refuse to give consent, the school system must initiate a due process hearing and have a hearing officer rule to proceed with the evaluation. Again, see Chapter 9 for a full explanation of due process.

Taking a Look: The Evaluation Process

Forms requesting parental permission for evaluation are frequently overwhelming. Their technical language and bureaucratic style can generate great anxiety in parents. Most parents know very little about educational assessments, psychological evaluations, and audiological, speech, and language testing. For these reasons, some school personnel telephone parents ahead of time or set up conferences to talk with parents about the need for a complete evaluation of their child. They discuss the tests and procedures to be used in order to help parents gain confidence in the evaluation process. Nonetheless, if you have not been aware of your child's learning problems, the letter and form requesting your permission for evaluation may still be intimidating. And, even if you have suspected your child may need special education services, the formal language and the "fine print" can be confusing. A sample letter requesting parents' permission to evaluate their child follows:

What should you do when faced with the school's request to evaluate your child's learning needs? Maybe, you think, the school knows best. So you sign the form, grant permission for your child's evaluation, and then wonder if you did the right thing. You may be relieved the school is finally going to do something. Or maybe you refuse to grant permission for evaluation and again wonder if you made the right decision.

Neither of these responses may be the most helpful to you or your child. What you need is a greater understanding of the evaluation process and a knowledge of specific actions you may take in response to the request to evaluate your son or daughter. You need some information about the rights and responsibilities of the people involved in your child's evaluation. Knowing what to do will reduce your feeling of helplessness and begin to let you and your child "do" something about evaluation, as opposed to being "done in" by evaluation.

Mr. & Mrs. Austin	RE	Evaluation
1519 S. West Street	SCHOOL	Westview Elementary
Alexandria Va. 22355	ID NO.	10094

Dear **Mr. & Mrs. Austin**:

As we have discussed, the following individual evaluations are essential in understanding your child's particular needs.

Audiological	X
Educational	X
Psychological	X
Sociocultural	X
Speech and language	
Vision	X
Medical	X

The evaluations may include conferring with your child, testing of general ability and educational achievement, and/or an evaluation of feelings.

If you have any questions about the evaluations or why they are necessary, please call **Ms. Pilerton** at **624-5525**. When the evaluations are completed, an opportunity will be provided for you to discuss the results. You also may have access to these and any other educational records pertaining to your child.

We are not able to proceed with these evaluations until we have your permission to do so. Please return the attached form to me, at the above address, within ten working days after receipt of this letter. You do have the right to refuse to give your permission. Should you refuse to give permission, the   County Public Schools has the right to appeal your decision.

If a recent medical examination is required, the examination may be scheduled through a private physician—at your own expense—or through the   County Department of Health Services—free of charge. If you wish to schedule a free medical examination for your child, please contact **County Health Dept.** at **524-6660**.

If you would like to be informed of the time, date, and place of subsequent meetings held to discuss your child's educational needs, contact **Ms. Pilerton** at **624-5525** who will inform you of the local screening and eligibility committee meetings.

Sincerely,

Marcia J. Pilerton
Principal
/ct

Attachment

cc: Cumulative File

PARENTAL PERMISSION FOR EVALUATION

I GIVE PERMISSION for the   County Public Schools
to proceed with the following evaluations for my child,

      Sara Austin   :
     Name of child

Audiological	X
Educational	X
Psychological	X
Sociocultural	X
Speech and language	
Vision	X
Medical	X

I understand that I have the right to review my child's school
records and to be informed of the results of these evaluations.
I understand that no change will be made in my child's educational program as a result of these evaluations without my
knowledge. I understand that I have the right to refuse to give
permission for these evaluations.

I have arranged to have a medical examination for my child through:
(Please check if
a recent medical ☐ A private physician ☐ County Department of Health Services
examination is
required)

_____   _____
       Date   *Signature of Parent*

I DO NOT GIVE PERMISSION for the   County Public Schools
to proceed with the evaluation of my child,_____.

I understand that I have the right to review my child's school
records. I understand that the   County Public Schools
may use established procedures to obtain authorization to
proceed with the evaluation and that if the   County
Public Schools appeals my decision, I will be notified of my
due process rights.

_____   _____
       Date   *Signature of Parent*

cc: Cumulative File

The Evaluation Process: Purposes, Activities, and Professionals

There may be many reasons why a child's physical, social, or intellectual development is slower than others his age. Some children merely mature more slowly than their peers; time will find them "catching up." In some instances, a child's home environment and family or cultural background may cause learning to proceed at a slower-than-average rate. Other children may have physical impairments that interfere with their development. Perhaps they have a visual or hearing problem. Still other children may have mental retardation, learning disabilities, or emotional problems. Any and all of these conditions could interfere with a child's general educational and developmental progress.

The purpose of the school's evaluation process is to identify your child's learning difficulties. While attempting to determine the source of the learning problems, information is also obtained concerning your child's present developmental and academic abilities. This information is helpful in understanding the nature of your child's problems and in planning his future educational programs.

School systems use many different tests and materials to evaluate children. In fact, P.L. 94–142 requires that the evaluation be conducted by a "multi-disciplinary team," a group of professionals with expertise in different areas. In some states the types of tests used in evaluation are specified by state regulations and vary according to the child's suspected disability. Basically, however, all tests and materials may be grouped into five categories, or as schools sometimes call them, *assessment components*. Not all states require that each component be completed for every child. Therefore, it is important that you check your state and local procedures to see which components are required. The five categories that are often used and the professionals who gather information for each category are:

1. **The educational component.** An analysis based on selected tests that identifies your child's current educational

performance and specific instructional needs in such academic areas as reading, math, spelling, and language performance. Specific tests may be given by the classroom teacher, when qualified, and by educational diagnosticians trained in using these tests.

2. The medical component. An assessment from a physician indicating general medical history and any medical/health problems which might impede your child's learning. Although many parents obtain this assessment at their own expense, each school system maintains a list of physicians and clinics where free medical examinations are available.

3. The social history component. A report developed from interviews with parents, teachers, and others describing your child's background and behavior at home and in school. The report is usually prepared by a school social worker who interviews the parents at home. If parents wish, however, they may request that the interview take place elsewhere—for example, at school.

4. The psychological component. A report usually written by a school psychologist and based upon numerous tests and the psychologist's observations and interpretations. The psychological testing assesses your child's general intelligence, social skills, emotional development, other thinking skills, and his ability to coordinate eye and hand movements. If your child's learning or behavioral needs are complex, this component may also include an evaluation by a clinical psychologist or a psychiatrist.

5. Others. Assessments in other areas which may be necessary to complete the picture of your child. Areas of development that may be assessed include your child's communication skills, such as imitating sounds, cooing, responding to language, or talking; his social skills, such as separating from parents and getting along with others; and his movement skills, such as rolling, raising his head, walking, and using his hands. In addition, your child's brain and central nervous system functioning may be assessed through a neurological examination, and his senses and perception may be evaluated through hearing, vision, and other tests. For very young children and infants, the purpose of the evaluation is the same as for older children: to identify their strengths and weaknesses as a basis for planning the services they need. Your pediatrician can give you guidance regarding specific tests necessary to provide a comprehensive understanding of your child's strengths and needs.

Formal Evaluation Requirements

All school systems are required by P.L. 94–142 and by state laws to follow certain procedures when evaluating a child.

First, the administrator of special education must inform you in your native language and primary means of communication— vocal, sign language, or Braille—of:

1. the school's intent to evaluate your child;
2. your rights as parents pertaining to special education for your child; and
3. the need for your consent prior to the initial evaluation and your right to notification of any subsequent evaluations.

Second, the school system must ensure its evaluation procedures provide for the following:

1. your written consent prior to the initial evaluation;
2. the assignment of surrogate parents if you are not available to protect the interests of your child;
3. confidentiality of all evaluation results;
4. an opportunity for you to obtain an independent evaluation of your child if you believe the school's evaluation is biased or invalid;
5. an opportunity for you to have a hearing to question evaluation results with which you disagree;
6. an opportunity for you to examine your child's official school records; and

7. testing that does not discriminate against your child because of racial or cultural bias or because the tests are inappropriate for a person with your child's disabilities.

Third, the school system must make sure its testing procedures meet these requirements:

1. The tests and evaluation materials are administered in your child's native language and primary means of communication.
2. The tests must be professionally approved for the specific purposes for which they are used.
3. The tests must be given by trained professionals according to the instructions of the publishers of the tests and materials.
4. Tests and evaluation materials that assess a wide range of educational and developmental needs and capabilities should be used in addition to tests designed to provide a single general intelligence quotient.
5. Tests should be selected and administered so as to ensure that they accurately assess the child's aptitude, achievement level, or other factors they are designed to measure, rather than reflecting the child's disabilities.
6. The evaluation should be undertaken by a team or group of persons from several professional backgrounds, including at least one teacher or other specialist with knowledge in the area of your child's suspected disability. Your child should be assessed in all areas related to the suspected disability, including, where appropriate, health, vision, hearing, social and emotional status, general intelligence, academic performance, communication skills, and motor abilities.

These are the minimum requirements school officials must meet when evaluating your child's need for special education services. The regulations of your state and local school district may include additional procedures. For example, your school may provide for a conference between you and the evaluation team members to discuss the results of your child's testing. Before proceeding with the evaluation for your child, review your school's rules and regulations carefully. Remember, if you believe your school system has not fulfilled the evaluation requirements as stated above and in your school's procedures, you can take various steps to protect your child's right to a thorough, accurate evaluation. Chapter 9 outlines these due process and complaint procedures in detail.

Parent Action-Steps for Evaluation

Now you know, generally, the purposes, the activities, and the professionals involved in the evaluation of a child, as well as the general requirements that school systems must satisfy. But your interest is not a general one. Your interest is in the particular evaluation being proposed for your child. With this specific concern in mind, "Parent Action-Steps for Evaluation" were developed for you to follow in each of the four phases of the evaluation process: (1) giving or refusing permission to evaluate; (2) activities before evaluation; (3) activities during evaluation; and (4) activities after evaluation.

For each phase of the process, you will find a series of actions and accompanying steps you may take to participate in your child's evaluation. This list of action-steps suggests activities other parents have found helpful when entering the evaluation phase of the special education process. Some of the actions and steps are applicable to testing conducted by private or public agencies outside the school system rather than in a school setting. Other steps are appropriate for young children rather than older students. You will want to undertake only those actions and steps that: (1) make sense to you; (2) are appropriate to the age and developmental level of your child; (3) will help you make a confident decision; and (4) will give you a feeling of managing, rather than being managed by, the evaluation process. You need not, and should not, take all the actions and all the steps outlined. Look over the listing and choose those actions and steps to follow which will be most helpful to you and to your child in assuring that the evaluation is fair and thorough. In making your selection, you will want to keep in mind your family's needs, and your child's age, disability, and past experience with evaluations.

Phase I: Giving or Refusing Permission to Evaluate

After the school system has notified you in writing of its intent to evaluate your child, you must decide whether to give or refuse permission for this evaluation. School system regulations prescribe the amount of time you have to respond, usually within ten days of notice. To help you decide, you may wish to:

ACTION A: Explore your feelings about this evaluation by

1. talking to your spouse, a friend, or a helping professional such as a teacher, counselor, or advocate;
2. recalling what was difficult and what was helpful in previous evaluations, unless, of course, this is the first one.

ACTION B: Learn more about your local evaluation process by

1. asking the director of special education or your school principal to identify the person in the school system most responsible for your child's evaluation;
2. obtaining all relevant written policies and procedures from the person responsible for the evaluation, the school's public information officer, or the department of special education;
3. obtaining parent handbooks and pamphlets on evaluation;
4. making a list of all your questions;
5. meeting with a knowledgeable person—an experienced parent, a school representative, an advocate—to discuss evaluation.

ACTION C: Learn more about the evaluation planned for your child by

1. requesting in writing from school officials the reasons for this evaluation;
2. requesting a detailed plan for evaluation, to include:
   a. areas to be evaluated;
   b. tests or portions of tests to be used;

    c. reasons for selecting tests;

    d. qualifications of persons giving tests;

    e. statement as to how the evaluation will be adapted to compensate for your child's suspected disability.

ACTION D: Assess the appropriateness of the tests by

1. consulting a knowledgeable person such as another parent, an independent professional, or a school psychologist;
2. reviewing literature on evaluation. (See annotated bibliography in Appendix D.)

ACTION E: Explore the independent evaluation alternative by

1. learning about your right to an independent evaluation, as described in Chapter 4;
2. learning your school's procedures for providing independent evaluations;
3. talking with parents whose children have had independent evaluations;
4. consulting a psychologist, diagnostician, or other professional in private practice.

ACTION F: Explore the consequences of refusing evaluation by

1. talking to the principal and teachers about alternatives to special education at the school;
2. discussing your concerns with the person in charge of the evaluation;
3. learning your school's procedures when parents refuse evaluation;
4. talking with knowledgeable professionals about your child's learning needs and the reasons you are considering refusing the school's evaluation.

Phase II: Before Evaluation

If, after completing the action steps just described, you decide to give permission for your child to be evaluated, you can take several steps to prepare for the evaluation. You may wish to:

ACTION A: Anticipate your child's needs in this evaluation by

1. talking with your spouse, your child's therapist or teacher, or an earlier evaluator about how your child handles evaluations, specifically his:
    a. reaction to strangers
    b. tolerance for testing demands
    c. ability to sit still for long periods
    d. response to doctors and other professionals
    e. fatigue threshold—how long until he gets too tired to work at his best
    f. need for an interpreter if non-English speaking or a user of sign language
    g. high and low points in the day;
2. reading pamphlets or articles on children and evaluations;
3. talking with your child about prior evaluation experiences and his thoughts about the new evaluation.

ACTION B: Prepare yourself for this evaluation by

1. talking to other parents about their experiences;
2. seeking tips on rough spots and how to work around them from an organization for parents of children with disabilities;
3. listing your practical concerns, such as:
    a. schedules
    b. costs
    c. child care
    d. transportation
    e. obtaining an interpreter
4. learning the evaluation facility's expectation for your involvement;
5. choosing among various roles you take, such as
    a. observer of your child
    b. supporter of your child
    c. information source about your child.

ACTION C: Plan for your child's evaluation with a representative of the evaluation facility or school's psychological services by

1. arranging for a meeting or a phone conference;
2. preparing for this meeting by listing your questions and concerns in priority order;
3. requesting information on, or clarification of, the evaluation process;
4. sharing your plans for your involvement;
5. raising concerns you might have over keeping the experience a positive one for your child.

ACTION D: Prepare your child for the evaluation by

1. talking together about the reasons for, and process of, this new evaluation;
2. giving your child opportunities to express his feelings and ask questions;
3. visiting the place where the evaluation will be conducted so your child will be familiar with the people and the surroundings;
4. planning together for a special activity when the evaluation is completed.

Phase III: During Evaluation

During the evaluation process itself, the actions and steps you select will be strongly influenced by your child's age and his past experience with evaluations. In many instances your child will be tested in school, during school hours, making it difficult or inappropriate for you to be present during the evaluation. When it is appropriate for you to be present, especially with an infant or preschooler, you may want to consider some of the following actions and steps. Keeping in mind your child's age, personality, and disability, you may wish to:

ACTION A: Ease your child into the situation by

1. allowing him to become familiar with the rooms in which he will be tested;
2. introducing him to the people who will be giving the tests;

3. reviewing the day's plan with him;
4. reassuring him that you will be available to him at all times;
5. encouraging him to ask questions and share worries.

ACTION B: Monitor the evaluation process by

1. requesting that the evaluation start on time;
2. inquiring as to any changes in personnel or tests to be used;
3. observing testing of your child whenever appropriate;
4. recording your impressions of your child's performance;
5. recording your impressions of each evaluator's interactions with your child.

ACTION C: Monitor your child's performance by

1. keeping an eye on his fatigue and stress levels;
2. staying with him during medical procedures—shots, blood tests, EEG;
3. asking for explanations of unexpected procedures.

Phase IV: After Evaluation

Parents and children usually have a need to feel that the evaluation is truly completed. There are a number of ways you and your family can wrap up the evaluation experience and begin to use the information gained from the evaluation for educational planning. You may wish to:

ACTION A: Help your child round out the experience on a positive note by

1. encouraging him to review the experience through storytelling, drawing pictures, or dramatic play;
2. discussing with him the people and activities he liked and disliked;
3. sharing your own feelings and perceptions of the experience;
4. informing him of the evaluation results—what was learned about his strengths and needs;
5. throwing an end-of-evaluation party!

ACTION B: Help yourself complete the experience by

1. recounting the experience to a friend or parent support group;
2. checking the actual evaluation experience against what you had planned or anticipated;
3. writing a letter to the evaluation facility describing your sense of the strengths and needs of the process;
4. giving yourself a graduation-from-evaluation gift!

ACTION C: Prepare for your parent conference with the evaluation team by

1. reading through your child's previous evaluation records, if he has been tested previously;
2. reviewing your information and notes on this evaluation;
3. asking the head of the evaluation team for the record of this evaluation, including individual reports;
4. analyzing the records by using the Four-Step Record Decoder described in Chapter 4;
5. noting your concerns in the form of questions to be asked at the parent conference;
6. asking someone to go with you to the parent conference.

To help you systematically negotiate the evaluation phase of the special education maze, a Parent Action-Steps for Evaluation Chart follows. The chart has space for writing each action and step you will take in the evaluation phase. At the end of the chart is a section for names, phone numbers, and dates related to those actions and steps. The chart allows you to plan steps you choose to take in your child's evaluation, to monitor the progress of the evaluation, and to maintain a record of how and when the evaluation was conducted and completed—all useful information.

The Evaluation Conference

Once the formal evaluation of your child has been completed, many school procedures call for a meeting or conference with you to explain the results of the testing. If the person in charge of your child's evaluation does not suggest such a meeting, you should request one. Unless you fully understand the results and conclusions drawn from the evaluation, you may have no idea whether your child needs or is eligible for special education services.

Your effective participation in all the remaining phases of the special education process depends in large part on how well you understand your child's learning problems. In order to work confidently with professionals during the upcoming meetings required to plan your child's special education program, you need to know the evaluation team's perspective of your child's current abilities and problems. Therefore, before attending any meetings following the completion of your child's evaluation, make certain someone has explained to your satisfaction the results and conclusions of the evaluation process.

PARENT ACTIONS STEPS
FOR EVALUATION CHART
(Worksheet)

Phase I: Giving/Refusing Permission to Evaluate

Action:_____

_____

Step: _____
Step: _____
Action:_____

_____

Step: _____
Step: _____
Action:_____

_____

Step: _____
Step _____

Phase II: Before Evaluation

Action:_____

_____

Step: _____
Step: _____
Action:_____

_____

Step: _____
Step: _____
Action:_____

_____

Step: _____
Step: _____

Phase III: During Evaluation

Action:_____

_____

Step: _____
Step: _____
Action:_____

_____

Step: _____
Step: _____
Action:_____

_____

Step: _____
Step: _____

Phase IV: After Evaluation

Action: _____

Step: _____
Step: _____
Action: _____

Step: _____
Step: _____

Action: _____

Step: _____
Step: _____

Important Telephone Numbers

_____

_____

_____

_____

_____

Important Dates:

_____

_____

_____

_____

FOUR

= ❖ ❖ ❖ =

School Records
and Reports
Journals of the Journey

To this point, you have collected information about your child's educational needs from two primary sources: from your own and others' observations of your child, and from observations made in the formal evaluation process. Chapter 2 helped you organize your personal observations into a clearly understandable framework, but what do you do with new information produced by your child's evaluation? Even when the results of the evaluation have been interpreted for you, you still may worry about remembering all that was said. Luckily, the school system does not depend solely upon the memory of its professional staff to recall specific children, their progress, and their needs. The memory of the school system is contained within its official records.

As a parent of a child with disabilities, you have special interest in knowing what is contained in your child's school records. This is true because of the significant information these records offer

Material in this chapter has been drawn extensively from *Your Child's School Records*, Washington, D.C.: Children's Defense Fund, 1986.

you about your child and also because of the emphasis schools place on these records when making educational decisions. If any information in your child's records is inaccurate, biased, incomplete, inconsistent, or just plain wrong, this material may well result in inaccurate decisions regarding your child's right to special education services. For these reasons you must know how to obtain, interpret, and correct these records and how to use them effectively in school meetings. This chapter will guide you through the corridor in the special education maze pertaining to school records.

Obtaining Your Child's Records from the Local School

Schools are required by law to maintain certain records and to make these records available to you upon request. In accordance with the federal *Family Educational Rights and Privacy Act,* also known as the Buckley Amendment, every school district must have a written policy governing the management and confidentiality of records. Further, the policy must include a procedure for parents to gain access to confidential records. The term "parent," as used in the Act, is broadly defined. It includes natural parents, guardians, anyone acting as a parent in the absence of the natural parent, and foster parents. Divorced or noncustodial parents have the same rights as custodial parents with respect to their child's school records unless a state law, court order, or binding custody agreement declares otherwise.

Getting copies of your child's school records should be virtually automatic. Begin by asking the school principal about the location of your child's various files or records. These will include a cumulative file, a confidential file and, sometimes, a compliance file. The principal will have the local school's *cumulative file,* which you will want to see and copy. Often the cumulative file contains little more than a profile card with personal identification data and perhaps academic achievement levels, some teacher reports, and report cards.

Also accessible to parents, the *confidential* file may be kept at your child's school, or in a central administrative office where the special education program offices are located. The file is called confidential because access to the information is limited to certain individuals. Your child's confidential record includes all of the reports written as a result of the school's evaluation; reports of independent evaluators, if any; medical records that you have had released; summary reports of evaluation team and eligibility committee meetings; your child's Individualized Education Program (IEP); and, often, correspondence between you and school officials.

Some school systems keep the report of eligibility meetings, correspondence between the parents and school officials, and other similar documents in a separate *compliance* file. The contents of the compliance file demonstrate that the school system has complied with time lines, notification, and consent regulations under P.L. 94–142. A good bit of detective work is sometimes required to understand your school system's individual filing system!

Once you know the location of the records, how do you best proceed to obtain copies of these files? If you want to get a copy of your child's records through the mail, you will most likely be required to sign a release-of-information form.

This can be obtained by calling or writing your school principal or special education director. Other school systems will send records upon receiving a written statement from parents requesting release of information. For this service, a school system can charge you only for the cost of reproducing and mailing the records, not for personnel time or other costs incurred by the school system.

Another way to obtain a copy of your child's records is by appointment. A telephone call to the appropriate office requesting a mutually convenient time for you to review and to make copies of the records often results in a school professional being on hand to guide you through them and to answer any questions. Again, your only expense will be the reproduction costs.

You might ask, "Wouldn't it be better if I go into the office unannounced to see the records?" In fact, there are several reasons why a surprise visit may not be the best strategy:

1. Perhaps you are concerned that if you give the school system prior notice, someone might remove parts of the records and then replace them following the appointment. Although isolated cases of schools removing material from files have indeed been reported, the good faith of both parents and school systems is needed in this area. Should problems develop, several procedures enable you to challenge and request removal of records of questionable value to your child.

2. Even if you do visit the office unannounced, school personnel are not required to show parents their children's records on demand. Often, however, they will accommodate you in an emergency. School systems are required to make records available within forty-five days. Most systems respond to a parent's request within two to five days.

3. A school office, like any office, is run most efficiently when the needs of the people working there are taken into consideration. If you arrive unannounced asking for services that involve the time of office staff, you can interrupt important routines and schedules. By asking for an appointment you continue to build the bridge of mutual respect and consideration needed in effective educational advocacy.

Records Open to Parents

Once you have gained access to your child's records, does this mean you can see any and all records pertaining to your child? Just what records is the school system legally required to show you?

Under the Buckley Amendment, schools must show parents all records, files, documents, and other materials that are maintained by the school system and contain information relating to their children. This includes all records referring to your child in any personally identifiable manner—that is, records containing your child's name, social security number, student ID number, or other data making them traceable to her. Excluded from the records schools must show you, however, are the following: (1)

notes of teachers, counselors, or school administrators made for their personal use and *shown* to nobody else (except a substitute teacher); (2) records of school security police when they are kept separate from other school records and used only for law-enforcement purposes within the local area, and when security police have no access to any other school files; and (3) personnel records of school employees.

Items (1) and (3) of these exclusions often cause parents concern. Frequently, parents whose children are evaluated by school psychologists want to see their children's test papers. Psychologists sometimes refuse to show parents these papers, claiming the tests fall within the personal-notes exemption or that the tests are copyrighted and cannot be disclosed to nonprofessionals. According to the Office of the General Counsel, U.S. Department of Education, test papers (protocols) completed in psychological evaluations and maintained in personally identifiable form are educational records under the Buckley Amendment. Therefore, upon your request, psychologists must show you the test papers and other materials completed by your child during her evaluation. To protect the future validity of the tests, however, psychologists cannot give you copies of these materials.

Similarly, parents often feel they should be able to examine the personnel records of their child's teacher to assess the teacher's academic qualifications and experience. But these records are exempt from such review under the Buckley Amendment and are not open to parental examination. (*Note:* If either the "raw scores" from your child's evaluations or the qualifications of your child's teachers become issues in due process hearings, you may obtain this information either from the files or from direct examination of witnesses during the hearing. More about this in Chapter 9.)

Examining and Correcting Your Child's Records

Even when you have your child's records in your hands, you may wonder what you've got. The language of the educators, psychologists, educational diagnosticians, and other school professionals often appears unintelligible at best and nonsense at worst. If this is the case for you, all you need to do is ask someone to help you. The law requires school personnel to explain the records to you when you do not understand them. Or you may take a friend or a knowledgeable professional with you to help review the records and explain confusing parts. When you do this, however, you will be asked to sign a form giving that person permission to see your child's records.

As you review the records, you may find places where information given about your child or family conflicts with your own assessments. If left unchallenged, this material could lead to decisions about your child's educational program that are not in his best interest. To prevent this from happening, you can follow two paths to address the problem. First, you can informally ask that school officials delete the material, giving your reasons for the request. Often school officials will honor the request and no problem arises. If difficulties do develop and they refuse to remove the requested material, your second approach to correcting the records is the formal hearing.

When you ask for a formal hearing, you should do so in writing, with a letter addressed to the school principal or the school official designated in your school's written procedures. Be certain to keep a copy of the letter for your files in the same way you will want to keep track of all correspondence with the school. The hearing you request will involve a meeting between you and school professionals, presided over by a hearing officer. The hearing officer in this case is usually an official of the school system who does not have a direct interest in the outcome of the hearing. The purpose of the hearing is to allow you and the school system to present evidence about the school record in dispute and to let the hearing officer determine who is right.

Under the Buckley Amendment, the school must schedule a hearing on any disputed records within a "reasonable" time, and you must be notified of the time and place of the hearing "reasonably" in advance. What is "reasonable" in your school system will be spelled out in your local school or state board of education regulations. These same regulations will also explain: (1)

your right to have someone, even an attorney, assist or represent you at the hearing; (2) the length of time the school system has to make its decision after the hearing; and (3) the requirement that the hearing officer include in the decision a discussion of the evidence and the justification and rationale for the decision reached.

Since the hearing officer at a records hearing can be a school official, parents might feel that the proceedings are not fair. Although unfair decisions have been rendered, more often than not the hearing officer will act impartially in deciding the issue. Even if parents are denied their request to have a record removed, further actions may be taken to reduce the negative impact of the disputed report.

The most effective way to handle this problem is to attach to the record a written explanation of your objections, detailing why you believe the material is inaccurate, biased, incomplete, or otherwise inappropriate. Because the school must, by law, keep your statement with the record, everyone who sees the record will be informed of your objection to its contents.

Besides amending the disputed record, you can take two other steps when you believe your "reasonable" requests to correct the records have been improperly refused. As soon as possible after the incident, you can send a letter of complaint to:

Family Educational Rights and Privacy Act
(FERPA) Office
U. S. Department of Education
400 Maryland Avenue, S.W.
Washington, D. C. 20202
Phone: 202/732-2057

This office is responsible for enforcing the Buckley Amendment and will look into your complaint. A second action you can take in some areas is to sue in court. Since most recent court decisions deny individuals the right to private suit under the Buckley Amendment, you should consult an attorney to see if such action is possible where you live. Both of these last options require significant time before action occurs. Therefore, if you use them, you should also amend the record in anticipation of having it removed later.

Finally, you should examine your own state laws regarding your rights to review, to control access to, and to correct your child's school records. State laws may provide parents with more rights in this area than does the Buckley Amendment. To determine if this is the case, you must first obtain and examine copies of the laws and policies regarding records in your state. Again, these laws and policies should be obtainable from your superintendent of schools or other designated officials.

Controlling Who Sees Your Child's Records

The Buckley Amendment prohibits schools from disclosing your child's records to anyone without your written consent. The only exceptions are:

1. school officials (including teachers) in the same district with a "legitimate educational interest," as defined in the school procedures;
2. school officials in the school district to which your child intends to transfer (but only after you have had a chance to request a copy of the records and to challenge their contents);
3. certain state and national education agencies, if necessary for enforcing federal laws;
4. anyone to whom a state statute requires the school to report information;
5. accrediting and research organizations helping the school, provided they guarantee confidentiality;
6. student financial aid officials;
7. people who have court orders, provided the school makes "reasonable" efforts to notify the parent or student before releasing the records;

8. appropriate people in health and safety emergencies such as doctors, nurses, and fire marshals.

According to federal law, police, probation officers, and employers cannot see or receive information from your child's records without your consent. The exception to this rule is where your state has a law, passed before November 19, 1974, *requiring* (not just permitting) schools to give them this information. If such a law exists in your state, your school can provide this information without your consent.

With the preceding exceptions, schools must have your permission to release material from your child's records to anyone other than yourself. When requesting release of the records, the school must tell you which records are involved, why they have been requested, and who will receive them. Likewise, if you want someone outside the school system to see your child's records, you will be asked to sign a release granting such permission. All these precautions have been instituted to protect your privacy and that of your child.

When Your Child Reaches Eighteen or Goes to Postsecondary School

When your child reaches the age of eighteen or enters a postsecondary educational institution such as a vocational-technical school, a college, a university, or trade school, most rights to records previously available to you are transferred to your child. The only parts of her record your child will not have the right to see are your financial records, any confidential letters or statements of recommendation placed in her educational records before January 1, 1975, and any statements or confidential recommendations your child has waived the right to see. This means if you wish to see the school records of a son or daughter who is eighteen or who is attending postsecondary school, he or she must first sign a waiver permitting this action.

Public Law 94–142 gives parents of disabled children special consideration when transferring record rights. The law grants states the authority to develop individual policies which take into account the type and severity of the child's disability and the child's age when transferring record rights from parents to their children. Thus, if your child with disabilities has reached age eighteen or is about to reach eighteen and is in secondary school, you should ask the director of special education if your state has a policy that allows you continued access to your child's records. If your state does not have such a policy, you and school personnel may want to develop a waiver form which your child can sign allowing you continued rights to review, to control access to, and to seek changes in those records.

When You Move

In today's society, people are always on the move. Your child's school records, of course, will move with you. To be certain your child's new school receives only relevant and current records, you should examine the records and identify specifically the material you want forwarded. Most school systems will honor your request and send only the information you want released. Should the school wish to send material you want withheld, you can initiate the hearing procedure described earlier to prohibit its action. In any case, before you move, *always* review your child's school folder. You will want to eliminate the irrelevant, inaccurate, and dated material or attach your critique to those records you believe should have been removed but were not.

Because of the importance of your child's records in determining special education eligibility, you should review and correct them annually, whether or not you move. You should also be certain you have a duplicate copy of all the material in the official files. In this way if the records are lost, as they easily can be in a large school system, you will have copies to replace them.

A Final Note: Thick Records

Classroom teachers have been heard to comment, "When I see a thick set of records of a child new to my class, I know trouble is coming." This is another reason for your diligence in reviewing annually your child's records. Many reports, especially those written several years previously, give little if any information that will be useful in current decisions about your child. A careful weeding out of irrelevant documents can help to avoid the "thick record syndrome."

The Four-Step Record Decoder

When you have obtained the school's records, often a stack of documents an inch or more thick, what will you do with them? How can you begin to make sense of all this material written about your child? You have already organized your home observations of your child into the framework of the Developmental Achievement Chart; now you will organize the school's observations of your child by employing the Four-Step Record Decoder. The decoder helps you organize, read, analyze, and evaluate your child's school records.

Organize

1. After obtaining the complete set of records from the school system, separate the documents describing your child (teacher reports, psychological evaluations, social history, IEPs, etc.) from other documents or correspondence of an administrative nature (the minutes of an eligibility committee meeting, consent forms, etc.). The other documents and correspondence help you keep track of your contacts with the school system.

2. Make an extra copy of the records. In this way you will have an original and a copy you can mark, cut, paste, and use however it will help you.

3. Arrange each set—descriptive reports and other documents—in chronological order.

4. Secure the pages in a folder with a clip or in a loose-leaf notebook so that if you drop them you won't have to back up three steps.

5. Number each report and make a chronological list that can be added on to as new records are generated. The list might look like this:

EDUCATIONAL REPORTS OF SUSAN MARTIN

REPORT	DATE	PERSON REPORTING
1. Psychoeducational evaluation	5/03/89	Katherine Conner
2. Teacher's report	5/89	Cathy Porterman
3. Social history report	5/12/89	Patricia Roberts
4. Psychiatric evaluation summary	6/08/89	Dr. Gerald Brown
5. IEP	6/14/89	Katherine Conner
6. Psychological evaluation summary	8/23/89	Dr. Ronald McPherson
7. Teacher's report	9/14/89	Dru Dunn
8. Psychologist's memorandum	9/14/89	Barbara Hager

Read

1. Read through the entire record to get overall impressions and tones of the school's view of your child.
2. In the margins of your working copy, put a question mark beside the statements or areas of the reports you do not understand or with which you disagree.

Analyze

1. Now reread the reports and underline the phrases or sentences you feel best describe your child's strengths and those that describe your child's problems. Put an "S" in the margin opposite a description of your child's learning strengths; a "P" opposite the problems. When you come to a phrase or sentence reporting your child's learning style, write "LS" in the margin.

2. Using a worksheet similar to the one on pages 75 and 76, place these phrases or sentences about your child's strengths and problems within the developmental categories of movement, communications, social relationships, self-concept/independence, perception/senses, thinking skills, and learning style.
3. After each piece of data put the *source* and *date*. Often you will find trends beginning to emerge. The same observation, said in similar language, may occur in several reports over a period of time.
4. List *recommendations* made by each evaluator or teacher in the last section of the analysis sheet. Recommendations might include services needed, classroom environment, class size, type of school setting, recommendation for further testing, specific teaching materials, or equipment.

Evaluate

Using the question-mark notations you have made in the margins and your overall sense of the records from your analytical work with them, evaluate them against the following criteria:

ACCURATE. Do the reports and portions of the records correspond with your own feelings, perceptions, observations, and assessments of your child?

COMPLETE. Are all the documents required by the school system for the eligibility, Individualized Education Program (IEP), and placement decisions available in the file? For example, medical report, social history, psychological examination, educational report, and others as may be required by your local or state guidelines.

BIAS FREE. Are the reports free from cultural or racial bias? Do they take into consideration the effect your child's disability might have had upon the outcome of the results of the tests?

NONJUDGMENTAL. Do the reports reflect a respect for your child and your family? Do they avoid the use of language that judges rather than describes? Examples of judgmental statements include: She is fickle. He is incorrigible. Examples of descriptive statements include: She is inconsistent in stating what she likes and dislikes. He will not respond to directions to stop disruptive behavior.

CURRENT. Are the dates on the records recent enough to give a report of your child's present behavior and functioning? Records generated within the past three years are generally useful for making good decisions. Older ones should be used with caution.

UNDERSTANDABLE. Is the language used meaningful, clear, and understandable to you? If technical terms (jargon) are used, have they been defined or made understandable to the non-specialist? (Example of an unclear statement: "She appears to have a psychological learning disability, calling for treatment involving a moderation of the special focus on interpersonal sensitivity she has received so far." What does that mean?)

CONSISTENT. Is there consistency among the descriptions of your child given by each evaluator or teacher? Or do you find contradictions and differences of opinion? Considering the record as a whole, does it make sense and lead to the given recommendations?

An example of the analysis sheets of the Record Decoder Sara's parents worked out are found on pages 77 and 78.

By completing your own Record Decoder analysis sheets, you will become thoroughly familiar with your child as seen through the "close-up lens" of her school records. The information contained in these records provides the basis upon which crucial decisions will be made concerning your child's education. The importance of organizing, reading, analyzing, and evaluating your child's school records cannot be overemphasized. Therefore, before continuing to the next phase of the maze, make sure the information in your child's file paints an accurate picture of her.

Four-Step Record Decoder

Data	Source	Date
MOVEMENT Strengths Problems		
COMMUNICATIONS Strengths Problems		
SOCIAL RELATIONSHIPS Strengths Problems		
SELF-CONCEPT/INDEPENDENCE Strengths Problems		

Four-Step Record Decoder   (continued)

Data	Source	Date
SENSES/PERCEPTION Strengths Problems		
THINKING SKILLS Strengths Problems		
LEARNING STYLE Strengths Problems		
RECOMMENDATIONS:		

Four-Step Record Decoder

Data	Source	Date
MOVEMENT		
Strengths		
1) She can catch a bounced ball.	1-3) Mr. Terrance Adaptive P.E. Specialist	1/89
2) She can kick a stationary ball.	1-2) Mrs. Lathrum - psychological test	1/89
3) walks forward on a four foot walking board	3) Mr. Terrance - PE	2/88
Problems	4) Mrs. Thurong - PE Teacher Report	11/89
1) fine motor - trouble drawing and integrating complicated figures		
2) gross motor - large for her age - gives appearance of being uncoordinated		
3) difficulty in integrating motor skills to form motor plan/act		
COMMUNICATIONS		
Strengths	1) Mrs. Ford - speech therapist	6/89
1) Sara has significant improvement in syntax	2) Ms. Chase - spec. ed. teacher report	6/89
2) She eagerly participates in class using appropriate vocabulary		8/87
Problems	1) County Health Dept. report	5/88
1) The problem may be in processing or word finding	2) Ms. Lacey - sp. ed. teacher report	1/88
2) There is a lag in expressive language - difficulty expressing ideas.	3) Mrs. Ford	
3) Poor word finding skills, poor sequencing skills, poor auditory memory and association skills.		
SOCIAL RELATIONSHIPS		
Strengths	1) Ms. Chase - Sp. ed. teacher report	6/89
1) She seems happy, is generally accepted by classmates - has maintained friendships in school.	2) Ms. Lathrum - psychological test	1/89
2) Sara is people oriented, although on an observing type basis.	1) Mrs. Lacey - sp. ed. teacher report	5/88
Problems		
1) She frequently tells peers what to do, and makes negative comments about herself when she makes mistakes.		
SELF-CONCEPT/INDEPENDENCE 1) She works well in a small, structured, positive environment and needs to continue to build a positive self image.	1) Ms. Chase - sp.ed. teachers report	4/89
Strengths	1-2) Ms. Lathrum - psychological test	1/89
Problems		
1) Sara's biggest difficulty is that she feels different, abnormal and rejected.		
2) Extreme need for nurturance and to feel good about herself.		

Four-Step Record Decoder (continued)

	Data	Source	Date
SENSES/PERCEPTION Strengths	1) On Bender-Gestalt test she could copy figures and make them recognizable, despite difficulties she experienced with integration and distortions	1) Dr. Hazlitt, private psychologist	3/89
Problems	1) She doesn't remember details from pictures she sees or stories she has read. 2) On Bender-Gestalt her planning is haphazard and unorganized, her production inconsistent	1) Ms. Chase, Sp.ed. teacher's report 2) Ms. Lothian, psychological test	6/89 1/89
THINKING SKILLS Strengths	1) In reading, her decoding skills are excellent. She has a good sight vocabulary. 2) She has learned addition and subtraction facts- is now learning 2's, 3's, 5's and 10's in multiplication	1) Ms. Chase-sp.ed. teacher report 2) Teacher's report	6/89
Problems	1) She has difficulty following multiple oral directions. 2) Her poor memory has caused problems with remembering math processes.	1-2) Ms. Chase-sp.ed. teacher report	6/89
LEARNING STYLE Strengths	1) She needs a small, structured environment	1-2) Ms. Chase- sp.ed. teacher report	6/89
Problems	2) She is eager to complete her work but often perseverates on favorite assignments 3) Her planning is haphazard and unorganized	3) Ms. Lothian, psychological test	1/89
RECOMMENDATIONS:	1) Helping her break down oral and written directions, repeating them to her, and having her repeat them are helpful techniques. 2) In reading use sight approach, context clues, language experience stories.	1) Ms. Lothian, psychological test 2) Ms. Lacey, sp.ed. teacher	1/89 1/89

Evaluation Troubleshooting

After you have reviewed your child's latest evaluation reports and examined past evaluations in the school file using the Four-Step Record Decoder, you will conclude one of two things. Either you agree that the evaluation results are accurate, complete, consistent, and up to date; or you believe they are deficient in some respect. If you believe the evaluation materials are satisfactory, you move to the next corridor of the special education maze—eligibility determination. But what if you think the evaluation findings are inadequate? What steps do you take next?

You can select one of two paths in attempting to correct the defects you find with the evaluations. One path is informal—you informally ask school officials to remove the faulty evaluation from the record, or undertake additional evaluations, or add materials you provide to the file, or possibly just clarify for you the deficiencies you see in the evaluation findings. Should this approach fail, you can seek to resolve your difficulties through a more formal approach.

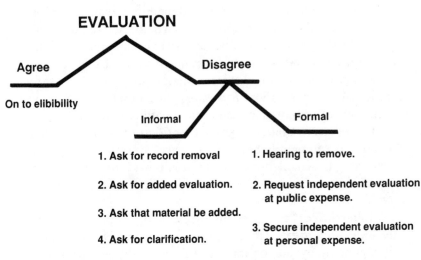

EVALUATION

Agree

Disagree

On to elibility

Informal

Formal

1. Ask for record removal

2. Ask for added evaluation.

3. Ask that material be added.

4. Ask for clarification.

1. Hearing to remove.

2. Request independent evaluation at public expense.

3. Secure independent evaluation at personal expense.

If your problem involves earlier evaluations that are now a part of your child's official school file, you can seek to amend the records by employing the formal process for correcting records described earlier in this chapter. When your concern is the inadequacy of the school's most recent evaluation, you can request that an independent evaluation of your child be made at public expense.

Both federal and state law provide parents the opportunity to obtain an independent evaluation of their child when they believe the school's evaluation is inadequate. An independent evaluation is one made by professionals *not employed by the school system.* Some local school systems maintain a list of professionals or organizations whose personnel meet the licensing criteria for conducting independent evaluations. Sometimes these evaluations may be conducted by the county or state departments of health or mental health. The steps you should follow to secure an independent evaluation are outlined in your state regulations. *But remember!* An independent evaluation paid for at public expense *does not* mean that you, the parent, can choose whomever you wish to make an evaluation of your child. Don't run out and have an evaluation made and send the bill to your school system. If you want an independent evaluation at public expense, begin by requesting one from the director of special education.

Will school officials agree to an independent evaluation? Not always. On the other hand, before they can deny your request, they must hold a due process hearing as described in Chapter 9 and must prove to the hearing officer the appropriateness of their evaluations. Otherwise, the school system cannot deny your request for an independent evaluation. *Remember!* You don't have to prove that the school's evaluation results are incorrect before asking for an independent evaluation—you are entitled to an independent evaluation if you merely believe the school system's findings are inadequate. If school professionals don't wish to agree to the independent evaluation, *they must initiate the hearing procedure to justify denying the request.*

An alternative to the independent evaluation at public expense is the independent evaluation at private expense. If you can obtain an independent evaluation at public expense, why would you ever want to pay for one out of your own pocket? There are several reasons. First, you can personally choose the professionals who will make the evaluation. This often gives you greater confidence in the findings and allows you to select the specialist most appropriate for working with your child. Second, when you pay for your own evaluation, you can control who sees the results. When an independent evaluation is made at public expense, the findings must be considered by the school system in making educational decisions regarding your child. Further, the independent, publicly financed evaluation may be presented as evidence in a due process hearing. If you feel that the independent evaluation is also incorrect, you have no way to stop its being used by the school system or the hearing officer. In contrast, if you pay for the evaluation of your child, you determine how those results are used and who gets to see them. Thus, if you conclude that the results accurately describe your child, you may submit the results for consideration by the school system or a hearing officer. If you are not confident of the findings, you do not have to submit them to the school or at a hearing unless required to do so by the hearing officer.

Although there are many benefits to paying for your child's evaluation, you must weigh these benefits against several potential costs before deciding to have your own evaluation. One major cost is the dollar outlay itself. Complete educational evaluations may cost $600 to $800 or more. When the evaluation merely confirms the school's findings, it may still be beneficial—it gives more reason to believe the initial testing results—but it is an expensive procedure for securing such confirmation. Still another cost occurs if you introduce findings from your own specialists, and these findings are given little or no significance by school officials or the hearing officer. The reason sometimes given for downplaying the importance of such evaluation data is reflected in the comments made by one school official in a due process hearing. According to that official, "Parents can shop around until they find a psychologist or other professional who will say exactly what they want to hear." If the school official or hearing officer with whom you are working has this attitude, the benefits of the evaluation you pay for may not equal their costs.

One last word about obtaining your own evaluations. Never have the evaluation results sent to school officials before you have examined them. On more than one occasion parents have done this to save time, only to discover that the evaluation results worked to their child's disadvantage. Therefore, discuss the evaluation findings with the professionals who developed them first. Then, and only then, decide whether you want the results sent to the school system or the hearing officer.

FIVE

= ❖ ❖ ❖ =

The Eligibility Decision
Passport to the Maze

You have passed through the educational planning cycle's first two phases—referral and evaluation. You have gathered data at home and examined your child's school records with the Four-Step Record Decoder. Now comes phase three—*eligibility*.

The eligibility decision is usually made by a committee. The committee is known by different names in different states; for example, Eligibility Committee, Multidisciplinary Team (M-Team), Placement Advisory Committee (PAC), or Admission, Review, and Dismissal (ARD) Committee. The exact name for this committee and its composition and procedures will be found in your local or state regulations. Some states require, and many encourage, parent participation in the eligibility committee meeting. Whatever the practice in your school system, you will want to be involved in this important meeting.

The procedure followed by the committee to determine your child's eligibility for special education is simple to describe in theory, and often impossible to describe in practice. In theory, here is how the committee operates. Most state regulations for special education include a series of "definitions of handicapping conditions." These definitions vary from state to state. Typical of some states is the following list of handicapping conditions for which eligibility is determined: autistic, deaf, deaf-blind, hard of hearing, visually handicapped, mentally retarded, multihandicapped, orthopedically impaired, other health impaired, seriously emotionally disturbed, severely and profoundly handicapped, specific learning disabled, and preschool developmentally delayed.

Each of these conditions is then defined in the regulations. For example, "mentally retarded means significantly subaverage general intellectual functioning, existing concurrently with deficits in adaptive behavior and manifested during the developmental period, which adversely affects a child's educational performance." If you don't understand this definition or any of the others, which may be equally obscure, ask the school professionals to translate them for you. A translation of the preceding definition of "mentally retarded" might read as follows: "An IQ remaining below a score of 70 for several years. In addition to the low IQ score, the child also shows problems in language, social skills, and other behaviors, all of which have adversely affected the ability to learn."

Remember, when you don't understand the definition of the handicapping condition your child is believed to have, ask to have the definition clarified. You may be surprised to learn that school personnel are themselves sometimes uncertain as to the exact meaning of the definitions. If this is the case, it is important to keep asking until you find someone who can explain the definition to your satisfaction. In this way you can ensure that your child's learning problems are accurately identified.

Each member of the eligibility committee receives copies of the evaluation reports and other relevant information contained in your child's official school file. The evaluation reports will either suggest the presence of one or more handicapping conditions or imply the absence of conditions severe enough to require special education services. The job of the eligibility committee is to compare the results and conclusions of the evaluation against the definitions of handicapping conditions. If the results correspond with one or more of the definitions, your child will be eligible for special education services. Should the committee conclude that the results of the evaluation do not meet the eligibility criteria, your child will be found ineligible for special education. In either case, you will be notified in writing of the committee's decision.

Eligibility in Action: A Case Study

Robert Boswell is seven years old. When he was two, his parents first noticed that his development was slow. Robert always has taken longer and expended much more effort to learn most of the things his brothers and sisters seem to pick up with ease. He has speech problems and uses only short, simple sentences. From the time he entered school, he has received private speech lessons. Because of Robert's continuing problems in school, his teacher suggested he be evaluated for special services. Mr. and Mrs. Boswell agreed with the recommendation and signed permission for the evaluation to take place.

Tests of general intelligence showed Robert to have an IQ of 105. Other tests showed him to have difficulties in coordinating his eyes and hands when copying geometric figures; problems coordinating his hands to catch a ball and his feet to stand on one leg; and difficulty in remembering things he had heard or read. Academic achievement tests found Robert to be more than two years behind his peers in reading and arithmetic.

In the state where Robert lives, the regulations governing special education define *specific learning disability* as:

a disorder in one or more of the basic psychological processes involved in understanding or in using language, spoken or written, which may manifest itself in an imperfect ability to listen, think, speak, read, write, spell, or do mathematical calculations which adversely affects the child's educational performance. The term includes such conditions as perceptual handicaps, brain injury, minimal brain dysfunction, dyslexia, and developmental aphasia. The term does not include children who have learning problems which are primarily the result of visual, hearing, or motor handicaps, of mental retardation, of emotional disturbance, or of environmental, cultural, or economic disadvantage.

When the eligibility committee compared Robert's evaluation reports with the preceding definition, they found that the results matched the definition. He displayed problems in language, reading, and arithmetic. The evaluation results indicated he had difficulty copying various shapes and was unable to distinguish left from right. These and other results showed he had "perceptual handicaps," as well as problems with his movement or motor control. None of these problems could be explained by mental retardation—his IQ, at 105, was in the normal range. Emotional problems, visual or hearing deficits, or environmental, cultural, or economic disadvantages were not found to be the source of Robert's problems. All the signs of the evaluation pointed to language problems and perceptual difficulties. Robert was therefore declared eligible for special education services because of his specific learning disabilities.

Had Robert's IQ fallen below 70, his handicapping condition would probably have been identified as mental retardation. With an IQ in this range and the other characteristics found in the evaluation, his learning problems would have matched those in the definition for mental retardation given earlier in this chapter. He would still have been eligible for special services, but he would have been eligible because of his mental retardation rather than because he had specific learning disabilities.

In the preceding case, the child was found to have only one major handicapping condition. But what happens if evaluation results indicate that a child has two or more handicapping conditions; for example, specific learning disabilities and emotional problems? Usually the eligibility committee will try to identify the primary handicapping condition—the condition most responsible for inhibiting the child's educational growth. If both conditions contribute equally to the child's learning problems, the committee may declare the child multihandicapped and eligible for special education. The identification of the primary disability and the secondary problems will determine the types of special education and related services the child requires.

Role of Parents at the Eligibility Meeting

School systems differ significantly in the extent to which they allow parents to participate in eligibility meetings. Some invite parents to attend the meeting, present their views, be accompanied by professionals to give expert opinions, ask questions of committee members, and be present when the committee takes its final vote. At the other extreme are school systems that fail even to notify parents when the eligibility committee is going to consider their child's case.

Your state and local regulations describe the procedures your school system must use and the time lines it must follow. Regardless of how the regulations read, you should ask to be notified, preferably in writing, when the eligibility committee plans to meet. Most likely a specialist in a certain disability area, the coordinator of special education, or one of the professionals who tested your child will be designated the *case manager.* The case manager produces an overall picture of your child's educational needs from the individual team members' findings and often is the team's representative at the eligibility meeting. Ask that person to notify you of the eligibility committee's meeting time and place. Let him know you would like to discuss your opinions with the committee and participate with the committee as they make their decision. The school system may balk at allowing you to sit with the committee as it discusses your child's case and makes its final decision. While you would hope public schools would not choose to work in such a closed manner, they still may do so. Federal and state laws tend not to require parent participation in final decisions on eligibility. The spirit of these laws, however, is one of openness and increased parent participation. Therefore, more and more school systems are opening eligibility meetings to parents and allowing them to present their opinions. In fact, some states' procedures combine the eligibility determination meeting with the Individualized Education Program meeting, thus requiring parent participation.

When you attend your child's eligibility meeting, you should take the following steps:

1. Get another person—spouse, friend, or professional—to attend the meeting with you. At the eligibility meeting you will find anywhere from four to ten school officials in attendance. If you attend by yourself, you may feel threatened and overwhelmed. You should acquaint the person accompanying you with what you plan to do at the meeting. That person should then make sure you do what you said you would do. He should also be another pair of "ears" at the meeting—listening to what is going on and bringing to your attention any important points you may have missed. Be certain to inform the committee ahead of time that this person will be coming with you to the meeting.

2. After the participants in the meeting introduce themselves and before the official business of the meeting gets under-way, pass around a picture or two of your child for everyone to see. Or, if possible, have your child briefly meet the committee members. Your goal is to help the committee realize that your child is more than a manila folder filled with papers and reports. You want the committee to know that this is a real person—your son or daughter—whose educational needs are in their hands.

3. As the meeting opens, ask the chairperson what procedures will be used, who the voting members are, whether you may stay for the entire time including the deliberations and decision making, what the final outcomes from the meeting will be (i.e., will a decision on eligibility be made now or

later), and when you will be informed officially of the decision. This step is very important since it assures that everyone will proceed with the same expectations for the meeting, thus eliminating much confusion.

4. Present your opinions to the committee in a statement which you have developed prior to the meeting. Most of the material for your presentation may be drawn from the analyses you made using the Developmental Achievement Chart and the Four-Step Record Decoder.

   a. Begin with a carefully written opening statement in which you set forth your conclusions regarding your child's handicapping condition and cite all relevant evaluations and records supporting your point of view.

   b. Describe your child's learning style as well as the developmental problems related to his disabilities.

   c. Refute or explain, where necessary, contradictory data, biases, etc. that you have found in the evaluations and records.

   d. Identify the special education program and services you believe are required to meet your child's learning needs and to build on his learning strengths. Again, cite relevant evaluations and reports supporting these recommendations.

5. In many instances you may wish to bring to the meeting professionals, teachers, and others who have worked with and know your child. Prior to the meeting talk with these people to find out how their opinions and views would add to your case. Ask them to come if you think it would help. You would then develop your presentation to allow them to discuss their views at the appropriate times. Inform the school professional in charge of the meeting that these experts will be accompanying you.

6. Finally, if you can stay during the committee's deliberations, listen carefully to the committee's discussion. If committee members appear to be using biased, inaccurate, incomplete, or out-of-date material or to be making incorrect statements, intervene and explain your concerns. In all these matters remember that diplomacy and tact throughout the meeting will serve you well.

Points of Contention in the Eligibility Meeting

Two major points of contention can arise between parents and school systems as a result of eligibility meetings. One problem occurs if the committee finds the child ineligible for services and the parents believe the child is eligible.* The other problem surfaces if the committee finds the child eligible, but says the child's handicapping condition is something different from what the parents believe it is. For example, the committee may conclude that a child is primarily emotionally disturbed, but the parents feel the child is primarily learning disabled. Or the committee may conclude that the child is mentally retarded while the parents believe his hearing impairment is the major cause of his learning problems.

For parents and children, either of the preceding problems is serious. Both could possibly lead to ineffective educational programming for the child. Therefore, parents should participate actively in the eligibility meeting and not wait for such difficulties to occur before entering the special education maze. By following the suggestions made to this point, you will often be able to head off conflicts. And if that is accomplished, you are halfway through the maze. If, despite your active participation, either of these problems does occur, you may challenge the eligibility

---

* A problem could arise if the eligibility committee found a child eligible for special services but the parents refused to permit their child to receive those services. Under these conditions the school system could request a due process hearing to force the parents to allow their child to receive special education. In practice, however, if parents refuse permission for their children to receive special services, most school systems will not fight that decision through a hearing.

committee's findings through a conciliatory conference or administrative review within the school system or through an impartial due process hearing. (More about these procedures in Chapter 9.) *But don't forget,* if your child is declared ineligible for services, or if you feel the committee has "labeled" your child incorrectly, you do not have to accept these results. *You can appeal these decisions.*

A Final Look at Evaluation and Eligibility

Evaluation and eligibility determination are key phases in the special education cycle. An accurate, perceptive evaluation will pinpoint your child's specific learning problems and in many instances may identify the causes of those difficulties. A valid evaluation, therefore, is essential to a fair and reliable determination of your child's eligibility to receive special education services.

Evaluation results, unfortunately, do not always provide clear, precise insights into your child's learning problems and their causes. When this is the case, the eligibility meeting takes on an even greater importance in your child's educational future. During this meeting, school professionals will review evaluation results, other records, and verbal testimony. They will then interpret what this often confusing information means for your child's future educational placement. You cannot allow this meeting and these decisions to take place without your active participation. By following the previous suggestions for obtaining and interpreting school records, for evaluation troubleshooting, and for participating in the eligibility meeting, you will be able to exert maximum personal influence in the decision-making process. You will have an active voice in your child's educational planning and even if your opinion does not prevail, your systematic planning for the meeting lays the groundwork for seeking a remedy through the appeals procedures described in Chapter 9.

SIX

═ ❖ ❖ ❖ ═

The Individualized Education Program
Road Maps, Sign Posts, One-Way Streets

You have gained your passport to the maze! With the help of the valuable information you developed by observing your child and analyzing her school records, you have successfully passed through the referral, evaluation, and eligibility stages. Now you turn a corner into another corridor of the special education maze. In this corridor, you will begin planning for the specific special education and related services to be included in your child's education program. Here again, you will use your written materials to provide information for your child's Individualized Education Program, or IEP.

What is an IEP?

An Individualized Education Program (IEP) describes the special education and related services specifically designed to meet the needs of a child with disabilities. The program is developed at one or more IEP meetings, and its provisions are detailed in writing in an IEP planning document. In this chapter you will find a description of the IEP *document*—the written plan for your child's own special education program. The six required parts of an IEP are outlined and examples illustrating ways in which parents can contribute to each of the parts are provided. The concepts of least restrictive environment and appropriate education are also discussed. Chapter 7 explores the various aspects of the IEP *meeting*, including when and how the IEP is developed, procedures followed during the IEP meeting, and alternative approaches for participating in creating your child's Individualized Education Program.

The IEP Written Document

As a parent, you play a vital role in developing the IEP planning document—the written description of the program tailored to fit your child's unique educational needs. The IEP is developed *jointly* by parents, educators, and, on many occasions, the person for whom the plans are being made, your *child*. Goals and objectives for your child, based on her current levels of functioning, are outlined by everyone involved in planning and providing services. In addition, the IEP specifies the educational placement or setting, and the related services necessary to reach those goals and objectives. The IEP also includes the date the services will begin, how long they will last, and the way in which your child's progress will be measured.

The IEP is more than an outline of, and management tool for, your child's special education program. The development of the IEP gives you the opportunity to work with educators as equal participants to identify your child's needs, what will be provided to meet those needs, and what the anticipated outcomes may be. It is a commitment in writing of the resources the school agrees to provide. Periodic review of the IEP serves as an evaluation of your child's progress toward meeting the educational goals and objectives jointly decided upon by you and the teachers. Finally, the IEP serves as the focal point for resolving differences you may have with the school system. For all of these reasons, the Individualized Education Program—both the document and the process through which it is developed—is a crucial part of special education—indeed, the cornerstone of special education. Let's take a look at the document itself and what it contains.

IEP Part 1: A Description of the Child

The first component of the IEP answers the question, "Who is this child?" After all, everyone involved in your child's education must come to know the person described in her written program. Basic identifying information, such as name, age, and address, is included. This section of the IEP also contains a description of your child as she is right now. It shows her current level of educational and behavioral performance and describes the effect of her disability on performance in academic and non-academic areas. This information is written in a box or space on the IEP document labeled *Present Level of Functioning and Academic Performance*, or simply *Present Level*, or something similar, depending upon your local school system's IEP format.

You have already collected information necessary to contribute to a description of your child's present level of performance. In Chapter 2, Strengthening Exercise #2, you filled out a column in the Developmental Achievement Chart labeled *Can Do* in each of the developmental areas. In Chapter 4, in the Four-Step Record Decoder, you recorded *strengths* and accomplishments in each developmental area. The *Can Do* and *Strengths* are the information sources for your child's present level of functioning. The following chart presents examples parents have gathered from each source.

DEVELOPMENTAL ACHIEVEMENT CHART
Can Do

- sets the table completely and correctly
- catches the bus, transfers to the subway, and gets to school on time
- follows a recipe to bake a cake
- rolls over from front to back
- skips rope when others turn the rope

FOUR-STEP RECORD DECODER
Strengths

- follows two commands
- knows the multiplication table through the 5's
- consistently uses the "m" sound to indicate need for "more"
- on Peabody Individual Achievement Test (PIAT):
  Reading recognition 2.3 grade level
  Reading comprehension 1.6 grade level
  Math 2.0 grade level
- uses a head pointer on the typewriter to spell words

Besides providing information about your child's development, in Part 1 of the IEP you have the opportunity to contribute your very important information about your child's unique learning style. Be sure to include written descriptions of your child's way of approaching a learning situation. A new teacher may need weeks or months to discover the way in which your child learns best. You can help the teacher and your child avoid some frustrations by including in the "present level" such descriptions as:

- He needs a quiet, secluded place for concentrated work.
- She learns quickly when working in a small group of children.
- He understands and learns better what he hears rather than what he sees.
- She imitates other children and learns from them.

These descriptions of *Can Do*, *Strengths*, and *Learning Style* are the substance of the first part of the IEP. Listing test scores, numerical attainment of 4th grade, IQ 94, age equivalent of three years, or simply naming your child's handicapping condition is insufficient. Descriptive statements are required in order for everyone involved in teaching your child to know her. The description of her present level of performance must be as complete and accurate as possible, for it is the foundation upon which the second part of the IEP, goals and objectives, is built.

IEP Part 2: Goals and Objectives

In the second section of the IEP, you and the other members of the IEP team set goals and objectives that will help your child to master those skills or behaviors you believe she should attain. These goals and objectives for your child's special education program are based upon her present level of functioning described in Part 1 of the IEP.

Before thinking about goals and objectives for your child, a look at the process of setting goals is in order. We set goals for ourselves and for others all the time. What are goals? Simply stated, goals are results to be achieved. You set goals for what you would like to do. You might set a goal to buy a new car, to lose ten pounds, to take a family vacation, or to plant a vegetable garden. In order to set specific goals, you must answer many questions. For example, to plan a vacation you might consider:

Who will go with you? The whole family? Should we invite the grandparents?
What will you do? Go camping? Visit relatives? Swim in the ocean?
How will you get there? By car? By bus?
Where will you go? To the mountains? To the beach?
When will you go and how long will you stay? Early summer? Late summer? To stay forever?

After you and your family have made these decisions, you could write the following goal for your vacation plans:

Goal: My family will drive to the mountains to camp for one week beginning August 4.

This goal for a family vacation contains five necessary ingredients or parts. It answers *who?* will do *what? how? where?* and *when?* These five basic parts are necessary for all clearly stated goals.

In order to reach the goal of the family camping vacation, you must take many smaller steps. You choose a state park to camp in, arrange annual leave from your job, borrow a tent, find a kennel for Rover, and take many other interim steps to make it possible to go to the mountains. These smaller steps are *objectives.*

Goals and objectives for an IEP are structured much the same as described above. Goals are an expression of results to be achieved in the long run; objectives are the intermediate steps necessary to reach the long-range goals. Annual goals written on an IEP state what your child is expected to do in one year. Each goal must be written as:

1. a positive statement that . . .
2. describes an observable event.

A well-written goal not only tells what skill your child will achieve but also is written in such a way that you and others can observe the achievement. Many IEPs contain vague goals whose outcomes are not observable or measurable.

Poorly Written Goals

— Bonnie Jean will improve her self-concept.
— Edward will communicate better.
— Jamie will grow stronger.
— Kevin will learn to write.
— Nina will be cooperative.

None of these poorly written goals fulfills both criteria of being (1) a positive statement that (2) describes an observable skill. None of these poorly written goals contains the five essential parts:

Who? ....will achieve?
What? ....skill or behavior?
How? ....in what manner or at what level?
Where? ....in what setting or under what conditions?
When? ....by what time? an ending date?

A well-written goal contains all five parts.

Well-written Goals
— Edward will use sign language to communicate self-help language in his classroom and speech therapy by June 30.
— Nina will prepare and present an oral report in social studies with two regular education classmates by May 7.

Each of these well-written goals is a positive statement describing an observable skill. They answer the questions of who? will do what? how? where? and when? When goals and objectives are written carefully and specifically, you and everyone else involved in teaching your child will hold the same expectations for her.

As mentioned above, objectives are intermediate steps taken to reach the long-range goal. Just as there are specific interim tasks necessary to make your vacation run smoothly, there are small steps or accomplishments your child needs to make in order to reach the annual goals written on her IEP. Short-term objectives are the steps to be taken between the "present level of performance" and the "annual goal." Short-term objectives contain the same five basic parts as annual goals—the who, what, how, where, and when.

An example of a well-written goal, based upon the present level of performance, with appropriate short-term objectives, is found below. This goal, written by Jamie's parents and teachers, is in the developmental category of movement.

ANNUAL GOAL. Jamie will walk upstairs, using one foot per tread, without assistance, at home and at school, by June 1.

PRESENT LEVEL OF PERFORMANCE. Jamie walks steadily on flat ground but goes up the stairs on her hands and knees.
OBJECTIVE 1. Jamie will walk upstairs with two feet per tread, holding the handrail and an adult's hand, by October 15.
OBJECTIVE 2. Jamie will walk upstairs with two feet per tread, holding only the handrail, by December 1.
OBJECTIVE 3. Jamie will walk upstairs one foot per tread, holding the handrail and an adult's hand, by March 15.

The goal and each of the objectives fulfill the requirements for well-written goals and objectives. They describe milestones for Jamie's accomplishment that can be observed within a specific time frame as she works toward the goal of climbing stairs unassisted.

You may have many questions as you think about goals and objectives for your child. For example:

1. *How can I know if a goal is reasonable to expect of my child? Does it demand too much or not enough of her?*

The answer to this question lies in part with the IEP meeting. A group of people, including parents, specialists, and past and present teachers who are knowledgeable of the child and knowledgeable of child development and handicapping conditions, are brought together in the IEP meeting to discuss reasonable expectations. Goals are set while looking at present levels of performance—what she can do now—at the rate your child has been developing thus far, and at the sequence and timing of normal growth and development. These considerations are helpful in setting appropriate goals and short-term objectives. You, or the teacher, do not have to set goals and objectives alone. A group works together.

2. *Should goals and objectives be written for all aspects of her education?*

Goals and objectives are required for all special education services, including vocational education. If your child has been declared eligible for related services such as speech therapy or a special adapted physical education program, goals and objectives must be written in each specialized area. "Bonnie Jean will receive speech therapy" or "Bonnie Jean will be in adaptive P.E." are not acceptable ways to describe the services. Goals must be written to describe what she will accomplish in language or physical development. For example, if Bonnie Jean's present level of performance in language describes her use of two-word phrases, an example of a goal might be: "Bonnie Jean will speak in three-word sentences using noun, verb, object construction in the classroom and speech therapy by May 15." This goal, built on her present level of functioning, serves to alert all teachers and her parents to work consistently toward the next step in her growth in communication skills.

3. *Must goals and objectives be written on the IEP for the parts of her program in the regular education classroom?*

Generally, goals and objectives are required only for special education services. Goals and objectives cover those areas of development in which your child has special problems. However, if any changes or modifications are necessary for your child to participate in a regular education program, those modifications must be described in the IEP. This requirement applies to all regular classes in which your child might enroll— vocational education, social studies, science, art, music and physical education. For example, if a visually impaired student needs to use a tape recorder in a lecture class, or sit close to the lecturer, this adaptation must be noted in his IEP.

A related question is whether the regular teacher is required to be informed of the contents of a student's IEP. The policy of the U.S. Department of Education states that the regular education classroom teacher should have a copy of the IEP, or at the very least be informed of its contents.* In some instances school systems have gone beyond the minimum requirements. They require the regular education teacher to participate in the development of the IEPs for special education students in their classrooms. At the very least, parents should request the active participation of the regular educators. In addition, the school system should provide the special educator or other specialist time to consult or give assistance to the regular classroom teacher.

In practice, school districts vary as to how much information flows between regular teachers and special education teachers. As parents, you will want to talk to each of your child's teachers to make sure they are informed of her educational needs. You may find it necessary to request a joint conference with all of your child's teachers and specialists in order to coordinate the various aspects of the IEP.

4. *Is it necessary for parents to develop knowledge and skills to write goals and objectives?*

Some parents have found they are able to acquire this skill by understanding the essential requirements for writing goals and objectives and by applying them to their child. Other parents prefer to leave the actual writing of goals and objectives to the educators who have the training and experience to develop them. They are careful, however, to know in which developmental areas they feel their child needs special attention. Knowing how goals and objectives are structured, they are able to critique and offer suggestions concerning the goals and objectives written by the educators. In either case, the better you understand the nature of goals and objectives and your child's abilities and problems, the more effective you will be as a member of the educational planning team. With your help, goals and objectives can be written very specifically for your child's needs and can allow you and her teachers to assess her rate of growth and her developmental progress.

---

* "Department of Education Policy Interpretation: IEP Requirements," *Federal Register*, March 31, 1981.

IEP Part 3: Special Education Placement

It is all well and good to have specific goals and objectives for your child—but goals and objectives are not enough! Next come decisions concerning placement. Where, or in what educational setting, can these goals and objectives best be met by your child? Part 3 of the IEP describes the special education placement to be provided your child, and the amount of participation she will have in the regular education classroom.

In years past, children with special education needs were placed in classrooms solely on the basis of disability groupings. For example, children with physical disabilities such as cerebral palsy, or children able to move about only with the help of a wheelchair, were placed in classrooms in which all students had physical disabilities. Similarly, students who had learning problems associated with Down syndrome or other mental retardation were automatically grouped with students with the same disabilities. The IEP requirements under P.L. 94–142 call for changes in the ways of grouping children. The IEP focuses the attention of parents, teachers, administrators and therapists on ability as well as on disability. Goals and objectives are formulated in order to use the student's learning strengths to overcome or compensate for the disabilities. Clearly, the intent of P.L. 94–142 is to determine a student's placement only after the IEP goals and objectives have been worked out mutually with parents, educators, and, very often, the student. The placement decision is then made on the basis of the strengths and needs of the student, by choosing a learning environment in which the educational goals and objectives can best be carried out.

But, you ask, on what criteria is this placement decision based? Two equally important factors must be weighed and balanced as you participate in making the placement decision:

1. the appropriate educational program; and
2. the least restrictive environment.

The words of the Education for All Handicapped Children Act herald these two provisions which are the heart of the new opportunities for our nation's disabled children.

> It is the purpose of this Act to assure that all handicapped children have available to them . . . a free appropriate public education which emphasizes special education and related services designed to meet their unique needs. To the maximum extent appropriate, handicapped children, including children in public or private institutions or other care facilities, are educated with children who are not handicapped.

What is meant exactly by the words "appropriate education"? How will you know if your child is receiving an appropriate education?

For years after the passage of P.L. 94–142, parents, educators, and even judges disagreed as to what was required under the law to meet the standard of an appropriate education. Then in 1982 the U.S. Supreme Court provided some clarification when it concluded that an "appropriate education" means the provision of personalized instruction with sufficient related services reasonably calculated to permit a disabled child to benefit from special education. While programs and services that provide only minimal academic achievement do not meet the requirement of an appropriate education, the Supreme Court stated that an "appropriate education" did not require programs and services designed to maximize a child's potential. State legislative standards, on the other hand, may exceed the federal requirements. Massachusetts' law, for example, requires the "maximum possible development in a least restrictive environment consistent with students' special needs."

The Supreme Court's clarification is important for you because it reinforces the idea that an appropriate education is personalized to the individual needs of your child. Children in special education are not to be given identical programs just because they have the same disabilities. Further, an appropriate program requires that your child receive programming and services that are reasonably calculated to permit her to benefit from them. This means that the proposed program and services must be designed in terms of content, procedures, and duration to lead to the student's development. Finally, a program which would appear to result in only minimal academic achievement would also fail to meet the standard of an appropriate program.

The planning activities you have completed for evaluation, eligibility, and the development of IEP goals and objectives will help you to develop the personalized education program to which your child is entitled. Your close work and contact with teachers and other school professionals during these activities will allow you to determine whether your child's program and services will reasonably allow her to develop beyond a minimal level in the coming year. As the year progresses, you will be able to assess the appropriateness of the program by comparing your child's development with anticipated goals and objectives. Should your child's progress appear minimal or non-existent after a period of months, you may well question the appropriateness of the program. This situation might call for a special meeting of the IEP committee, as will be discussed in the next chapter.

Once you have designed an appropriate program for your child, you must next determine the least restrictive environment in which this program can be provided. The least restrictive environment for a child with disabilities is defined by the extent to which the child will be educated in the public schools with students who are not disabled. Rather than being in separate special education classrooms with special teachers, more and more children with disabilities are now being integrated into regular classrooms. The special education teachers and specialists work alongside the regular education teachers. In these integrated classrooms, all children,—both disabled and non-disabled—ideally experience the benefits of friendships and of learning from one another. Further, following graduation from school, young people with disabilities are more often ready to move into community jobs and independent living if they have had opportunities to work and learn with their nondisabled peers.

For these reasons, P.L. 94–142 requires opportunities for disabled students to participate in all nonacademic and extracurricular activities on a nondiscriminatory basis and in the least restrictive environment. These activities include meals, recess, athletics, and special interest groups and clubs. You will want to make sure your child is able to take advantage of these activities with children who do not have disabilities.

Some school systems emphasize that any student with disabilities can be successfully placed in a regular education learning environment if appropriate program modifications and related services are provided. Nevertheless, most school systems follow an approach for placing children which has predominated for many years. This approach uses the "continuum model" of services devised by Evelyn Deno.* Deno developed a diagram describing the various combinations of educational placements typically available to children in special education. This diagram, found below, can assist you in thinking about placement for your child which is both educationally appropriate and least restrictive.

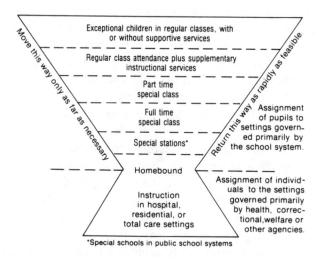

---

* Evelyn N. Deno, *Educating Children with Emotional, Learning and Behavior Problems* (Minneapolis, Minn.: University of Minnesota, Leadership Training Institute/Special Education), 1978, p.109.

The continuum model illustrates the variety of settings in which a child with disabilities may be served. The tapered design is used to indicate the considerable difference in numbers of children likely to be involved at the various levels of service. At the top of the chart is the least restrictive setting for a student in a special education program. At this level, the student spends all day in the regular classroom with related services provided either within that classroom or in a therapy setting. As stated above, this type of setting is being used more often than ever before for students with all types of disabilities and with all degrees of severity of problems. Moving down the continuum, you find the child spending more of her time with other students who also are disabled. As the progressive narrowing of the diagram indicates, the most specialized, most restrictive facilities are needed by very few children.

To use the continuum model, you begin at the top of the diagram and ask, "Is the regular classroom, or the regular classroom with related services, the learning environment in which my child's goals and objectives will best be met?" This type of special education setting is now considered appropriate for many children who previously might have been excluded from participation in the regular classroom with nondisabled children. For example, Juanita uses a wheelchair to move about. In past years she was assigned to a separate classroom for children who are physically disabled. This year, however, her goals and objectives indicate regular classroom placement with the related service of physical therapy twice a week. The school building in which she will attend eighth grade now has ramps for her to move to various levels of the building. Juanita's program was based on both factors:

1. **The appropriate educational program.** The IEP goals and objectives include physical milestones, academic achievements, and social/emotional growth. Juanita will receive the related service of physical therapy for thirty minutes twice a week to assist in her physical development.

2. **The least restrictive environment.** Juanita's goals and objectives can be realized in the regular education program, which provides maximum time for Juanita in a classroom with children who are not disabled. She will be separated from her eighth-grade classmates for only one hour each week for physical therapy. Her therapy requires equipment that cannot be brought into the regular classroom.

In every special education placement for every child, the appropriate education and the least restrictive environment must be given equal consideration. Many people have misinterpreted the least restrictive environment to mean that all children with disabilities will be put into the mainstream, or regular education classroom. The least restrictive environment concept, however, must always be coupled with what is appropriate education for each individual child. For Sally, a fourteen-year-old girl who needs instruction in feeding herself, in learning to sit, and in basic self-care, the appropriate education in the least restrictive environment might be in a special class all day. The maximum extent of her involvement with children who are not disabled might be with peer tutors from regular classrooms. Other contact with nondisabled students might come from her attendance at assembly programs, music classes, and daily lunch in the cafeteria.

In a few situations, public school systems find that they simply do not have the programs or services required to provide a child with an appropriate education. For example, financial reasons may make it impossible for the school system to hire or to contract with professionals to deliver these programs. In other instances, there may be a shortage of certain professionals within a community or there may be only one child who requires highly specialized services. Even in situations like these, P.L. 94–142 requires school systems to provide the child with a free, appropriate public education.

When there are no public programs within the state to meet the child's educational needs, school systems place children in private day or residential schools. These private placements are legally more restrictive than special schools in the public school system because they separate the child both from her nondisabled peers and her public school classmates. According to P.L. 94–142, the private school placement is considered a last alternative placement for a child to receive an appropriate education. The law requires that before employing this placement option, school officials and parents should explore every way possible for delivering a free, appropriate education within the public school system. If an appropriate education cannot be provided within the public schools or through other public institutions within the state, then the school system has a duty to provide the child with an appropriate education in a private school at no expense to the parents.

For many years, the framework provided by Deno's continuum model of special education services has helped parents and school personnel plan for each child's individualized education. By moving down the diagram *only* as far as necessary for appropriate education, each child with disabilities can be assured of education in the least restrictive environment.

Below are three examples of special education placements planned for children in IEP meetings.

EXAMPLE 1. Robert will be in the regular education classroom throughout the school day. The itinerant teacher for children with visual impairments will provide talking books, consultation with the teacher about classroom adaptations, and individualized instruction for Robert on a one-to-one basis.

EXAMPLE 2. Martha's reading, arithmetic, spelling, and handwriting goals will be met in the learning disabilities resource classroom. She will participate in social studies, science, music, and art in the third-grade regular education classroom. Special physical education will be provided by a teacher trained in working with people with physical disabilities.

EXAMPLE 3. Claudia will attend a special school for her academic training and her self-care skills. Her program will include vocational training at community job sites in homemaking, gardening, and food service.

Although these three special education placements seem very different, they each fulfill two major requirements under P.L. 94-142. They are each specifically designed to provide one particular child an appropriate education in the least restrictive environment.

IEP Part 4: Related Services

In addition to the classroom setting for your child's special education program, the IEP describes related services to be provided at no cost to you, the parents. These services might include, but are not limited to, one or more of the following, as defined in the regulations for P.L. 94–142:

AUDIOLOGY

1. identification of children with hearing loss;
2. determination of the range, nature, and degree of hearing loss, including referral for medical or other professional attention for the habilitation of hearing;
3. provision of habilitative activities, such as language habilitation, auditory training, speech reading (lipreading), hearing evaluation, and speech conservation;
4. creation and administration of programs for prevention of hearing loss;
5. counseling and guidance of pupils, parents, and teachers regarding hearing loss; and
6. determination of the child's need for group and individual amplification, selecting and fitting an appropriate aid, and evaluating the effectiveness of amplification.

COUNSELING SERVICES

Services provided by qualified social workers, psychologists, guidance counselors, or other qualified personnel.

EARLY IDENTIFICATION

The implementation of a formal plan for identifying a disability as early as possible in a child's life.

MEDICAL SERVICES

Services provided by a licensed physician to determine a child's medically related handicapping condition which results in the child's need for special education and related services.

OCCUPATIONAL THERAPY

1. improving, developing, or restoring functions impaired or lost through illness, injury, or deprivation;
2. improving ability to perform tasks for independent functioning when functions are impaired or lost; and
3. preventing, through early intervention, initial or further impairment or loss of function.

PARENT COUNSELING AND TRAINING

Assisting parents in understanding the special needs of their child and providing parents with information about child development.

PHYSICAL THERAPY

Services provided by a qualified physical therapist.

PSYCHOLOGICAL SERVICES

1. administering psychological and educational tests, and other assessment procedures;
2. interpreting assessment results;
3. obtaining, integrating, and interpreting information about child behavior and conditions relating to learning;
4. consulting with other staff members in planning school programs to meet the special needs of children as indicated by psychological tests, interviews, and behavioral evaluations; and
5. planning and managing a program of psychological services including psychological counseling for children and parents.

RECREATION

1. assessment of leisure function;
2. therapeutic recreation services;

3. recreation programs in schools and community agencies; and
4. leisure education.

SCHOOL HEALTH SERVICES

Services provided by a qualified school nurse or other qualified person.

SOCIAL WORK SERVICES

1. preparing a social or developmental history on a handicapped child;
2. group and individual counseling with the child and family;
3. working with those problems in a child's living situation (home, school, and community) that affect the child's adjustment in school; and
4. mobilizing school and community resources to enable the child to receive maximum benefit from his or her educational program.

SPEECH PATHOLOGY

1. identification of children with speech or language disorders;
2. diagnosis and appraisal of specific speech or language disorders;
3. referral for medical or other professional attention necessary for the habilitation of speech or language disorders;
4. provisions of speech and language services for the habilitation or prevention of communicative disorders; and
5. counseling and guidance of parents, children, and teachers regarding speech and language disorders.

TRANSPORTATION

1. travel to and from school and between schools;
2. travel in and around school buildings; and
3. specialized equipment (such as special or adapted buses, lifts, and ramps), if required to provide special transportation for a handicapped child.

In the same way that present level of performance, goals, objectives, and classroom placement are individually determined for children during the IEP process, so, too, are related services. Part of your child's right to an appropriate education is the receipt of those related services necessary for her to benefit from special education. Once you and school professionals have determined through the evaluation process that your child needs certain related services and have included them in the IEP, the school system has a legal duty to provide those services. This duty exists even when the particular related services are not, for any reason, currently available within the school system. For example, if physical therapy, social work services, or language therapy were not provided by school employees but your child needed them to benefit from her program, the school system would have to provide these services by contracting with outside professionals.

As you think about possible related services the school might provide your child, many questions will probably arise. What kinds of services are needed? For what length of time each day or week? Who will provide the services? How can I ensure that the receipt of related services does not take my child from the classroom so often as to interrupt her regular school program? How can I make certain that therapists and teachers talk together so there is consistency in my child's program?

To answer these questions, you will need to discuss your child and her needs with teachers, therapists, administrators, and other school personnel. You may also find it helpful to ask questions of specialists outside the school system, discuss your child's need for related services with physicians, and talk to other parents whose children require similar services. Information and materials on related services available from the professional and other organizations listed in Appendix C may also assist you in answering these questions.

After you have accumulated information from a variety of sources, you will be able to weigh and balance the needs of your child for related services, the different ways and times for integrating services into your child's program, and the potential benefits your child will receive from those services. In this manner you can determine your priorities for your child's related services as you prepare for and participate in the IEP meeting.

IEP Part 5: Time and Duration of Services

You have moved through four stops along the IEP corridor in the special education maze. The fifth stop guarantees you won't get stuck in one place. In this section the starting times and duration for your child's program are determined. Once the goals and objectives are written and the services decided upon, the school system has a duty to begin these services without undue delay. Most states specify the number of days within which a program must begin once parents have signed permission for the program. At no time is a child to wait at home for special education services to begin, unless an agreement has been reached between you and the school system for a temporary homebound program. Occasionally, a temporary or interim placement is required, to which parents and the school system must agree.

Under ordinary circumstances, a date is determined in the IEP meeting for the beginning of each of your child's services. In addition, the expected duration for each service is recorded. The expected duration might be six weeks for a related service of counseling with a social worker, to be followed by an assessment of progress and a recommendation for either continuing this service or ending it. Or the expected duration may be a nine-month school year for such parts of the program as classroom placement.

In some cases children with severe disabilities might require more than the usual number of school days in order to receive an appropriate education. Children eligible for an extended school year are those who show significant regression during breaks in their education and who regain their losses so slowly that they would be unlikely to attain their potential level of self-sufficiency and independence without a sustained program. In each case, provision of additional schooling beyond the normal school year must be determined on an individual basis and written into the IEP.

In general, the long-term duration for services should be projected no further than one year. This is because P.L. 94–142 requires an annual review of the services provided in the IEP. Once a year at the IEP meeting, a review is conducted to determine whether your child's special education services are still appropriate and are provided in the least restrictive environment. This annual review, discussed more fully in Chapter 10, ensures that no child will be left in special education without a careful examination of her changing needs.

In addition to specifying the long-term duration of your child's services, Part 5 of the IEP should also include short-term, daily hours for each service. For example, "Jessica will attend speech therapy twice a week, on Monday and Thursday, from 10:00 to 10:30." Certainly parents will want to get specific information on the times and timing of all parts of their child's school program. Too often children who receive special services miss some of the most important parts of the instruction in the classroom. For example, when Willie went to the learning disabilities resource room for special instruction in math, he missed his reading group in the regular education classroom. He was falling behind in reading until his parents talked to his regular class teacher and the resource room teacher. As a result, both teachers adjusted their schedules in order to accommodate Willie's instruction in reading and in math.

IEP Part 6: Evaluating the IEP

How do you know if your child is making progress? To find out, you and your child's teachers periodically need to conduct evaluations to determine if short-term objectives are being met. Part 6 of the IEP—called "Objective criteria and evaluation procedures"—allows you to plan the dates these evaluations will take place, and the evaluation procedures that will be used.

The critical element in evaluation comes in writing clear, measurable, observable goals and objectives. When a goal such as "Suzy will improve self-esteem," is written, parents and teachers will be hard pressed to know when and how Suzy has arrived at this improved state of well-being. A specific annual goal for Suzy might be, "Suzy will demonstrate pleasure in her own accomplishments by planning and completing classroom projects on time by June 30." A short-term objective might be, "Suzy will choose two classmates, with whom she will cooperatively plan and complete an art project to illustrate a story in the fifth-level reader, by January 14." To evaluate the objective, parents and teachers might ask the following questions:

1. Was the art project completed on time?
2. Did Suzy read and comprehend the story?
3. Did the teacher observe and note incidents to illustrate Suzy's cooperation with classmates?
4. What indications show that Suzy made plans for the project? What were the materials chosen? Who took responsibility for what parts of the project?
5. How did Suzy demonstrate pleasure in her accomplishments? Did she urge her parents to come to open house to see it? Was she eager to show and tell about the project?

Specific goals or objectives such as those written for Suzy allow parents and teachers to ask critical questions about a child's growth and development. When Suzy completes the objective, her parents and teachers could conclude that she would have good feelings about her school work, about herself, and about her relationships with her classmates.

At least once a year, and at any other time when a teacher or parent requests it, a meeting is held to review progress toward goals and objectives. Very often in the space on the IEP for "objective criteria and evaluation procedures," you will see written "teacher-made tests" or "teacher assessment." You may wish to inquire about these tests. What will they be? When will they be given? Are there other ways of measuring progress? Tape recordings, examples of schoolwork, classroom observations, completed projects, standardized tests, and many other techniques are useful in evaluation. By using information from a variety of sources, the teaching team comprised of teachers, specialists, and parents can measure progress in a student's growth and learning.

A Planning Chart for the IEP

Now that you have passed the five stops in the IEP corridor, you may wish to make a copy of and complete the following chart to prepare for the upcoming IEP meeting. You will concentrate on those areas of development in which your child has particular problems and needs special services to help in overcoming or compensating for those problems. In the first column, write a brief description of the problem, followed by the "Present Level of Functioning" in the second column. Columns three and four are spaces for your ideas for long-range goals and short-term objectives to help your child with the problem. In the fifth column you can note the special education and related services that you believe can best help your child reach those objectives. Finally, the sixth column provides a space for your ideas for checking progress on the goals and objectives. Following the blank chart, you will find an example of an IEP Planning Chart filled out by Sara's parents before they attended her IEP meeting. A sample of Sara's IEP is found on pages 122 and 123.

Conclusion

Once your planning is completed, you will be well prepared to attend the IEP meeting. The work you have done in filling out the IEP Planning Chart will lay the foundation for your active, informed participation in the important decisions to be made about your child's education. The next chapter will show you how best to use your valuable insights into your child's growth, development, and learning style so you and your child's teachers can plan an appropriate special education program.

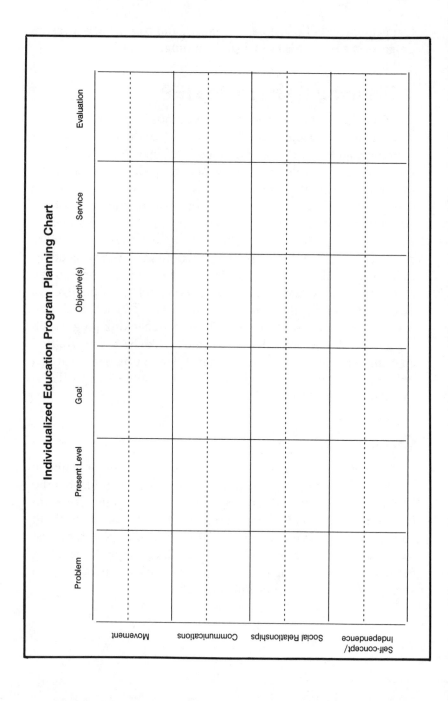

Individualized Education Program Planning Chart

	Problem	Present Level	Goal	Objective(s)	Service	Evaluation
Self-concept/ Independence						
Social Relationships						
Communications						
Movement						

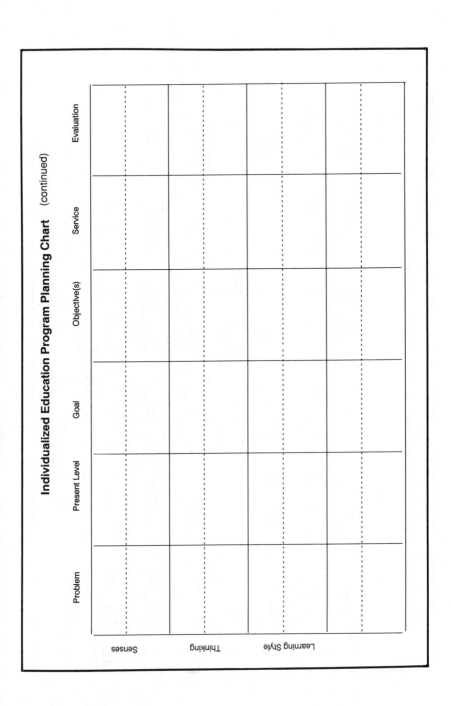

Individualized Education Program Planning Chart (continued)

	Problem	Present Level	Goal	Objective(s)	Service	Evaluation
Senses						
Thinking						
Learning Style						

Individualized Education Program Planning Chart

Sara

	Problem	Present Level	Goal	Objective(s)	Service	Evaluation
Movement	Uncoordinated	She gives up in the middle of an obstacle course	To find her way across an obstacle course	1) Practice skills for individual sections of course 2) understand what to do on entire course	Adaptive PE	By June 30 she will complete obstacle course unassisted
Movement	Trouble drawing human figures	Draws simple shapes and people figures	To draw more complex figures in a recognizable way	1) Draw shapes using a stencil 2) Draw shapes without using stencil; add on features	Special ed classroom and reg. ed. art class	By June 30 Sara's human figure will include 18 specific features
Communications	Can't think of common words	Forgets names of common household items - toothbrush, ketchup, radio	To increase her ability to use the right words	1) Work with new vocabulary words 2) Use new words correctly and spontaneously	Special ed Classroom	Tape recorded observations
Communications	Poor Sequencing Skills	Talks about daily activities with no attention to the proper order	To tell about her day or weekend in sequential order	1) Sara will talk about single experiences 2) She will keep an activity calendar	Speech/ Language Therapy	Tape recordings Compare to goal tape
Social Relationships	Frequently tells peers what to do	Insists her friends play Barbie dolls or she won't play	With a classmate will plan a project in a "give and take" way	1) Plan with a friend under adult direction and praise 2) Work with classmate independently	Special ed. Classroom	Observation of Spec. ed. teacher
Social Relationships	She feels different from others	Asks why she is in special classes and her sister is not	Sara will describe ways she is same/ different from a friend	1) Describe same/ different clothing 2) Identify some different personality traits	Special ed. and regular classes and home with family and friends	observation notes
Independence/ Self-concept	Makes negative comments about herself when she makes mistakes	She says "I hate myself" when she does something wrong	Sara will praise herself verbally for a job well-done.	1) She will smile when praised 2) Imitate a shoulder shrug when she makes mistakes	All teachers and family	Teacher and parent observations
Independence/ Self-concept	Always wants mom to be around	Sits and waits alone on front porch for long periods if mom is not home on time.	To make independent decision to go to neighbors when she gets home from bus alone.	1) Make a chart/ decision plan for alone time 2) Explain plan to teacher and neighbor	Spec. ed. teacher home and neighbor	Parent Observation Chart Completed

Individualized Education Program Planning Chart

Sara (continued)

	Problem	Present Level	Goal	Objective(s)	Service	Evaluation
Senses	Doesn't remember details of picture	Remembers vaguely the whole picture but not details.	To look at picture and describe more than 2 details	1) Identify missing details in picture by drawing them in 2) She will name missing details	Spec. ed. classroom	Oral Test
Senses	Difficulty following Oral Directions	Follows one direction at a time	To carry out 3 directions given at one time	1) Follow one command correctly 2) Repeat directions aloud before acting	Spec. ed. Classroom Speech therapy home	Informal teacher made tests
Thinking	Disorganized way of retelling a story she has read	Tells about story in a disorganized way; no attention to proper order.	To understand and tell main ideas in short stories	1) Describe main character 2) Decide on main ideas 3)	Spec. ed. classroom Oral Book report time	By June, she will present an oral book report and accurately tell main ideas.
Thinking	Does not understand value of coins	Confuses nickels, dimes and quarters; both value and name	To buy something and count the change	1) Learn the name and value of each coin 2) Count money with mixed change	Spec. ed. Classroom	Demonstrate use of money
Learning Style	Haphazard planning	Leaves one homework subject to start another; then leaves both unfinished	To plan alone how to do her school work	1) With adult help, she will learn to break tasks into small steps 2) Make her own charts	Spec. Ed. Classroom	Completed planning charts Successful accomplishment
Learning Style	Very concrete - not able to think abstractly	Doesn't understand jokes or puns that are the least bit subtle	To learn to tell a joke	1) Read a riddle, explain meaning to teacher 2) Tell riddle from memory	Speech/Language therapy	Tell the class a joke or riddle

INDIVIDUALIZED EDUCATION PROGRAM

Student Name Sara Austin DOB 10/8/80
Student ID# 72348
Current Assignment Queensbury School
4th grade

DATES
Initial IEP 9/86
Current IEP 9/89
IEP Review 6/90

EXCEPTIONAL EDUCATION ASSIGNMENT(S):	INITIATION DATE	ANTICIPATED DURATION	PERSON RESPONSIBLE
Learning disability resource room 15% of time/week at Queensbury School	9/89	6/90	Roberta Chase

(Location / Program / Organization / Time)

RELATED SERVICES:			
Speech and language therapy ½ hr. 3x/week	9/89	6/90	Phyllis Find
Occupational therapy ½ hr. 2x/week	9/89	6/90	Paul Cecil

EXTENT TO WHICH STUDENT WILL PARTICIPATE IN GENERAL OR
VOCATIONAL EDUCATION: 85% in general education
                        program

REQUIRED SPECIAL AIDS, SERVICES, OR EQUIPMENT:
N.A.

Subject Hours/% of time	Subject Hours/% of time
English, Social Studies,	Art/Music 1 hr./week
& Science 20 hrs/week	

Vocational Education
Physical Education X Regular ___ Adaptive

IN ATTENDANCE AT IEP MEETING:

	Signature	Date		Signature	Date
LEA Representative (Title: Principal)	Louis Fischer 9/89				
Parent(s), Guardian(s) or Surrogate Parents (s)	Nina Austin 9/89	Robert Austin 9/89			
Student					
Teacher(s)	Anna Chase 9/89				
Evaluator(s)					
Other(s)					

Student Name **Sara Austin**
Student ID# **72348**
Exceptional Education Assignment **LD Resource Room**

PERFORMANCE OR SUBJECT AREA: Math

PRESENT LEVEL: Adds and subtracts 2 digit numbers
Counts to 50 by 5's
Identifies penny, but confuses nickels, dimes, quarters

ANNUAL GOAL:
Sara will be able to make change for a dollar using pennies, nickels, dimes and quarters by June.

EVALUATION OF SHORT-TERM INSTRUCTIONAL OBJECTIVES

SHORT-TERM INSTRUCTIONAL OBJECTIVES	Criterion for for Mastery	Evaluation Procedures and Schedule to be used	Results/ Date
1. Sara will discriminate between the 4 different coins.	Accurately name the coins — 100%.	Teacher observation using real coins by Oct. 29.	
2. Sara will identify the coin and its value.	Write number value under picture of coin.	Worksheets on coins completed accurately in independent work by Jan. 1.	
3. Sara will make change for a dime in three ways.	Demonstrate with real coins.	Teacher observation by March 1.	
4. Sara will make change for a quarter in three ways.	Use pennies, nickels & dimes to make a quarter accurately — 100%.	Teacher observation by April 6.	
5. Sara will purchase a box of crayons at school store and count change.	Purchase completed with 100% accuracy.	Crayons and correct change given to teacher by May 27.	

NOTE: Additional performance or subject area pages would be completed for Sara Austin's IEP.

= ❖ ❖ ❖ =

SEVEN

The Individualized Education Program Meeting

Selecting the Route

Your child's Individualized Education Program (IEP) is the cornerstone of his special education program. The IEP meeting is an opportunity for you and the school system to combine your separate areas of expertise and jointly come up with the appropriate education program for your child.

Because your contributions to the IEP meeting are so important, P.L. 94–142 requires schools to follow specific procedures and time lines to ensure your participation. The school district must tell you, in writing, and in ways that you can understand, when the meeting will be held, its purpose, and who will attend. The school also has to schedule the IEP meeting at a time that is agreeable both to you and the school personnel involved. This meeting must be held within 30 calendar days of the date the school finds your child eligible for special education services. Additionally, IEP meetings must be held at least once a year; more often if requested by a teacher or parent.

Building on the suggestions given in Chapter 6, the following section offers hints for preparing for the meeting and for making your contributions once you are there. Each time you are notified of an IEP meeting, you may want to reread this section to decide which of the many suggestions made you will want to follow as you prepare for the meeting.

Some Thoughts on Preparing for and Participating in an IEP Meeting

Considerations Prior to the IEP Meeting

1. Upon notification of the IEP meeting, call the person who is to direct the meeting and find out (a) who will attend the meeting, if that information is not included in the notification, and (b) how long the meeting will last.

2. The minimum number of people required to be at an IEP meeting is *three:* (a) a representative of the public school qualified to provide or supervise the provision of special education, (b) a teacher, and (c) a parent. Other individuals may be invited by the parents or the school system. Your child can be included if you feel it is appropriate. If anyone who provides services such as speech therapy to your child has not been invited to the meeting, ask that he be invited. If he cannot attend, make arrangements to meet with him and obtain his ideas to include in the final IEP document.

3. If you feel the time allotted for the IEP meeting may be inadequate to discuss all your concerns, make arrangements to meet a second time or to make the first meeting longer.

4. Referring to your personal observations, the Record Decoder, and the IEP Planning Chart, make notes on the goals, objectives, and evaluation criteria you want included in your child's IEP. Alternatively, you may wish to design

your own IEP to bring with you to the meeting, using the sample IEP in the previous chapter as a guide.

5. For each developmental area, rank order the goals and objectives you want your child to achieve.

6. Talk with other persons—teachers, parents, professionals, and so on—about the special education and related services they feel your child needs. Identify and write down in rank order the special education and related services you want your child to receive.

7. Determine the extent to which you feel your child should participate in regular education programs in light of his learning style and special education needs.

8. Develop a written agenda of everything you want to discuss at the IEP meeting including your rank ordering of goals and objectives, the extent of your child's participation in the regular education program, and the special education and related services you want your child to receive.

9. If school officials are working with your child for the first time, develop a plan for making your child's presence felt at the beginning of the IEP meeting. Telling a short anecdote or bringing photographs of your family, tape recordings, examples of schoolwork, or your child himself can help people unacquainted with him realize that he is far more than a stack of papers!

10. While you and the school professionals will most often agree about your child's IEP, you might want to think of potential areas of disagreement and develop plans to address those problems.
    a. Identify the data in the records and elsewhere supporting your position on the potential problem areas.
    b. Identify the data in the records and elsewhere supporting the school's position.

    c. Identify information to counter the school's position.

    d. Develop alternative proposals for achieving your goals and objectives for your child which school officials might accept more readily.

    e. Prior to the IEP meeting, determine the minimum special education program and related services you will accept for your child before appealing the IEP.

11. Determine the role you feel most comfortable assuming during the meeting.

    a. *Very assertive role:* taking charge of the meeting early and guiding it. If you choose a very assertive role, a way to ensure that your own agenda is covered is to have it carefully written out and even rehearsed with your spouse or others who support your point of view. To help guide the meeting in the directions you wish, provide a copy of your agenda for each member of the IEP team.

    b. *Assertive role:* allowing school officials to lead the meeting but ensuring that all items on your agenda are covered completely to your satisfaction.

    c. *Less assertive role:* permitting school officials to lead the meeting and pressing only for a few specified items.

12. Ask someone to attend the meeting with you. Often it is very helpful to have someone else to listen, take notes, and support you. Discuss with him prior to the meeting what you hope to do in the meeting and what you want him to do.

Considerations During the IEP Meeting

1. If school officials are working with your child for the first time, take steps at the beginning of the IEP meeting to make your child's presence felt in that meeting, as previously suggested.

2. Ensure that each item required for an IEP is fully discussed. These include:
   a. a description of your child's present level of educational performance in all areas, including movement, communications, social relations, self-concept/independence, senses/perception, thinking, and learning style;
   b. a statement of annual goals and of short-term objectives for each of those goals;
   c. a statement of the special education and related services to be provided to meet each of the goals and objectives;
   d. a statement of the extent to which your child will be able to participate in regular educational programs;
   e. the projected dates for starting services and the anticipated duration of the services; and
   f. a statement of the objective criteria, evaluation procedures, and schedules for determining, on at least an annual basis, whether your child is achieving his short-term objectives.

3. Whether you have chosen a very assertive, assertive, or less assertive role, make sure that everything you want to discuss is covered to your satisfaction. If the school personnel begin the meeting by reviewing their recommended goals and objectives, anticipated services, and evaluation criteria for your child, you should follow their discussion by identifying how these items relate to the IEP you envisioned before the meeting. Where you agree with the proposed program, express your agreement and check off the item from your list. Where disagreements arise, explain your objections and try to reach an acceptable solution. If disagreements cannot be resolved immediately, make a note of those areas, express your desire to come back to these issues later, and move on to new goals and objectives.

   An alternative approach is for you, the parents, to begin by reviewing the elements of the IEP you have developed and to have the school people comment on each item either as you bring it up or after you have finished your presentation. Then you can proceed to manage areas of agreement and disagreement as described above.

4. As the meeting progresses, keep participants focused on the elements of the IEP and on your child. Do not let the discussion wander off to unrelated matters.

5. As the discussion comes to an end, review the agenda of concerns you developed prior to the meeting. Make certain that everything on your agenda has been covered. If you disagreed earlier over any aspects of your child's IEP, return to those matters now and seek to resolve them.

6. At the conclusion of the meeting you will probably be asked to sign the IEP document. Your signature may have a different meaning in different school systems. Sometimes parents are asked to sign the IEP merely to indicate their presence at the IEP meeting. When this is the case, you should sign the document as requested. Remember, however, that your signature in this case does not mean you agree with the IEP as written.

In some school systems, your signature on the IEP indicates your agreement with the document and your consent for proceeding with the proposed placement. Certainly if you are satisfied that the IEP meets your child's needs to the fullest extent possible, you may now signify agreement by signing the IEP or the permission for placement document, whichever your school system requires. If, however, you want to examine the IEP without time pressure, tell the school officials you would like to review the IEP over the next day or two. Request that they provide you with a copy and tell them exactly when you will give them your final decision regarding the program and placement described on the IEP. And if you do not accept portions of the IEP, identify clearly to the school officials those portions that you find unacceptable. If they will not change those items, tell them you want additional time to consider the IEP. Ask them to give you a copy, and tell them exactly when you will make your final decision.

7. Whether or not you request extra time to examine your child's IEP, review this final checklist before signing the IEP or permission for placement document:

   a. Does the IEP accurately and fully describe your child's present level of educational performance in all relevant developmental areas? Does it accurately portray your child's learning style?

   b. Do the annual goals describe the skills you would like your child to develop within the next year?

   c. Are annual goals written to build on your child's present level of educational performance?

   d. Is there at least one annual goal and short-term objective for each related service your child will receive?

   e. Are goals and objectives written as positive, measurable statements?

   f. Do goals and objectives contain the five essential parts of who will do what, how, where, and when?

   g. Do the annual goals and short-term objectives meet the priorities you have established as essential for your child?

   h. Are all special education and related services clearly identified along with projected dates for beginning services and the anticipated duration of the services?

   i. Does the IEP clearly describe the extent to which your child will be able to participate in regular educational programs?

   j. Does the IEP include appropriate and understandable criteria and evaluation procedures and schedules for determining, at least on an annual basis, whether the short-term instructional objectives are being achieved?

k. Have you asked all teachers and therapists who are providing services to your child whether they agree with the IEP and will provide these services? If these professionals attended the IEP meeting, they will have already answered these questions. If they did not attend the meeting, you should talk with them before signing the IEP.

8. If you do not find the IEP totally acceptable, decide which of the following actions you will take:

a. Sign the IEP or permission for placement document but note which parts of the IEP you find objectionable and indicate in writing your plan to appeal those parts. This option should allow your child to receive the special education and related services on his IEP pending appeal of the part to which you object. (See Chapter 9 for information about ways to resolve disagreements with the school.)

b. Refuse to sign the IEP or permission for placement document and indicate in writing your intention to appeal the IEP. Before doing this, ask what educational services your child will receive if you follow this option.

c. Sign the IEP or permission for placement document and indicate in writing the parts with which you disagree but write nothing about a plan to appeal. This option at least puts you on record as feeling that the IEP does not adequately meet your child's needs.

Visiting Placement Options

Before you agree to a classroom placement for your child's special education program, you will want to visit the school. Occasionally there is more than one classroom within the school system appropriate to meet the goals and objectives and to provide the related services outlined in your child's IEP. In the same way you offered educators unique, valuable knowledge of your child during the evaluation, eligibility, and IEP phases, you will also be able to give them particular insight into the kind of environment suited to your child's learning style. By visiting school classrooms, talking to administrators and teachers, eating in the cafeteria, and observing playground activities, you can assess the educational program with the needs of your child in mind. You will be able to ask questions and perhaps offer suggestions about adjustments or modifications necessary to respond to your child's unique ways of learning.

Many parents feel uncertain when they visit schools. They wonder what to look for as they observe school programs. The outline below serves as a guide for your observations. It provides questions to ask and guidelines to follow in assessing the activities, materials, methods, and physical layout that make up the classroom environment. This guide can assist you in deciding if the suggested placement is compatible with your child's educational needs and his learning style. It can also help you decide if the classroom environment will enable your child to build on his strengths, allowing him to learn in ways he does best. You should find this guide useful when you visit a school or classroom before giving permission for your child to be placed there; you should also find it valuable when you have questions and concerns at parent-teacher conferences.

Guidelines for Placement Observations

Classroom Organization

A. PHYSICAL ENVIRONMENT
   1. Layout
      a. How is furniture arranged? (Desks lined up in rows? Tables and chairs for small group work?)
      b. Are there large open areas or is the room divided into smaller components?

      c. Is the furniture the right size for the students? Is special equipment available (e.g., chairs with arm supports, individual study carrels, balance stools, bathroom fixtures at appropriate levels, etc.)?

      d. Where is the classroom located in relationship to the cafeteria? The bathroom? Outdoor areas? The special services?

2. General atmosphere
      a. Is the general atmosphere relaxed or formal? Soothing or stimulating?

B. DAILY ACTIVITIES
1. Sequence of activities
      a. What is the daily schedule? Do children seem to understand the schedule?
      b. Are related services scheduled at times that do not interrupt a child's participation in the ongoing school work?
      c. How does the teacher indicate that one activity is over and another beginning?

2. Consistency
      a. Is the schedule generally the same every day?

3. Variety
      a. Does the daily schedule include active times and quiet times?
      b. Is there provision for daily outdoor activity?
      c. How frequently does the teacher change the pace of activities?

C. SOCIAL ENVIRONMENT
1. Peer interactions
      a. Are children allowed to interact spontaneously with one another? When? How often?
      b. Does the teacher encourage children to cooperate with one another? During school work activities? During free time?

2. Teacher-child interactions

    a. How does the teacher relate to the children?
    b. Does the teacher tolerate and adjust to individual children?
    c. Does the teacher enter into conversations or play situations with children?
3. Values
    a. What values do the teacher and the children seem to hold? Success? Creativity? Social manners? Enthusiasm? Docility? Physical prowess?

Curriculum

A. GOALS AND PRIORITIES
1. What developmental areas are included in the curriculum (i.e., movement, communications, social relationships, independence/self-concept, thinking skills, etc.)?
2. What developmental areas receive emphasis in the classroom? What is *not* a curriculum priority? Where do academics fit in? Are life skills emphasized?

B. MATERIALS
1. Are the teaching materials concrete or abstract?
2. Are the teaching materials appropriate to the developmental level of the children?
3. Do the materials teach through various senses—vision, touch, hearing? Through movement?
4. Are the materials physically accessible to children?
5. Are the materials designed to interest children?

C. METHODS
1. Groupings
    a. Do children work individually, in small groups, or as a total class?
    b. Are the children grouped homogeneously (all at the same skill level) or heterogeneously (different skill levels in the same group)?

     c. Are the groupings different for different curriculum areas?
2. Teaching style
     a. Does the teacher take a highly structured approach leading all learning activities? Or does he also allow for spontaneous learning situations?
     b. Does the teacher work individually with children or does he focus more on groups?
     c. Performance expectations
         (1) Does the teacher expect all children to perform at approximately the same level?
         (2) Does the teacher expect children to wait for their turns or to volunteer answers spontaneously?
         (3) Does the teacher expect children to listen to and follow group verbal instructions?
         (4) Does the teacher expect children to work independently? Without interrupting with questions for the teacher?

Conclusion

Now that you have negotiated the maze to a special education placement, you might be wondering where all of this hard work on behalf of your child and his education is leading. At this point you might be feeling that your child will never be ready to leave school. Yet that day will indeed arrive, and much more quickly than you now believe. It is never too early to begin exploring passageways in the maze that lead after school years to your child's maximum independence in work life, living arrangements, recreation, and community activities.

In the following chapter you will learn about the concept of career education for special-needs children. By integrating career education into your child's IEP, you and school professionals may work together to prepare your child for his life as an employee, citizen, and contributing member of society.

EIGHT

=== ❖ ❖ ❖ ===

Transition
Pathways to the Future

Can my daughter really learn to live away from home? Will she have a job in the community? What are her chances for further education after she leaves the public school system?

No matter how young your child is, these and many other questions most likely have already come to your mind. As your child grows older, your family will continue to be faced with many perplexing concerns regarding her future. These concerns often cause increasing anxiety about what life will hold as the years go by.

With your hands full just coping with day-to-day life, planning to address future concerns is often difficult to do. Without a crystal ball to provide a vision of what lies ahead, you may question whether you have anything to gain by putting forth the time and effort required for such planning. The answer is a resounding "yes." Whatever your child's disability, steps you take now can help create a more positive future for both you and your child.

Probably the best way to reduce the anxiety and stress associated with future uncertainty is through careful planning, beginning early enough in your child's school life to use the resources of the school to assist you. You have an important role to play to ensure that your child with disabilities—as with all of your children—will have as independent and self-sufficient a life as possible. This chapter will help you understand the concept of career education and the ways in which career planning can assist your child in moving toward a future of maximum independence.

Hopes and Facts

Families of children with disabilities are now accustomed to the educational entitlements provided by P.L. 94–142 and its amendments, including a free, appropriate, public education in the least restrictive environment. These families frequently assume, or just hope, that similar entitlements to publicly funded services will continue for their sons and daughters when they graduate from or leave the school system. This is not the case. Once a young adult with disabilities leaves the school system, there is no guaranteed program that takes up where P.L. 94–142 leaves off; no current federal or state laws provide all young adults with disabilities with rights to continuing education, or to the housing, jobs, or support services needed to help them live independently.

Schools, parents, and communities have been working hard in recent years to address the problems of young people who leave school at age eighteen or twenty-one with nowhere to go. The U.S. Department of Education, Office of Special Education and Rehabilitative Services, has provided leadership in these efforts by funding model programs to remove obstacles that traditionally keep people with disabilities from obtaining jobs. During the 1980s, the Department of Education declared a national priority to develop independent living alternatives for young people with disabilities and to ease their transition from school to work. As a result of these activities, the nation's school systems are now required to provide all students in special education with plans for the transition from school to the world of work. In addition, planning among students, parents, special educators, vocational educators, adult service system representatives, and employers is helping to pave the way toward a broad range of community jobs.

Laws enacted by the United States Congress complement the Department of Education's strong initiatives to provide effective transition from school to work. One such law is the Carl D. Perkins Vocational Education Act, P.L. 98–154. It assists states in providing vocational education—instructional programs that teach particular occupational skills. Specifically, the Perkins Act extends the rights of secondary students under The Education for All Handicapped Children Act, including provisions for the Individualized Education Program and the least restrictive environment, to vocational training. The Perkins Act provides funding to state educational agencies to ensure that vocational education in the public schools will not be segregated. Regular vocational education classes in the schools must be open to all students, with federal funds set aside to finance any special adaptations needed to make materials and classrooms accessible to students with disabilities.

Section 504 of The Rehabilitation Act of 1973 provides further assurance that students with disabilities will meet no discrimination within public school programs. Section 504 requires the adaptation and program modifications that may be needed by students to participate in federally funded programs, including vocational education. Its provisions enable young men like Peter, for example, to take auto mechanics. In the past, the mild mental retardation that prevented Peter from reading the manuals required in the course would also have prevented his taking the course. Today, however, using tape recordings of the manuals to assist him in learning the materials in the course, he is able to participate fully in vocational education.

While vocational education may be an important part of your child's educational program, it must be viewed in relation to her overall school program and her general plans for the future. Transition planning requires far more than placement in vocational education classrooms. Students, their parents, and educators need to begin early to identify areas of interest and the suitability of certain careers. Participation in career education can help them in this important endeavor.

Preparation for Life after School—Career Education

Career education is the broader context of which vocational education is only a part. Career education is the process that prepares your son or daughter to participate in the worlds of work, family, recreation, and the community. When parents and educators include career education in a student's school program, they are helping to prepare that student to succeed in jobs, to participate in community activities, and to enjoy as independent a life as possible upon leaving the public schools. This chapter, however, will explore only the *employment* aspects of career education—the importance of working, the development of good work habits, the exploration of different types of jobs, and the learning of actual job and daily living skills. These aspects of career education are illustrated in the following pages using the experiences of the Connors family.

Career education advances through four sequential, but sometimes overlapping, stages. The stages include: (1) career awareness/orientation; (2) career exploration; (3) career preparation; and (4) career placement, follow-up, and continuing education.

Career awareness, the first stage of career education, is an ongoing process. In this stage, children become aware of different jobs, begin to see themselves as future workers, and learn positive attitudes toward work. Often this awareness begins at home when children are asked to do chores or to care for themselves. In fact, parents who require that their children, regardless of disability, pick up clothes and toys, wash and dress themselves, help with table setting, take out the garbage, or otherwise contribute to family life, give them a head start in developing work attitudes.

The appropriate time for beginning the career awareness stage depends more upon a student's developmental level than her grade level in school. For example, children with mild mental retardation may be ready for career awareness as early as kindergarten, while children with more severe disabilities may not be ready for this stage until the 5th to 10th grade years.

Examples of activities for the *career awareness/orientation phase* include:

- creative playing of various workers' roles
- taking field trips to see people at work
- hearing talks by former students who are working
- visiting businesses where people with disabilities are employed

Career awareness often develops so gradually that parents may not realize right away that their child is in this stage. For example, when Mary Connors was a small girl, her parents noticed her special sensitivity to other people. Mary understood others' feelings and was able to respond to them even though she couldn't express herself in language that was easily understood. She had a large family of dolls, and the Connors' cats and dogs were her constant companions. She often pretended to be a nurse or veterinarian with her dolls and pets. Her family gave Mary every opportunity they could to be with other children and adults and to help with household chores, especially when company was coming. As Mary grew older, she took on more and more responsibility for one of the pets. Although they did not realize it at first, Mr. and Mrs. Connors were playing an important part in Mary's career awareness development. As the years went by, they began to perceive her interests and strengths as ones that might lead to a possible career for Mary.

Career exploration is the second stage of career education; like career awareness, it is also a lifetime endeavor. This stage is usually a part of the middle school years, but once again, when it begins depends more on the student's developmental level than her grade level. During this stage students have opportunities to look firsthand at different types of work. Opportunities for "hands-on" experiences give students an understanding of the world of work and of their own abilities and needs. Examples of activities for the *career exploration phase* include:

- planned visits to a variety of work sites in order to understand job requirements
- interest testing
- practice of specific job skills (alphabetizing library book check-out cards, putting machinery parts together)
- summer jobs

Mary Connors entered this stage at about the age of twelve, when her mother decided to encourage her continuing interest in caring for others by arranging for her to work with a teenage family friend as a baby sitter's helper. When her friend Carla had a sitting job, Mary would accompany her and help in the activities associated with putting the young children to bed. A few years later, when Mrs. Connors' father became ill and moved into their home, Mary took responsibility for many of the personal and home care needs of her grandfather. At the same time, Mary was involved at school in various career exploration activities. With her class she visited a florist, a hospital, a pet training school, a retail dress shop. In each of these places she and her classmates observed people at work and heard them talk about their jobs. She was learning some of the requirements for certain occupations. Both in her school work and her home activities she began to see job possibilities. Her family and school teachers encouraged her ongoing interest in caring for others.

Career preparation is the third stage of career education, usually occurring during the later school years. At this stage students begin to develop specialized skills and gain knowledge about particular jobs and careers. Students' personal interests, aptitudes, and abilities are more clearly identified, and are matched with courses that offer a variety of experiences in and out of the classroom.

Vocational education is an important activity within the career preparation stage. As mentioned earlier, vocational education refers to instructional programs that teach specific occupational skills such as photocopy production, janitorial services, laboratory work, and pet grooming. These programs are discussed in more detail later in the chapter.

Examples of activities for the *career preparation phase* include:

* working as assistants to school employees
* reading newspaper want-ads
* holding part-time jobs in the community
* participating in work-study programs
* filling out job applications

In Mary Connors' case, her experiences in child care and in caring for her grandfather gave her a head start when she reached her teenage years and had access to a vocational program in her school. She began a work-study program at the high school that allowed her to spend part of her day in the community participating in a special nursing assistant program. Students in this program worked in a variety of settings providing care to others for several hours each day. First, Mary worked with the nurse in an elementary school, keeping the equipment clean, putting fresh sheets on the cots, and staying with young children as they waited for the nurse. Six weeks later, she worked in a nursing home alongside a skilled nurse's aide. Her final work experience during that school year was at the pediatric unit in the local hospital, learning to make beds, to sterilize toys and equipment, and to be a companion for young sick children.

Career placement, follow-up, and continuing education is the final stage of the career education process. This stage of development requires the involvement of family, schools, and often several community resources to help the student find satisfactory employment. Guidance, counselling, and other support services may also be required to help young people with disabilities make decisions about job placement and further education. Once students leave the public schools, public or private adult service agencies continue to provide, to a limited degree, job training programs and support services.

What do students do when they graduate from high school? Depending upon the options in the community and the nature of a person's disability, the following types of opportunities may be available.

1. **Adult Day Programs.** These programs take place in settings with other disabled people. Traditionally, these programs serve more severely disabled individuals and provide training in personal care, community living, and vocational skills development. Such programs are run by public service or consumer agencies and may be called Intensive Developmental Centers, Work Activity Centers, or Developmental Centers.

2. **Sheltered Employment.** Sheltered employment programs provide a work environment in a supervised setting. As in the adult day centers, sheltered workshops are segregated, serving only workers with disabilities. Worker productivity is supposed to equal at least fifty percent of that of a non-disabled worker. Workers do contract work such as preparing bulk mailings, refinishing furniture, or assembling bicycle brake parts. Each worker is paid on a "piece rate" basis according to the number of items he or she completes.

3. **Supported Employment.** Supported employment is paid employment for workers with disabilities who need ongoing support to get and to keep a job. Supported employment provides jobs for people with severe disabilities so they can work in the community outside of segregated, sheltered work settings. The employee with disabilities works either individually or as a part of a small work crew, always integrated, however, into the mainstream of work life. A job coach provides support by helping the employee to improve her job skills, interpersonal relations, or any other job-related needs. Salaries for supported jobs are at or above the minimum wage. Examples of supported jobs include grounds keeping, working in medical laboratories to keep equipment ready for the scientists, or assembling electronic circuit boards.

4. **Transitional Job Training.** A relatively short-term program designed to help an individual obtain a job, or to develop the work habits and learn the skills needed for a particular job, is called transitional job training. This type of training is conducted by schools or by Rehabilitative Service Agencies through work-study programs. In transitional job training, a young person with disabilities might work temporarily at a clerical job within the school before moving on to a permanent job in an office.

5. **Post-Secondary Education.** Education after high school can take place in a vocational school, community college, college or university, or through an apprentice program. Today, many colleges and universities provide specialized programs and support services for students with disabilities.

6. **Competitive Employment.** This option covers everyday jobs, paying wages at the going rate, in settings with non-disabled workers. Jobs can be either on a part-time or full-time basis.

As discussed earlier, there is no one right time for beginning any of the four stages of career development. In fact, some students with disabilities may not go through all four stages. For example, young people with severe and profound disabilities may learn job skills in paying and nonpaying job settings without having first participated in career awareness and exploration programs. These individuals may benefit from further career exploration later on.

Whether or not your child is able to take part in all four stages, career education provides a road map that can help you find the school services that will best prepare your child for adult life. Working together with your child's teachers and school specialists, you can develop appropriate IEP goals and objectives for career education. It is important to note, however, that career education does not replace a student's academic program. Work-related skills and experiences may be included in the academic program, or they may be taught at a separate time during the day. Mary Connors' parents are using the IEP process to ensure Mary's participation in both school and community-based job training. In this way Mary will be ready to enter the world of work when she leaves the public high school.

Parents Provide Unique Information—The Personal Profile

You can help prepare your child for the transition from school to work by collecting and organizing information that provides a realistic picture of her employment related strengths, training needs, and requirements for ongoing support on the job. In particular, you need to gather information that gives a sense of your child's work personality—of her personal traits, interests, aptitudes, abilities, and employability skills. Many families have found it helpful once again to organize their information in a written form, through the use of the Personal Profile. With information organized and written down, you will be prepared to share your knowledge in a concise, timely manner. The Personal Profile is organized around the following components:

Personal traits are distinguishing qualities or personal characteristics. Examples include:

1. prefers an orderly environment;
2. is generally messy;
3. enjoys group activities;
4. likes to be alone;
5. is curious about the way things work;
6. follows the lead of others;
7. takes initiative.

Interests are feelings of liking or wanting to do something. Examples include:

1. watching and participating in sports;
2. enjoying arts and crafts;
3. listening to music;
4. caring for animals;
5. preparing food;

6. working outdoors.

Aptitudes/Abilities are capacities for learning and doing. Examples include:
1. following directions;
2. using small tools;
3. matching names, numbers, colors;
4. using math skills;
5. using communication skills;
6. judging shapes and sizes.

Employability skills are the behaviors and attitudes that enable a person to function in the role of a worker. Often an individual's personal traits are translated into employability skills. Examples include:
1. dependability (e.g., arrives on time, keeps regular attendance, keeps schedule);
2. interpersonal relations skills (e.g., works without interfering with others, cooperates with supervisor, communicates adequately with co-workers);
3. personal grooming (e.g., keeps self clean, clothes neat, and hair cut and combed).

To begin building a bank of information about your child's work personality, think back to the information in Chapter 2 describing parents' observations of their children. You will be surprised how quickly some of these personal traits, interests, aptitudes/abilities, and employability skills will come to your mind. The most important source of information about your child's employment strengths, needs, and aspirations, however, is your child herself. By talking with or observing her, you can identify times when she has enjoyed a sense of accomplishment or the good feelings about herself that are the result of a job well done. Such experiences could include school projects, volunteer work, leisure activities, or family events. Your child can be her own best advocate!

To help you organize your information, the Personal Profile form is shown on pages 149 and 150. The form describing Mary Connors is found on pages 151 and 152. The three columns on the first page are headed Traits, Interests, and Aptitudes/Abilities. There are spaces for you to write your impressions of your child in each column. After you record examples of behaviors, there is space for you to write the source of your observations. Sources might include teachers' reports, your own observations, or the results of formal testing. Identifying the specific sources of your observations can help you to build your information bank and to plan with school professionals and adult service providers for your child's transition from school to work.

Below the three columns on the first page of the Personal Profile is space for you to describe the supports your child might need to obtain and perform a job. For example, a young man who is a "neatnik" can be a great help in keeping a workplace orderly. He might need support and assistance, however, in knowing when to clean certain areas of an office. Or a person who has the aptitude/ability for understanding verbal directions might need support and help when communicating with other workers.

The second page of the Personal Profile is for your record of the employability skills that will enable your child to function in the role of worker. These behaviors and attitudes are the major ones that employers seek. Employers believe that technical skills can be taught. What they are looking for are employees with attitudes, values, and habits such as self-discipline, respect for authority, willingness to try, and careful grooming. Just as on the first page of the profile, spaces are provided for your observations, the sources of the observations, and the supports that will be required. Examples of supports needed might be grooming reminders, a blinking alarm clock, or guidance in moving from one activity to another.

Personal Profile

Traits	Interests	Aptitudes/Abilities
Observations:	Observations:	Observations:
1.	1.	1.
2.	2.	2.
3.	3.	3.
Sources of Observations:	Sources of Observations:	Sources of Observations:

Supports Needed:

Personal Profile (continued)

Employability Skills

Observations:

1.

2.

3.

Sources of Observations:

Supports Needed:

Personal Profile

Mary

Traits	Interests	Aptitudes/Abilities
Observations:	**Observations:**	**Observations:**
1. Shy with people she doesn't know, but loyal to family, friends, dogs and cats!	1. Caring for animals and dolls.	1. Remembers what people like -- favorite foods, etc.
2. Persistent in solving problems when left alone.	2. Trying on new clothes and jewelry.	2. Helps to feed pets at home
3. Cautious when trying new things.	3. Teenage magazines and TV programs	3. Can change babies' diapers and help young children put on coats and boots.
Sources of Observations:	**Sources of Observations:**	**Sources of Observations:**
Conversations with Carla	Speech therapist uses teen magazines to encourage conversation.	Counselors from Rec. Dept.
Teacher's report		Our observations
Our observations of Mary untangling the dog's leash		

Supports Needed:

Guidance in knowing which jobs to do when.

Assistance in making decisions about how to respond to a young child's cry.

Help with tasks that require finger dexterity, such as opening cans, using a knife, etc

Personal Profile

Mary
(continued)

Employability Skills

Observations:

1. Friendly -- she gets along with other people whether she really likes them or not.

2. Dresses well -- wears the right outfit for the right occasion.

3. Understands and observes daily and weekly schedule -- but flexible when the schedule changes.

Sources of Observations:

We let her wake up with the alarm and get ready for school each day. Teacher reports she works well with her classmates on art projects.

Supports Needed:

When changes in routine are necessary, she needs advance preparation. A communication board or other help to talk with and understand others. Time to think about and try out new tasks before she is expected to do them

Once you have gathered and organized information on the Personal Profile form, you will be prepared to provide others with important insight and understanding relevant to your child's future as a worker. Your information will prove invaluable as you participate in transition planning meetings conducted by the school, work with counselors from vocational rehabilitation, and meet with potential employers. The practical insight and information provided by young people, their parents, and other family members are vital when planning successful transitions from school to the workplace.

Planning Transition with the Schools

As you consider ways to plan for your child's entry into the work world, the logical place to begin is with the school. By using the school system's resources wisely, you can go far in preparing her for the transition into the work world. You, your child, school professionals, and people from adult service agencies all possess important knowledge and perspectives. You need to work as a team to develop the skills, opportunities, and support services that will be necessary for her to participate successfully in work and community life.

Up to this point, the chapter has considered only the ways in which *parents* can assemble information in order to seek transition services and employment for their child. The *school*, however, also has an obligation to assess the vocational needs and abilities of its students. Vocational assessment is a related service that should be written into the IEP when a student reaches the junior high or early high school years. To obtain a picture of a student's aptitudes and interests as they relate to career education and to employment, a multi-dimensional battery of tests is given. Many school systems have their own procedures for conducting formal vocational assessments, while others work cooperatively with rehabilitative service agencies to provide them. No matter where the assessment is conducted, however, its purpose is to help you and school personnel with vocational planning for your child.

Vocational assessments provide information about a particular student in order to design, implement, and evaluate an appropriate vocational program. They may also be used to provide information necessary to determine eligibility for certain programs or services, such as those provided by school vocational programs or vocational rehabilitation agencies. In addition, they should help the student explore career possibilities, assist teachers in determining the student's skills and learning styles, and target those areas where the student can benefit from further training.

Vocational assessment generally consists of three major components. First, *work sampling* tests a student's "hands-on" performance in certain simulated and actual work environments. The more closely the work sample resembles an actual job, the more easily a student and the evaluator can judge whether or not such a job would fit the student's abilities and interests. Examples of work samples include assembling gears for bicycles or filing papers in alphabetical order. Second, *standardized tests* evaluate such areas as the student's interests, aptitudes, manual dexterity, clerical ability, and mechanical ability. These tests are designed to give some prediction of how a student is likely to perform in jobs calling for certain interests and skills. Third, *behavioral observation* is a systematic way of observing, recording, and interpreting the behavior of a student as she works. Most vocational educators agree that skilled observation of a person on the job gives a far better idea of the person's vocational abilities than any standardized tests or work samples. Therefore, in many schools vocational assessments include observations of students in a variety of community-based work settings over a period of months. From these observations, the vocational evaluator gains a broad picture of the student's interests and abilities. These experiences also provide a real work environment in which students can practice work behaviors and learn the expectations of various jobs.

Ideally, a vocational assessment should use a combination of work samples, standardized tests, and behavioral observations to develop a picture of your child's vocational interests and potential. Parents or professionals, however, should never allow vocational assessments to be the sole factor in determining the suitability of a job or career pathway. Employers and adult service providers recognize that vocational training alone seldom fully prepares a person for a job. If you wait until a young person is "ready" for a job; if you wait until she has learned in school all the requirements for a job; if you wait until some service provider has prepared her to move from a sheltered, segregated job to a job in the community; the day may never come. It is now widely acknowledged that young people with disabilities are able to get and to keep jobs for a longer period of time if they are placed in jobs that interest them, are trained on the job, and then are given the supports that they need to keep the job. Today, in contrast to earlier years, the overall philosophy of career education for children with disabilities has changed from "train and place" to "place, train, and support."

More and more school systems are recognizing the importance of beginning to plan the transition from school to work and community life early in a student's high school years. They are requiring formal transition plans involving the students, parents, school professionals, and adult service providers. By systematically combining the family information with that of the school system, families will help to ensure that the many agencies involved in employment and other life activities for young adults with disabilities will be well informed and better able to provide assistance. Your family can use the Career Education Planning Chart, found on pages 157 through 159, as an informal transition plan to work with school personnel, employers, and adult service providers. The Chart can be attached to your child's IEP or to the written plan developed by a counselor from the Department of Vocational Rehabilitation.

Career Education Planning Chart

The Career Education Planning Chart is divided into seven parts. Part I is the "Summary of Individual Functioning." In this section, you and your son or daughter can write a statement summarizing the information about traits, interests, aptitudes/abilities, and employability skills you have gathered on the Personal Profile.

Part II is a "Summary of Career Education Recommendations to Date." Based upon observations summarized in Part I and upon other observations made in the home, community, and at school, you can write your initial thoughts and suggestions for a career education program. In Section B you can note recommendations made by school personnel in your child's school or vocational assessment records.

In Part III you set priorities by ranking the areas of career education you believe need attention at this time. If you decide that two areas are of equal importance for your child—for example, career awareness and career exploration—career education goals and objectives will need to be developed in both areas.

"Goals and Objectives for Career Education" can be written in Part IV. The process for writing them is the same as for the IEP. Vocational educators or other teachers familiar with career education can assist you in formulating appropriate goals and objectives for the areas of career education to be addressed. The Career Education Planning Chart prepared by Mary Connors and her parents is found on pages 160–162. On this chart you can see typical career education goals and objectives.

In Part V you can note any "Program and Course Modifications" necessary for your child to participate fully in a vocational program. For example, to help compensate for a physical disability, a student might need certain adaptations to the computer equipment she uses.

Part VI allows you to identify the "Services Needed to Meet Goals." In this section you write the name of the agency which will provide the services, the contact person at the agency, the specific services, and the responsible funding party. For example, if your child needs to learn to use public transportation, vocational rehabilitation may provide and pay for that training. Finally, you may list everyone you believe should assist in developing the plan for career education in Part VII. Their agencies and telephone numbers will help you as you need to contact them for meetings or for information.

Career Education Planning Chart

Date_____

Student's Name_____

Current School Placement_____

I. **Summary of Individual Functioning**

Using information on the Personal Profile, write a summary statement to describe your son/daughter.

A. Traits:_____

_____

_____

B. Interests:_____

_____

_____

C. Aptitudes/Abilities:_____

_____

_____

D. Employability Skills:_____

_____

_____

II. **Summary of Career Education Recommendations to Date**

A. Parents' Recommendations:_____

_____

_____

B. School and Agency Recommendations:_____

_____

_____

1.

III.   Career Education Priority Areas

Rank areas as High Priority (I), Moderate Priority (2), or Low Priority (3). Areas may be assigned equal priority.

<u>Rank</u>

A.   Career Awareness/Exploration

B.   Employability Skills
(Training in skills generally needed to
obtain and maintain employment but not
targeted to a specific job or occupation.)

C.   Career Preparation/Vocational Education
(Training in skills needed for a
targeted job or occupation.)

IV.   Career Education Goals and Objectives

A.   Career Awareness/Exploration

Goal:

Objective:

Objective:

B.   Employability Skills

Goal:

Objective:

Objective:

C.   Career Preparation/Vocational Education

Goal:

Objective:

Objective:

V.   Program and Course Modifications

2.

VI.   Services Needed to Meet Goals

Agency	Contact Person	Services	Agency Responsible for Funding the Services

VII.   Agencies and people who might be a part of developing the plan for career education.

Agency	Person	Telephone Number
_____	_____	_____
_____	_____	_____
_____	_____	_____
_____	_____	_____

3.

Career Education Planning Chart

Date _October 3, 1989_

Student's Name _Mary Connors_

Current School Placement _Middle County High School_

I. **Summary of Individual Functioning**

Using information on the Personal Profile, write a summary statement to describe your son/daughter.

A. Traits: Mary is shy with strangers, but very loyal when she knows people. Although cautious in trying new things, she is persistent in solving problems when given enough time.

B. Interests: She likes to take care of other people and animals. She plays well with young children. She likes clothes, teen magazines and TV shows.

C. Aptitudes/Abilities: She is a good helper with pets, with young children at the Rec. Dept., and her grandfather. She senses other peoples' needs and moods and remembers what they like.

D. Employability Skills: She is friendly even when she doesn't like someone. She is careful about personal grooming and follows schedules and routines. She needs help communicating with others.

II. **Summary of Career Education Recommendations to Date**

A. Parents' Recommendations: Career exploration in the areas of childcare, health care and geriatric care.

B. School and Agency Recommendations: Mary should try coaching younger children in special education programs.

1.

VI.   **Services Needed to Meet Goals**

Agency	Contact Person	Services	Agency Responsible for Funding the Services
Recreation Department	Elizabeth Shoemaker	Child-care training program	Recreation Department
Middle County Public Schools	Andrew Chitty	Speech / language	Middle County Public Schools

VII.   **Agencies and people who might be a part of developing the plan for career education.**

Agency	Person	Telephone Number
Middle County Public Schools	Mr. Andrew Chitty	384 - 0021
Recreation Department	Elizabeth Shoemaker	384 - 6329
Department of Vocational Rehabilitation	Gregory Suterland	386 · 4883

2.

III. **Career Education Priority Areas**

Rank areas as High Priority (l), Moderate Priority (2), or Low Priority (3). Areas may be assigned equal priority.

		Rank
A.	Career Awareness/Exploration	*1*
B.	Employability Skills (Training in skills generally needed to obtain and maintain employment but not targeted to a specific job or occupation.)	*2*
C.	Career Preparation/Vocational Education (Training in skills needed for a targeted job or occupation.)	*3*

IV. **Career Education Goals and Objectives**

A. Career Awareness/Exploration

Goal: *Mary will supervise a small group of children at her after school program.*

Objective: *Mary will help a small group of children set up snack time.*

Objective: *Mary will organize and play a group game with kids outdoors.*

B. Employability Skills

Goal: *Mary will re-supply the snack cupboards for the after school programs.*

Objective: *Mary will inventory the cups and napkins and bring more from the stockroom to the cupboards.*

Objective: *Mary will inventory the juice and crackers and ask the kitchen workers for more.*

C. Career Preparation/Vocational Education

Goal:

Objective: *Mary is not ready for this yet.*

Objective:

V. **Program and Course Modifications**

Language/communication system for co-workers and supervisor. Picture cards showing sequences of proper responses to children.

3.

You can use the Career Education Planning Chart not only to plan services for your child but also to monitor services once they are in place. Remember, no plan is permanent. Your child's career education plan can be changed as your child's needs change. By taking the time and effort to write your ideas and hopes on the Career Education Planning Chart, you will find that the planning meetings with school officials and adult service providers will be more productive and will lead toward greater work opportunities for your child.

Vocational Education Placements

When your child reaches the career preparation stage, you will want to consider the school's vocational education programs. These programs offer numerous valuable benefits, especially when they provide opportunities for training in community-based work settings rather than in traditional, school-based settings. For example, young people who participate in work experience programs learn the requirements to obtain and to keep a job. Work experience programs also provide students with real skills developed in real jobs. Furthermore, students in these programs find their skills to be more lasting, enjoy earning money, and also develop work histories necessary when later applying for employment.

The more traditional vocational education programs available to special education students lie on a continuum from the least restrictive setting, where disabled and non-disabled students learn together, to very restrictive programs serving only students with disabilities. Rodney's experience with vocational education is typical of disabled students served in less restrictive placements. Rodney's interest in automobiles started when he was a very small boy. He was in special education classes throughout his school years, but always went to the vocational education wing of the high school whenever he had free time and hung around the automotive classes. In planning for Rodney's career education, his parents advocated for his placement in the Automotive Program. Although they were aware that his learning problems would most likely prevent him from becoming a certified auto mechanic, they asked the school to modify the program so Rodney could learn basic automotive skills. Rodney participated in the regular vocational training classes, learning skills in the area of auto mechanics to match his interests and abilities. Among the skills Rodney learned were changing tires, removing worn tires from their rims, and putting on new tires. When Rodney graduated from high school, he went to work at a local tire company.

In contrast to Rodney, many students in self-contained special education classes receive their vocational education in segregated settings. Often these vocational classes simulate work activities involving such skills as stuffing and sorting mail. More and more vocational training, however, is being conducted outside of traditional classrooms. For example, Robert Boswell's vocational training has included helping to keep the school bus fleet in readiness for the next run. Each day he and other classmates go to the bus yard and help clean the buses to prepare them for the next day. Robert enjoys this skill training very much.

Each school system is required by P.L. 94–142 and the Carl Perkins Act to have a variety of vocational placements for their special education students. Together, parents and school professionals can devise creative programs for students with disabilities.

Looking toward the Employment World

When young adults leave school, where do they go for further education, training, or employment? Opportunities for further schooling or for work differ from community to community. Many families find that the best avenues into the work world for their child with disabilities are the same as for their non-disabled children. What has been called the "self, family, friends network" can be used.* Calling upon family connections and contacts is one of the surest ways to explore work and training options for young adults. For example, one family in the paint and hardware business

---

* Hasazi, S., H. Preskill, L. Gordon, and C. Collins. "Factors Associated with the Employment Status of Handicapped Youth," paper presented at the American Educational Research Association, New York, NY, 1982.

created jobs not only for their own disabled family member but for other workers with disabilities as well.

A second way to explore opportunities for work, training, or further education is to seek out community service agencies and organizations serving people with disabilities. Your state's Department of Rehabilitative Services or Vocational Rehabilitation, the Department of Mental Health and Developmental Disabilities, and, of course, the Department of Education can direct you to programs which assist young people in obtaining and keeping a job. Support, advocacy, or educational groups such as the Association for Retarded Citizens, United Cerebral Palsy, and the Association for Children and Adults with Learning Disabilities may also provide important information on post-school programs and services. These and other organizations are listed in Appendix C of this book.

Remember that all communities do not offer their workers with disabilities every type of employment option available—adult day programs, sheltered employment, transitional job training, supported employment, and competitive employment. Planning effectively for your child's life after high school, however, requires the exploration of options that are available well in advance of your child's graduation or twenty-first birthday. Since eligibility criteria for adult services vary from agency to agency, you and your son or daughter are well advised to visit several of these post-secondary placement options in your community in order to understand the requirements for entry into each type of placement. By advance planning you can use the school years, the IEP process, your child's network of family and friends, and the assistance of public and private agencies to help prepare the way for a smooth transition from school to the workplace.

Conclusion

Career education provides a systematic introduction to the world of work for young people with disabilities. Through participation in the career awareness, exploration, preparation, and placement stages, students learn the importance of work, the broad range of work options, the relationships among various job roles, and the personal and economic benefits of being a worker. You, as a parent of a young person with a disability, have an important role to play in your child's career education. It is essentially the same role enacted by parents of any other young person. You are preparing your child to be as independent and self-supporting as possible.

Because of the obstacles most young people with disabilities face, however, your role in planning the transition from school to work becomes more critical. By planning for your child's career education program, you can assist her in gaining the skills, confidence, and positive attitudes needed to participate as fully as possible in the world of work.

NINE

=== ❖ ❖ ❖ ===

Due Process

Detours

As you and your child participate in the special education cycle, you may sometimes find yourself disagreeing with observations, conclusions, and recommendations school people have made concerning your child and his educational program. And school people may not always agree with ideas you have about your child, either. In these situations, how are disagreements settled? Does the school system have its way by default? Must you seek appointment or election to the school board to exercise enough influence to have your way? Fortunately, a procedure known as the *due process hearing* exists to resolve differences that develop as you negotiate the special education maze.

This chapter describes the conflicts that may be resolved through due process, the procedures and steps followed in a due process hearing, and the benefits and costs involved in such a hearing. In most instances the hearing process should be the parents' last resort for obtaining a free, appropriate public education for their child. The experiences of parents and educators demonstrate that problems are usually resolved more quickly and satisfactorily in an informal setting, beginning with the teacher, and, if necessary, moving on to include principals and other administrators. To encourage the informal resolution of disagreements, school systems usually provide you with the opportunity to participate in an administrative review or conciliatory conference prior to going to a formal due process hearing. Nevertheless, if all the informal approaches have failed to produce the results you believe are right for your child, you need not give up on your efforts for change. At this point the due process hearing offers another opportunity for you to secure the educational rights to which your child is entitled.

Conflicts Resolvable through Due Process

Educational advocacy for children with disabilities has its legislative foundation in the Education for All Handicapped Children Act enacted by Congress in 1975 and since passed in similar form by all state governments. This law, and the six other federal statutes known collectively as the Education of the Handicapped Act, or EHA, establishes broad guidelines for local schools to follow in providing special education and in protecting the rights of parents and children entitled to those services. While state and local laws and regulations may be more detailed in their provisions than P.L. 94–142 and related federal statutes, their provisions cannot conflict with the federal law. For this reason, this chapter focuses primarily on due process procedures and the due process hearing described in the Education of the Handicapped Act. Should you have to use these procedures, however, you will also need to read and understand the procedures followed by your state and local school jurisdictions. These procedures may be readily obtained from your local director of special education.

P.L. 94–142 not only describes the due process hearing procedure for resolving conflicts in obtaining special education for your child, but it also identifies the specific conflicts that may be resolved by this process. You may initiate the due process hearing procedure only when you believe the school system has not fulfilled a duty it is required to perform under the law itself. Just what are these duties P.L. 94–142 requires of school systems?

1. School systems must provide a *free, appropriate public education* for all children with disabilities aged three through twenty-one, unless state law prohibits or does not authorize the expenditure of public funds to educate nonhandicapped children aged three through five or eighteen through twenty-one. In these states, a free, appropriate education is only required for children aged six through seventeen. As of the 1990 school year, however, P.L. 99–457, a 1986 amendment to P.L. 94–142, *requires* states to extend all the rights and protections of P.L. 94–142 to disabled children ages three through five or lose federal funding for various preschool special education programs. Because P.L. 94–142 and its amendments specify only the minimum requirements that states must satisfy, some states provide a free, appropriate education for disabled children younger than three and older than twenty-one. Check your state laws and regulations to determine the policy in your state. This education is to be provided completely at public expense.

2. School systems must ensure that disabled and nondisabled children are educated together to the maximum extent appropriate. Children with disabilities are to be placed in special classes or separate schools "only when the nature and severity of the handicap is such that education in regular classes," even if supported with supplementary aids or services, cannot be achieved satisfactorily. This is the legal provision mandating the education of children with disabilities in the *"least restrictive environment."*

3. School systems must set forth in writing in the *Individualized Education Program*, the specially designed education and related services your child will receive to meet his unique educational needs.

From the school's perspective, the preceding three items are duties the law requires them to perform. From the child's and parents' perspectives, these are rights P.L. 94–142 gives to the child. To guarantee that these rights are exercised, the law outlines further duties for school systems and further rights for children and parents.

4. School systems must give reasonable *written notice* to parents before they evaluate or place a child, change his special education placement, or refuse to take such actions. The notice must contain a full explanation for the school system's decision and be communicated to the parents in their native language and in a manner they can understand.

5. School systems must *obtain parent consent* before the initial evaluation is conducted and before the child is first placed in a special education program on the basis of the IEP. After the initial placement, parents must be notified in advance of any changes, but their consent is not required. Parents can, however, initiate a due process hearing to challenge changes with which they disagree. Should parents refuse to allow the initial evaluation or initial placement of their children in a special education class, school officials may also request a due process hearing to override the parents' objections. Actions of this nature, however, are usually taken by school personnel only in extreme situations. Such an action might be taken when they believe special education is required to protect the physical or mental health of the child or others in the school environment.

6. School systems must *provide an evaluation of the child, using a multidisciplinary team,* which includes at least one teacher or other specialist knowledgeable in the area of the suspected disability. A child's handicapping condition cannot be determined solely on the grounds of one test or the observations of one professional.

7. School systems must *ensure that evaluation tests are nondiscriminatory.* Tests and other evaluation material must be free of cultural bias. They must reflect accurately the child's aptitude or achievement level and not be biased by the child's impaired sensory or speaking skills or by other

disabling conditions. A brief explanation of the tests to be used and the information they provide must be made available to the parent.

8. School systems must *make available to parents for inspection and review all records* used in the evaluation, placement, and IEP processes as well as those records that are a part of the child's official school file. These records must be maintained in strict confidentiality. (See Chapter 4 for a complete discussion of your rights regarding school records.)

9. School systems must provide, with one exception, for the child to have an *independent evaluation* at public expense if the parents disagree with evaluation results obtained by the school system. The exception arises when school officials believe their evaluation data are accurate and sufficient. In these cases, school personnel may request a due process hearing to prove their claim. If the hearing officer does not agree with the school system, an independent evaluation at public expense will be ordered for your child. Should the hearing officer uphold the school's position, however, you will be unable to secure a free, independent evaluation. But remember, unless school officials request and hold a due process hearing to validate their evaluation data, they cannot deny your request for an independent evaluation. They have a duty to honor your request.

10. School systems must provide parents with *an impartial due process hearing* upon the request of parents who believe any of the preceding rights have been violated. (Conflicts concerning school records, however, do not require an impartial due process hearing. See Chapter 4.) The hearing must follow procedures described by state statute, regulation, or the written policy of the state education agency. Hearings conducted at the local school system level allow both the parents and the school system a right of appeal to the state education agency.

If you believe the school system has violated any of the preceding rights and you have been unable to resolve your differences informally, you can request a formal due process hearing by writing the local superintendent of schools. Remember, this process is not available to settle all disputes— only those arising from rights and duties provided in the federal law as outlined above or as set forth in your own state and local laws.

Examples of Conflicts Resolved in Due Process Hearings

1. Whether a child should be identified as learning disabled or emotionally disturbed (evaluation/eligibility).
2. Whether a child should receive related services such as speech or occupational therapy (appropriate services and IEP).
3. Whether a child should be placed in a self-contained classroom or a regular classroom with support services (least restrictive environment).
4. Whether a child should be placed at public expense in a private school (appropriate education and least restrictive environment).
5. Whether the Stanford-Binet intelligence test discriminates against young, nonverbal children (nondiscriminatory testing and the need for an independent evaluation).
6. Whether a child is mildly mentally retarded or moderately mentally retarded (evaluation/eligibility).
7. Whether a child is eligible to receive learning disability special education services (evaluation/eligibility).
8. Whether a child is receiving the program outlined in his IEP (appropriate education/IEP).
9. Whether a child's appropriate education requires more than the normal 180 school days—an extended school year (appropriate services and IEP).
10. Whether a child receives services at home or at a school (least restrictive environment).
11. Whether a child receives a vocational or academic education (appropriate education/IEP).

As you can readily see, each of the preceding conflicts centers upon some aspect of the child's right to a free, appropriate public education, outlined by an IEP, and provided in the least restrictive environment. Disputes like these represent the vast majority of conflicts brought to due process hearings. These are the areas most crucial in determining the educational progress your child will make. At the same time, decisions regarding these matters are ones where professionals may well disagree and where school systems may be forced to spend additional money if their opinions are not upheld. If you go to a hearing, the chances are quite good that it will concern issues of this nature.

Seldom are due process hearings required to force school systems to perform their procedural duties of providing notice of proposed actions, obtaining parental consent for testing, offering appropriate evaluations, or allowing parents to review their child's records. Usually schools have standard procedures for meeting these requirements. They develop form letters for notifying parents of actions they take or propose to take and for obtaining parental consent when necessary. They normally use teams for educational evaluation and try to avoid biased evaluation methods and tests. And they usually provide opportunities for parents to see records and to obtain independent evaluations when they disagree with the results of the school's evaluation. In the event you do have a conflict with the school system on a procedural issue, however, remember, you have a right to a due process hearing.

Conflicts Not Resolvable through Due Process Hearings

What about disagreements with the school system involving issues other than those outlined above? For example, what about other kinds of situations in which you believe your position is reasonable and that the school's position is unreasonable or just plain wrong? Often you may feel certain an impartial third person would see the situation your way. Unfortunately, a due process hearing cannot be used to settle all conflicts. The process is only available for resolving disputes directly related to the rights and duties of parents and school systems under P.L. 94–142.

Examples of Conflicts Not Resolved through Due Process Hearings

1. You want to attend the meeting where committee members will determine your child's eligibility for special services, and state law does not require your presence at that meeting.
2. You want your child to have a particular teacher, but school officials say there are other teachers with similar qualifications (and they are correct).
3. You find school personnel condescending and sometimes abrasive to work with. Although you have mentioned this to them, their behavior has not improved.
4. You want your child moved to another class because he has a personality conflict with the teacher, but the school will not approve the change.
5. You feel that school officials could move faster in placing your child, but they always use the maximum number of days legally allowed in making their decisions.
6. You dislike the school psychologist who will do your child's evaluation and would like another psychologist to do the testing. The school says no change can be made without violating the time guidelines set by the state education agency for completing your child's evaluation and eligibility determination. But you can request a hearing to challenge the results of these tests.

In each of these examples, the school system has discretion in making decisions or is not required by law to perform a specific duty. To make changes in these situations, parents must initiate informal negotiations with school personnel or lobby for help from the local school board, PTA, or other relevant groups. Due process hearings cannot be used to resolve issues of this nature.

What Happens at the Due Process Hearing

The purpose of the due process hearing is to allow an impartial third party, the *hearing officer*, to examine the issues upon which you and the school system disagree and to settle the dispute by making an unbiased decision. Hearing officers are usually appointed by the state education agencies and often are lawyers, educators, or other professionals familiar with special education. The hearing officer cannot be an employee of a public agency involved in the education or care of the child, nor can that person have a professional or personal interest that could adversely affect his objectivity in the hearing. Each state maintains a list of persons who may serve as hearing officers. Refer to your state and local regulations to determine how hearing officers are selected to hear individual cases.

P.L. 94–142 does not describe in great detail the procedures to be followed in due process hearings. Most states, therefore, have developed these procedures more fully in their own laws, regulations, and policies. States' laws differ over matters such as the degree of formality followed in the hearing; whether the hearing officer is a lawyer, educator, or other professional; whether the hearing is conducted by one hearing officer or a panel of hearing officers; and whether or not witnesses are allowed to hear the testimony of one another. Regardless of these differences, however, the basic outlines of a hearing can be described along with certain rights parents may exercise during the hearing.

Rights of Parents in the Hearing

As explained earlier, both parents and school systems may initiate due process hearings. Whichever party initiates the hearing, however, P.L. 94–142 gives you certain rights to employ before, during, and after the hearing. These include the rights:

1. To be accompanied and advised by an attorney or by a lay advocate, and by individuals with special knowledge or training with respect to your child's problems.
2. To present evidence, to confront and cross-examine witnesses, and to compel school personnel to serve as witnesses at the hearing.
3. To prohibit the introduction of any evidence at the hearing that was not disclosed to you at least five days before the hearing.
4. To obtain a written or electronic verbatim record of the hearing.
5. To obtain a written copy of the hearing officer's determination of the facts of the case and the decision reached.
6. To appeal the decision of the local hearing officer to the state education agency and, if desired, to bring suit in the appropriate state court or a district court of the United States.
7. To have your child present at the hearing.*
8. To open the hearing to the public.
9. To receive from the school system reasonable attorney's fees as part of your costs when the hearing officer or judge rules in your favor in a due process hearing or civil action. These costs may only be awarded when parents have been represented by an attorney. Furthermore, since in a few instances costs may not be awarded even when you win your case, you should ask your attorney to explain these exceptions before proceeding. (This right was added by P.L. 99–372, The Handicapped Children's Protection Act of 1986, one of the seven statutes comprising the Education of the Handicapped Act, EHA.)

Description of the Hearing

As mentioned earlier, hearings may be formal or informal, though hearing officers usually prefer informality—especially

---

* School officials also have rights 1 through 6, but only parents have rights 7 through 9.

when parents are not represented by an attorney. Parents may choose to be represented by a lay advocate—a person without a law degree but with specialized knowledge in representing children and parents in due process hearings and other proceedings. The participants in the hearing will be: (l) the parents, their counsel or advocate (where used), and the parents' witnesses; (2) the school system's representative, the school system's counsel (where used), and the school system's witnesses; and (3) the hearing officer. Also in attendance, but not participating, might be a court reporter—if the hearing is transcribed—and the public—if parents have requested an open hearing.

The sequence of events at a typical hearing varies from state to state and according to the formality of the proceedings. Basically, however, a hearing proceeds in the following manner.

Sequence of Events*

1. The hearing officer checks to be sure that all is ready to "go on the record," that is, the stenographer and/or recording equipment are ready.
2. The hearing officer will open the hearing, usually stating:
   a. the nature of the matter to be heard;
   b. the time, date, and place of hearing;
   c. the names of all parties and counsel, if any, and of the hearing officer;
   d. any factual matters already agreed to by the parties; and will
   e. ask for preliminary statements by the parties.
3. The party requesting the hearing, the plaintiff, makes the first opening statement, followed by the opening statement of the other party, the defendant. Opening statements should be brief, clear, and to the point. They explain your view of the case—the issue(s), the law, and the broad outlines of the facts. The purpose of the statement is to give the hearing officer a preview and an overview of what your

---

* Barbara Bateman, *So, You're Going to a Hearing: Preparing for a Public Law 94–142 Due Process Hearing* (Northbrook, Ill.: Hubbard, 1980), pp.18–20.

evidence is going to show. A good opening statement creates an impression of clarity, organization, and control.
4. The plaintiff calls his first witness.
5. The hearing officer swears in the witness and asks that his or her full name be stated for the record.
6. The plaintiff then proceeds with the questioning. If the witness can identify documents to be introduced into evidence, that will happen while the witness is on the stand. For example:

> *Plaintiff:* Your honor, we'd like to introduce this document, D-1. (It is numbered then, if not previously.) What is this? (showing D-1 to witness)

> *Witness:* This is a letter I wrote to the parents on November 15 stating why Jane was not eligible for special education.

> *Plaintiff:* (Shows copy to other counsel)

> *Hearing Officer:* Any objections?

> *Defendant:* No.

> *Hearing Officer:* D-1 is admitted into evidence.

7. The defendant cross-examines and/or questions the plaintiff's witness (optional).
8. The plaintiff again questions witness (optional).
9. The hearing officer questions the plaintiff's witness (optional).
10. Steps 4 through 8 are repeated for all plaintiff's witnesses, then for all defendant's witnesses.
11. Both parties make closing statements. A closing statement summarizes your case, emphasizing the strong points you have made and the weaknesses in your opponent's case. The closing statement, like the opening statement, is not

evidence. Rather, it is your effort to organize the case for the hearing officer so he views it as you wish it to be viewed. Keep it brief. Everyone, even in a short hearing, tends to feel tired and drained and anxious for it to be over.

12. The hearing officer and both parties, still on the record, discuss when written arguments or briefs, if any, are to be submitted, when the decision is to be rendered, and they check that all documents are properly marked and the hearing officer has copies, and so forth.

13. The hearing officer closes the hearing by announcing, "The hearing is closed."

According to P.L. 94–142, the local school system must ensure that within forty-five days after receiving a parent's request for a hearing: (1) a final decision is reached by a hearing officer, and (2) a copy of the decision is mailed to the parents. The decision of the hearing officer is final unless one of the parties appeals to the state education agency or brings civil action in court.

In practice, school systems may fail to meet the forty-five day time limit. When parents complain of these time violations at due process hearings, most hearing officers will criticize the school officials and direct them to comply with time requirements in the future. Seldom, however, will a hearing officer render a decision in favor of a parent merely because the school system has failed to observe legally imposed time guidelines. You can, however, file a formal complaint with the state education agency. Your complaint may lead to a review of the matter by the state education agency and instructions from that agency to refrain from violating these time lines in future cases. Failure to follow these instructions may ultimately result in the withholding of federal and state funds from the local school system. Therefore, local school systems usually will bring their procedures into compliance and will not violate parents' rights in future cases.

Decisions and Appeals

The hearing officer does not make a final decision at the time of the hearing. The maximum length of time the hearing officer has to render a decision is the number of days remaining in the forty-five-day period since the hearing was requested. In practice, most hearing officers attempt to reach a final decision and notify parents within two weeks of the hearing.

The hearing officer's duty is to make an independent judgment either affirming what the school system has done or proposes to do, or directing school professionals to take a specific action to correct a mistake they have made. This judgment clarifies the rights and duties of children, parents, and school officials as to exactly what must be done in order to meet the requirements of the law. The written decision must include the hearing officer's findings of the relevant facts of the case determined at the hearing and his recommendations for resolving the conflict. If you or the school system do not agree with the hearing officer's decision, you may appeal for another hearing with the state education agency, known in many states as the State Board of Education.

The review made by the state education agency will also be an impartial due process hearing. The official conducting this review will examine the record developed in the first hearing to identify the substance of the issues and to see that all procedures followed due process requirements. The reviewing officer may, at his or her discretion, provide the parents and the school system the opportunity to present additional oral or written argument, or both. Finally, the official may request a hearing to obtain additional evidence believed essential to render a fair decision. A formal hearing at this appeal may not be necessary, however, when the reviewing officer believes that sufficient evidence to decide the case has been provided in the original hearing. The decision of this official is final unless you or the school system bring a civil action in court.

Federal law requires the state education agency to render its decision and to notify parties of that decision within thirty days of receipt of the appeal. Some states shorten the time for action by requiring a decision within ten to fifteen days after the initial decision. You need, therefore, to check your own state regulations to determine the time limit in your state.

Should you or the school system believe that the decision of the state education agency is incorrect, P.L. 94–142 gives either party the right to file suit in the appropriate state court or in a federal district court of the United States. If a suit is filed, the court will receive and examine the records of the prior hearings; will hear additional evidence at your request or that of the school system; will base its decision on a preponderance of the evidence (meaning the side having more than 50 percent of the evidence in its favor); and will direct the losing party to do whatever is believed appropriate to remedy the existing problem. Since courts are heavily burdened already, legal action of this nature may take far too long to serve as a practical remedy for problems you may face with school officials.

Think Twice (Or More) before Requesting a Hearing

The decision to resolve your differences with the school system through a due process hearing should not be taken lightly. This step will ultimately involve significant time, money, thought, and physical and emotional energy from both you and school professionals. Consequently, it is seldom advisable to seek a due process hearing unless you have reached the point where you feel any further discussions with school officials are futile and the only way around the impasse is a hearing. Before you reach this point, use every possible means to resolve disagreements. Attend meetings. Request conferences with the teacher, principal, or special education director. Listen to and seriously consider all proposed solutions. Ask questions. And provide all the information you have to prove that your view or recommendation is correct. Prior to requesting a hearing, you may wish to try an intermediate step. In your state this step may be called an administrative review, a conciliatory conference, or mediation.

Final Steps before Requesting a Hearing

If you reach an impasse with school officials, most school systems provide for an administrative review, conciliatory conference, or mediation to resolve troublesome issues before going to a hearing. Usually one or more neutral third parties are brought in to hear the issues and to find an acceptable solution. These third parties are most often drawn from the ranks of schoolteachers and administrators not directly involved in the problem. Since these third parties are employees of the school system, many parents feel that a fair solution cannot be reached in these meetings. Experience with such conciliatory conferences, however, suggests that acceptable solutions frequently are developed when parents and school professionals work in good faith. If you find the outcome of these conferences unsatisfactory, however, you may still go forward with a due process hearing.

The procedures followed in administrative reviews, conciliatory conferences, or mediation are outlined in state and local laws and regulations. The authority of these committees varies. In some states, the conciliatory conference committee can make binding decisions for the school system. In others, the committee functions solely as a mediator attempting to help parents and school officials find an agreeable solution to their problems. Once again, you will need to examine your own state and local laws to determine the functions of this committee in your school jurisdiction.

If you wish to go directly to a due process hearing, you can choose not to work with the principal or special education director and can bypass a conciliatory conference or mediation. The school system cannot require such conferences as prerequisites to a due process hearing, nor can they use the conference to delay the due process hearing. The danger with skipping these intermediate steps is that doing so may prejudice your case. Most hearing officers and judges believe that parents should follow all possible means for resolving their problems before coming to them. So for the sake of your child's education, you need to work as closely as possible with the teachers, principal, and other administrative officials of your school system.

Factors to Consider and Weigh before Requesting a Hearing

As the previous sections pointed out, the decision to request a due process hearing to dispute some aspect of your child's special education program is a serious matter. For this reason, you should consider each of the following matters carefully and thoroughly.

First, do you understand clearly the position of the school system regarding the education of your child, and do you know what evidence—facts, reports, professional testimony—the school will present to support its position? At least five days prior to the hearing, you can obtain from the hearing officer a list of the witnesses and the documents the school system will present. Without this knowledge, you will be unable to determine what issue you are questioning at the hearing, your chance of winning the hearing, and, ultimately, whether or not you should request a hearing.

Second, are you absolutely clear as to what you believe is wrong with the school system's actions or decisions? Do you possess or can you obtain evidence demonstrating that the school's actions or decisions are incorrect? Unless you can articulate precisely where and why the school system is in error, you will be unable to gather evidence to support your case. Furthermore, unless you can submit evidence at the hearing to prove the school's error, the hearing officer cannot rule in your favor.

Third, do you know exactly what services, placement, or other actions you believe the school system should take to provide your child with a free, appropriate public education in the least restrictive environment? Can you obtain evidence to support these educational recommendations for your child? Hearing officers are often not educators. Therefore, it is not enough for you merely to show that what the school system is proposing is inappropriate. You will also need to convince the hearing officer of the correctness of your own educational recommendations. This requires additional research and evidence gathering.

Fourth, when you look at the evidence supporting your position and weigh it against the evidence supporting the school's position, which is more convincing? If the evidence for both positions is equally persuasive, the hearing officer will usually give the educational professionals the benefit of the doubt. Unless the evidence is well over fifty percent in your favor, you will have a very, very difficult case to win.

Fifth, where will your child be placed during the time required to conclude the hearing? Normally, your child will remain in the existing placement pending the outcome of the hearing. If you like your child's placement and the school is recommending a placement you do not like, you may want to request a hearing merely to keep your child where he is until your disagreement is resolved. But what if you do not like your child's current placement but still want to continue with the hearing?

If you wish to place your child in a private school pending the decision of the hearing officer, you should first obtain written agreement for such action from the school officials. If the private placement is upheld by the hearing officer, the school system will be directed to reimburse you. Similarly, if you move your child without the school's permission, you may still receive reimbursement if the hearing officer or court concurs that the placement you have selected is the appropriate placement for your child. If, however, you move your child to a private school, with or without the school's agreement, and your position is not upheld, you will have to pay the private school expenses yourself.

Sometimes even if you do not like your child's current placement, you may find there is no alternative to leaving him in that placement until the hearing is complete. Once the hearing officer announces a decision, the school system will place your child in the education program required by that decision—either the program you proposed, the program the school proposed, or yet a third alternative specified by the hearing officer.

Sixth, do you want a professional to represent your interests in the due process hearing? While you may be well informed regarding educational advocacy for your child, most parents find they are too emotionally involved to represent themselves effectively. Thus, they either obtain the services of an attorney or a lay advocate to prepare and present their case.

Whether you select a lawyer or a lay advocate, you should first make certain that anyone you are considering is experienced in the practice and procedures of special education due process proceedings. Otherwise, you will tend to increase your expenses as your attorney or advocate learns on the job, and reduce your chances of receiving competent representation. You can often find the names of experienced attorneys and advocates by contacting your state and local bar associations, organizations for persons with disabilities, members of the local special education advisory committee, or parent training and information centers in your community or state. (See Appendix B.)

The costs of representation in due process hearings are usually significant. Therefore, before hiring any representative, you should ask for an informal estimate of the costs he believes will be incurred. While the representative cannot be held to this informal estimate, you at least will have a general idea of the amount of money involved.

Although lay advocates may charge less for their services than attorneys, the Handicapped Children's Protection Act of 1986 makes the hiring of a lawyer more attractive should you win the hearing or a court action. Under this law, courts may award reasonable attorney's fees to parents or guardians of disabled children who have been the prevailing party in a due process hearing or civil action. These costs may be awarded only when parents have been represented by an attorney, not by a lay advocate. When costs are awarded, parents are reimbursed by the school system for most expenses involved in preparing and presenting their case. Costs may include travel expenses, fees for expert witnesses, transcripts, and the like. Should you lose your case, however, you remain solely liable for all the costs you have incurred. To understand fully your rights to reimbursement under this statute, you should consult an attorney familiar with your state and federal courts and laws.

Obviously, a decision to go to a hearing is a commitment of substantial time, money, and psychic energy. When two adults share responsibility for a child, *they should not go to a hearing unless both agree that such action should be taken.* Preparing for and participating in a hearing require the cooperation and support of all adults responsible for the child. If both do not agree that a hearing is the only route to go, neither will probably weather the hearing process very well.

The final factor to consider in deciding whether to request a due process hearing is the benefits that will result if you win your case. The most important benefit, of course, is that your child will receive an appropriate educational program designed to meet his specific educational needs. You could even put a dollar value on the benefit by determining how much a similar program would cost—if you could get it—from a private school. A second benefit is that you will have spared your child the harm that might have accompanied an inappropriate educational program. For example, the school system might have diagnosed your child as emotionally disturbed rather than learning disabled. If the school is wrong and is proven so, the benefit you receive is saving your child from the inaccurate label, "seriously emotionally disturbed."

Once you have examined the potential costs and benefits of a hearing and have weighed the chances of winning your case, you are ready to make a final decision. If the potential benefits are greater than the potential costs, you may well want to go to a hearing. If the potential benefits and costs are about equal, you may want to consider alternative ways to provide your child with what you believe is an appropriate educational program. For example, you may want to obtain private placement or services at your own expense. If the costs are much greater than the potential benefits, you will have to decide if you can afford those costs should the hearing officer rule against you.

The decision to request a due process hearing is not an easy one to make. By examining each of the preceding matters, you can understand more completely the implications of your choices and have greater confidence in the correctness of your final decision. One last suggestion—once you have considered all of the pros and cons you can think of, discuss them with friends, professionals, and others familiar with your situation. You will be amazed at how often someone with a fresh perspective will see potential costs and benefits that you have overlooked.

Final Thoughts

The impartial due process hearing has promoted the objectives of the Education for All Handicapped Children Act in two important respects. First, the existence of this process has put school officials on notice that their actions may be reviewed by impartial third parties if parents feel that mistakes have been made. The awareness of such a review has caused school officials to become more careful, discreet, objective, and open in their work with special children and their parents. Without the cloud of the due process hearing hanging over their heads, many school systems might lapse into the practices of prior years when parents' concerns were ignored or merely tolerated.

The second way due process hearings have advanced the goals of P.L. 94–142 is by actually correcting mistakes made by school systems. Considering the hundreds and thousands of children with disabilities which school systems serve each year, it is little wonder that mistakes are made. These mistakes, however, need not go uncorrected today. As parents learn how to exercise their children's and their own due process rights, they become more knowledgeable, influential educational advocates. This chapter has sought to inform you of how and when to use the due process hearing. In the final analysis, the due process hearing should be a last resort for correcting mistakes made by school systems. But because the due process hearing exists for parents to use, its use is needed less often. That is as it should be.

TEN

=== ❖ ❖ ❖ ===

Monitoring
Checkpoints

You have traveled a long way since first entering the special education maze. Referral, evaluation, and eligibility determination seem like dim shadows. Even decisions regarding placement and the IEP are less clear than the day they were made. But now your child is in the appropriate classroom, with appropriate services scheduled to be given. The maze is completed!

But wait, not so fast! All that you have done so far has been essential for your journey. But your task is not completed. Placing a child in a class, establishing educational goals and objectives, and scheduling services on an IEP are not the same as achieving those goals and objectives and receiving those services. Your next step involves periodic checking up on your child's progress. For example, you will want to know if she is moving toward those milestones you set as goals and objectives. Is she receiving the related services agreed upon? Is she spending time with children who are not disabled in the regular education classroom—in music or art class, at recess, and in the cafeteria?

You have completed your trip through the maze only when your child begins to realize her potential as a result of a free, appropriate public education in the least restrictive environment.

This trip is finished only when you monitor your child's IEP and the educational and developmental growth derived from the learning program spelled out in that document. This chapter gives suggestions for monitoring your child's special education program.

Why Monitor?

But why must you monitor your child's program and progress under the IEP? Can't you trust the school systems to live up to what they say will be done? Doesn't there come a time when you have to turn the educational reins over to the "experts"? And isn't now that time?

Yes, most school systems can be trusted to implement the IEP. Nevertheless, attempts to carry out the IEP may fall short for many reasons: lack of funds to hire occupational therapists, a teacher falling ill for several months, or a sudden increase in enrollment leaving less time to work with your child. These and other factors may result in your child's IEP not being implemented. *But they are not legitimate reasons for failing to implement the IEP.* If you know the IEP is not being carried out, you may immediately intervene to get it back on track. Likewise, if the IEP you have agreed to is being carried out to the letter but is ineffective, you may also intervene. But if you have not monitored the IEP, you may find yourself in the position of Mr. and Mrs. Green.

The Greens' son, John, had a major speech disability. The IEP for John, therefore, included individual speech therapy, twice a week, for thirty minutes each period. As the year progressed, the Greens saw little advancement in their son's speech skills. Still, they kept hoping progress would come, in time. At the end of the school year, the Greens met with John's teacher, Ms. Prizer. During their conference, Ms. Prizer proudly showed Mr. and Mrs. Green John's language board. The board contained letters of the alphabet, simple signs for frequently used words—I, go, open, close—and other communication symbols. Ms. Prizer explained that John would carry this small board with him throughout the day. When he wanted to communicate with someone, he would point to the appropriate symbols on his board. The Greens were impressed with this innovation, although somewhat surprised they had not learned of it before the end of school. When they asked Ms. Prizer how the board was used with John's speech therapy, they learned of yet another innovation in their son's IEP. "Oh," said Ms. Prizer, "John has not had speech therapy for seven months. When he showed no progress after two months of therapy, we decided to use the language board as an alternative to speech therapy to improve his communication skills."

Maybe the language board was more useful than speech therapy, but that is not the point. No change in your child's IEP should be made without school personnel notifying you. Unless you monitor your child's IEP, you won't know whether innovations are being made in her program. Yes, once the IEP is written you can turn the educational reins over to the "experts." But you should continue to monitor your child's educational and developmental progress.

Monitoring Practices and Techniques

Most parents approach the topic of monitoring the IEP with apprehension. They wonder, "Who am I to question what the educators are doing?" "How will I know whether the IEP is being implemented?" "What do I do if the IEP is not being followed?" Combine this uncertainty with the normal tendency to trust "authorities," and no wonder parents are hesitant at the thought of second-guessing school officials and teachers.

What can you do to overcome these understandably common fears? Your first concern should be to focus on selected aspects of the IEP to determine:

1. Is the educational plan being carried out?
    a. Is the classroom instruction following the IEP?
    b. Are the required related services being provided?
2. Is the plan working well for your child?
    a. Is the classroom setting truly appropriate for your child's needs?

b. Is your child making educational and/or developmental progress in school?

Having identified the questions to ask for effective monitoring, your second concern becomes finding the answers to those questions. Parents have found many techniques to be helpful when monitoring their child's IEP. The most frequently used methods include the following:

HOLDING CONFERENCES. Having individual meetings with your child's teachers, school administrators, tutors, therapists, and other professionals on a regular basis, or whenever there is an issue to be discussed. Keep a written record of the dates of meetings, topics discussed, and outcomes.

MAKING CLASSROOM OBSERVATIONS. Either visiting the classroom with the specific intent of observing some aspect of your child's learning activities, or volunteering in the class and at the school and using those opportunities to observe your child and her program. Keep a written record of when you make each observation and a detailed description of what you observe.

EXCHANGING A NOTEBOOK. Sharing comments, suggestions, observations, and the like with your child's teacher via a notebook which your child carries to and from school. Also included can be a checklist of important behavioral goals and objectives from the IEP.

JOINING GROUPS. Participating in your local Parent-Teacher Association and in local parent groups such as the Association for Children and Adults with Learning Disabilities (ACLD) and the Association for Retarded Citizens (ARC). These groups often provide excellent, up-to-date information on programs and school services relevant to your child's IEP.

TALKING WITH YOUR CHILD. Asking your child how school is going, what the most enjoyable activities in school are, and how much time she spends in speech or math. Keep written notes detailing your child's responses. Look over her homework, what she has to do and has done. Help her with homework. Note the length of time spent on homework and how much help you provided.

These are just a few of the techniques you might use to assess your child's program and progress during the school year. While the list is not complete, it provides a starting point from which you can begin to develop your own monitoring plan.

You and Your Child's Teacher

The single most important source of information on your child's progress is her teacher. The teacher talks with you after school, at the IEP meeting, and at regularly scheduled conferences. The teacher completes your child's report card and fills out the notebook you send back and forth. The teacher talks with the school psychologist, the physical therapist, and administrators about your child's needs and progress, and then the teacher talks to you.

The free flow of information between you and the teacher will depend mainly upon your relationship with one another. If the teacher perceives you as a concerned parent who also understands the needs and problems of teachers, and if you believe the teacher can teach your child effectively, you will probably receive plenty of up-to-date, specific information about your child's progress. But how do you as a parent develop this cooperative relationship with your child's teacher? You may wish to try some of the following suggestions:

1. Try to develop a personal relationship with your child's teacher. Some families feel comfortable inviting their child's teacher to dinner; others find regular telephone conversations helpful.
2. Give the teachers and specialists sufficient time to get to know your child before asking their opinions about her progress, problems, the appropriateness of her program, and so forth.
3. Convey to the teachers and specialists your understanding of the difficulties they frequently face in doing their jobs— be empathetic to their needs, too!

4. Prepare for conferences in advance by developing and bringing with you a list of questions, concerns, and comments. This saves everybody time and ensures that nothing important will be overlooked.
5. Let teachers and specialists know what is important to you in the education and development of your child.
6. Discuss and share your plan for monitoring your child's IEP, and follow through with that plan.
7. Discuss problems you believe have arisen in implementing the IEP with the teachers and specialists involved. Don't begin by going right to the school administrators.
8. Consider ways you might volunteer time or materials for the classroom.

Each of the preceding activities offers an excellent occasion for you to build bridges of trust and openness with teachers and other specialists working with your child. As these relationships are developed and strengthened, you will experience more and more confidence in your ability to know and understand your child's progress, and the extent to which her IEP is actually being implemented.

Observing in the Classroom

Besides communicating with the teacher, another useful way to monitor your child's educational progress is through classroom observation. Schools vary in their policies of allowing parents to observe classroom activities. How receptive teachers are to parent classroom visits also differs (another good reason for developing an open relationship with your child's teacher). In all cases, however, before you visit your child's classroom, check first with the teacher and then the school principal to determine the specific policy in your school.

Once you know the school policy on classroom visits, you are ready to prepare yourself for this monitoring activity. Following are several suggestions designed to increase the effectiveness of your classroom visit.

1. Give the teacher sufficient prior notice of your visit.
2. Before visiting the class, obtain general information about the classroom. (When does math come? When is recess scheduled? What books are being used?)
3. Decide what you want to observe (e.g., reading group, playground time) and then let the teacher know your plans.
4. Tell the teacher how long you plan to spend in the classroom.
5. Respect the teacher's routines and fit your observations within them when visiting the class.
6. Observe only your own child or interactions involving your child and other children or adults.
7. Keep your conversations with professionals or other adults to a minimum during your observation time.
8. After the classroom visit, make some notes describing your observations, impressions, and/or concerns.
9. Follow up your observation with a brief conference (or phone call or note) thanking the teacher for the opportunity to observe and sharing your findings, thoughts, and questions with the teacher.
10. Tell the teachers and specialists what you like about their teaching style—they'll be pleasantly surprised you noticed.

Whenever you go for a classroom visit, remember that many people, teachers included, can be uncomfortable when they are being observed. The tension created by not knowing why you have come to observe can cause unnecessary anxiety, and even real misunderstanding, between you and the teacher. Notifying the teacher of your desire to observe your child, explaining the purpose of your visit, and following up after the observation can relieve much potential tension. These steps should smooth the way for a productive classroom observation and an open relationship with your child's teacher. You might also want to explain to your child the reasons for your visit in terms that express your interest in her school activities, teachers, and classmates.

Being an Informed Consumer

Besides making classroom visits and communicating with your child's teacher, another helpful monitoring strategy is to become an informed consumer. Although you are not expected to be a special education teacher, physical therapist, or other special education professional, you can still learn many basic ideas important for monitoring your child's education. For example, you can learn about current teaching methods and therapeutic techniques as they relate to your child's disabilities. This information can be obtained in many ways: from parent groups and associations that conduct workshops; from special lectures or presentations; from individual professionals who are willing to share their knowledge with you; from the local PTA; from continuing education classes at local community colleges and universities; and from books, pamphlets, and magazines. In these and many other ways, you can become a knowledgeable consumer of the special education services in your local school system. And as an informed consumer you will also become an effective monitor of your child's educational program and progress.

Summing Up

Monitoring the IEP is hard work. Only time, energy, and careful thought can make it pay off. The jargon—"educationese"— found in many IEPs is often impossible to decipher. Educators know what they mean by "voice quality" or "voice intensity," for example, but parents may not. Make certain, therefore, to ask questions at the time of the IEP conference so you *do* know what the IEP means as well as what it says. This is basic to effective monitoring.

Not knowing if the goals and objectives are appropriate can cause difficulties also. Your own sense of your child's educational needs helps you here. Completing the Strengthening Exercises described in Chapter 2 will give you added confidence in evaluating the annual goals and short-term objectives suggested for your child's IEP. Monitoring by checking up on the dates of the short-term objectives can help you further in assessing the continuing appropriateness of your child's goals and objectives. Are the objectives being met on schedule? ahead of schedule? or not at all? Answers to these questions will lead you to others. For example, if the results are positive or negative, what accounts for those results? Is it the program, the teacher, or the classroom setting? The answers to all these questions may require some changes in your child's IEP.

Making Changes

What happens when your monitoring activities lead you to decide change is necessary? Where do you start the change process?

Elements of your child's IEP can be changed at any time through mutual agreement of the IEP members. But once you have approved an IEP, you should wait a reasonable time before deciding the program is not working or needs changing.

What is a reasonable time? In part, this depends upon your child's age, rate of development, and the educational skills being taught. If your child naturally develops slowly or the educational skill requires significant time to acquire, three to five months may be necessary before noticeable progress occurs. If development is rapid or the skill more readily learned, you may feel that changes should begin within one to three months. In either case, a useful approach would be to wait until the time specified in your child's IEP for assessing achievement of the initial short-term objectives. If these objectives are clearly not being met, a change in program, services, teachers, or some combination of the three may be in order.

The following diagram of circles suggests that the best place to begin your efforts to change your child's IEP is with her teacher or other specialists. If problems are resolved at this initial level, changes will often be immediate and on target. At this first level of change, the process for correcting problems is the least complicated—although it may not seem so. If your efforts to alter the IEP are unsuccessful at this level, you move out one circle toward the perimeter and seek change at the administrative level.

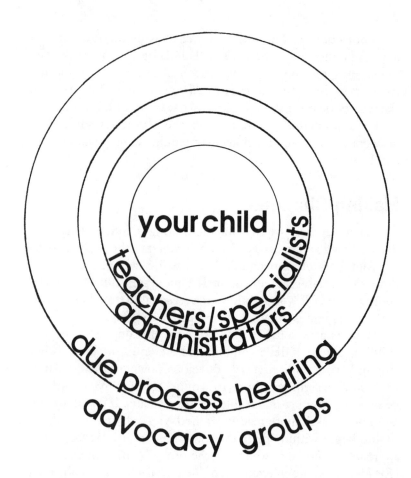

Your first attempts to work with school administrators in changing your child's IEP should be made informally. An informal request for an IEP change sent to the teacher or principal will often be all that is needed. Your request should be accompanied by a written explanation and monitoring data supporting reasons for your request. Should this fail to be sufficient, you can then initiate the administrative review or conciliatory conference procedures available in most school systems.

When satisfactory results are unattainable through the administrative process, your next step is to request a due process hearing. As pointed out in Chapter 9, you must consider this step very carefully before deciding whether to take it. In some instances, however, you may have no alternative. Therefore, even though several months may pass before a final ruling is made to change your child's IEP, the due process hearing remains a viable method for achieving potential change. Of course, if the due process proceedings all seem futile or their results seem biased and inaccurate, you can also seek changes through court action. Considering the time and cost involved in this action, however, its use should be reserved only for major IEP disagreements.

Where, then, does the last circle on the perimeter— political and legal advocacy—enter the IEP change process? This outer circle is often activated to force school systems to do something they currently are not doing, such as providing physical therapy or psychological counseling services. Or political and legal advocacy may also be employed to force school systems to do better and more extensively things they are doing on a limited scale; for example, providing vocational training or speech therapy. In both instances, parents work singly and jointly to persuade school administrators, school boards, city councils, and state legislators to appropriate additional funds for these activities. Or parents sue in court to force school jurisdictions, and indirectly, legislative bodies, to abide by the law and to provide appropriate services. Ideally, both political and legal advocacy can produce the same results—children receive the programs and services in the kinds and amounts appropriate to meet their educational needs.

Although both political and legal advocacy and due process hearings can be highly effective in obtaining educational change, remember: the further you move from the center of the circle, the importance of your child's individual educational needs becomes less and less the focus. Changes made by teachers are usually completed rapidly, with up-to-date information, and in an understanding environment. When IEP changes are generated at points further from your child, the decisions may be slow in coming, out of date, and made out of context. Again, this underscores the need for close relationships with your child's teacher. Begin and end with the teacher whenever you can. You will be miles ahead.

The School Checks Up: Monitoring by the School

The school system must conduct a formal review of your child's program as it is written in her IEP at least once a year. This process is referred to as the *annual review*. The annual review is an opportunity for you, your child's teachers, and other school professionals to look at the past year's IEP goals and objectives and evaluate how well they have been met. The annual review is a time not only to look at past progress, but also to consider next year's IEP goals and objectives.

Sometimes teachers or other school personnel may decide before the annual review that your child's progress is not satisfactory. If so, they usually will notify you, seeking additional information or even suggesting a conference. In some instances they may even request formal evaluations of your child. If this happens, the material you read on evaluation procedures in Chapter 3 will once again become relevant to negotiating the special education maze.

P.L. 94–142 requires the school system to conduct a complete evaluation of your child once every three years. This is called the *triennial evaluation*. The school system may choose, for legitimate reasons, to reevaluate your child before the end of three years, but in general schools have too few resources to evaluate your child very often.

There are several practical implications of the triennial evaluation you should keep in mind. First, because reevaluation occurs only every three years, your child will usually be placed in a particular program and left there for three years, unless something extraordinary happens or you personally request a change. Second, in the three years that elapse between formal evaluations, only the teacher, other professionals working with your child, and you will be monitoring your child's progress. Since even conscientious teachers and other school professionals have limited time to provide services, they often devote little effort to monitoring the results of their work. Therefore, if you don't monitor the IEP carefully, three years could go by before you discover that little or no progress has occurred. Your child cannot afford that time.

There is one other important implication of the requirement for a triennial evaluation that you should not overlook. Every three years you will be faced with a new eligibility determination decision. Pressures on school systems are growing to cut the costs of special education. In the face of these pressures, you must be prepared to present a clear, convincing case as to what, for your child, is an appropriate education in the least restrictive environment. By monitoring your child's IEP carefully and consistently and by following the steps outlined earlier in this book, you should be well on the road to presenting that compelling case for your child each time the triennial evaluation rolls around.

ELEVEN

=== ❖ ❖ ❖ ===

A Review of the Special Education Maze

Does the Maze Ever End?

Over the years parents have often been confused, frustrated, and generally perplexed in their attempts to understand how school officials make decisions about the education of their special children. As parents talk with teachers and administrators and hear of evaluation and eligibility procedures, IEPs, learning disabilities, and due process hearings, they often feel that schools have built a complex special education maze through which only educators can find the way. Parents frequently have not known how to take the first step toward negotiating this maze.

This book has been written for parents—and their special children. In the preceding pages you were introduced to the corridors of the special education maze—the circular process of referral, evaluation, eligibility, IEP, placement, monitoring, and, when necessary, due process procedures. Understanding this process gives you insight into the entry points for the maze, the rules and regulations for traveling through the maze, and potential strategies for negotiating the maze. The end result of your journey, it is hoped, will be that your child receives a free, appropriate public education in the least restrictive environment.

Federal and state laws have created the legal basis for ensuring that children with disabilities receive a free, appropriate public education. Local school systems and their teachers and administrators have the potential knowledge, dedication, and resources to carry out these laws. You, as parents, however, possess the one additional ingredient needed to blend these laws and resources together to produce an effective education for your child. This ingredient is your unique and loving knowledge of your child, what he knows, and how he learns. If this knowledge is not included in educational planning and programming for your child, the program ultimately developed may be inappropriate and, conceivably, ineffective. Your child cannot afford to lose days, months, and years in the wrong program. You do not want this time to be lost, or you would not be reading this book.

Emphasis throughout this book is placed upon the importance of parents acquiring the skills, knowledge, and values essential for becoming effective educational advocates for their children.

Educational advocacy is a means for parents to participate intelligently and collaboratively in decisions affecting the education of their children with disabilities. Educational advocacy offers you an approach for ensuring that your special knowledge of your child is reflected in the educational programs and the educational environment he encounters. Educational advocacy provides you with a plan of action for successfully negotiating the special education maze.

A New Experience with Each Trip through the Maze

The special education planning and programming cycle described in Chapter 1 is a recurring one. Each year the educational goals, objectives, and services outlined in your child's IEP are reexamined and revised as needed. Each time you travel through the special education maze, whether it is for the annual review or the more extensive triennial evaluation, changes will have occurred. You will find new school professionals working with your child; shifts in the laws, regulations, and policies pertaining to special education; and different strategies used by school officials to implement the rules of the maze. The fact that each trip through the maze is a new experience has significant implications for parent educational advocates.

First, each time the cycle begins, you must gather new data about your child; analyze the data; organize it for purposes of making evaluation, eligibility, IEP, and/or placement decisions; and prepare for and participate in the meetings where these decisions are made. All of this, of course, will be more easily accomplished when you have carefully monitored your child's program.

Second, since laws, regulations, policies, and practices change rapidly in the special education field, you should check annually with your state and local education agencies for any changes in these procedures that may have occurred since you last traveled the maze. Following this suggestion will ensure that you do not waste valuable time using outmoded procedures, and, more importantly, that you do not overlook any new rights or entitlements your child has been given over the years.

Third, because school personnel come and go as frequently as rules and regulations change, you should also continually update the key people chart found earlier in this book. By asking around, you should be able to learn something about the educational background and experience of these new people. And, by keeping your information about the educators in the special education maze up-to-date, you can help to foster the confidence and trust needed for successful collaboration.

Fourth, each year brings new problems and opportunities to local school systems. These problems and opportunities often are linked to changes in funding which may have either a positive or negative impact on educational programs. On the negative side, you might find fewer services, higher student/teacher ratios, and longer bus rides. On the positive side, some school systems are recognizing the value of strengthening the parent/professional partnership. One way they are doing this is by establishing parent resource centers in their school systems. Such centers offer training courses in educational advocacy for parents and provide information and referral to school and community services. Both positive and negative changes within local school systems will sometimes alter the ways in which school professionals view their duties for educating disabled children in accordance with federal and state law. By knowing the particular problems and opportunities confronting your school system, you will be better prepared to face any changes in strategy school officials may seek to implement.

Finally, since each trip through the maze is a new one, you will have to formulate new strategies and tactics to be sure they meet the changed conditions. Although you may have succeeded in obtaining an appropriate education for your child on one trip through the maze, past success does not promise continued success. Only thoughtful, careful, hard work can prepare you to be an effective educational advocate for your child. There is no substitute for diligent preparation for negotiating the maze.

Changing the Maze and the Rules of the Maze

You may find that no matter how skilled you become in negotiating the special education maze, your child's program never seems appropriate to meet his needs. Classes may be too large, related services unavailable, self-contained classrooms nonexistent, and transportation inconvenient. When these problems arise and due process procedures, short of court action, fail to correct them, educational advocacy has reached its limits of effectiveness. Legal and political advocacy must then be employed to bring about necessary changes.

Legal advocacy is best used when school officials interpret the law one way and you another. Although hearing officers in due process hearings may agree with the interpretations of school officials, their word is not final. Only the courts can definitively answer questions about the interpretation of laws. Courts clarify the meaning of federal and state laws; courts rule authoritatively on whether state and local education policies and regulations conform with federal and state laws. When you feel that state laws conflict with federal laws and school officials will not change their procedures to meet your objections, the courts offer one alternative for changing both the system itself and the policies and regulations governing it.

Yet another option for altering the special education system is political advocacy. In this type of advocacy, groups lobby legislative, executive, and administrative bodies in an attempt to change specific government budgets, policies, and procedures. The Council for Exceptional Children, the Association for Retarded Citizens, and United Cerebral Palsy are just some examples of the many groups that engage in political advocacy. The distinguishing feature of political advocacy is its emphasis upon changing specific elements of the special education maze—for example, procedures for evaluation, criteria for eligibility, budgets appropriated for special education, and certain rules for special education, such as the rights of parents to participate in various meetings. In contrast to educational advocacy, where the advocate is concerned only with the welfare of one child, political advocacy seeks changes either in the overall process or its encompassing rules and regulations in order to benefit all children with disabilities. This type of advocacy may be essential when the process itself is flawed or where the rules and regulations are inherently unjust or impractical. In these situations educational advocacy will prove insufficient and nothing short of political advocacy will assure a free, appropriate public education for children with disabilities.

Legal and political advocacy have their places, but their effects often are felt only in the long run. In the short run, your child needs immediate services and educational programs that meet his unique needs. Educational advocacy, as outlined in the preceding pages, is designed to assist you in meeting these short-run educational needs. As parents gain skill and experience in using legal, political, and educational advocacy, they will learn the situations in which each is most effectively employed—and will use them accordingly. But in the last analysis, when the special education system and accompanying regulations have been altered by legal and political advocacy, success in negotiating the newly designed system will ultimately depend upon parents' abilities to serve as educational advocates for their own children.

Through the Maze with Others

At many points in the special education planning cycle you have been encouraged to ask a friend to assist and accompany you in advocating for your child. This was true in evaluation, eligibility, IEP/placement, and due process proceedings. The purpose of this suggestion is at least twofold. First, another person can enhance your effectiveness as an educational advocate by serving as a source of ideas and suggestions and as a second pair of eyes and ears. Second, another person can provide the personal and emotional support most parents need to cope with the stress of traveling through the special education maze.

While the help and assistance of one or two friends can make you a more effective educational advocate, the combined efforts and support of numerous other parents can increase your effectiveness even further. By forming a team of parents committed to educational advocacy for their children, you will immediately increase your collective knowledge of the local school maze and decrease the debilitating feeling of isolation so often caused by coping alone with the intricacies and frustrations of the maze.

How do you start your own groups of educational advocates? One good place to begin is by having a number of concerned parents, not more than fifteen to twenty, study this book as a group. If you can enlist the assistance of special education teachers, school psychologists, or other professionals who work with children with disabilities, they may provide the group with expertise to explore in more depth selected topics—for example, evaluation, eligibility, IEPs, or due process procedures. But remember, this book was meant for you—the parent. Don't let professionals take over your course. The intent of the group study is to assist you as an educational advocate for your child. Any professional assistance you get should be oriented toward helping you incorporate your unique insights of your child into his special educational plans and programs.

A second starting point is for you to contact the Parent Training and Information Center (PTIC) in your state. These centers are funded under P.L. 98–199, the 1983 amendment to the Education for All Handicapped Children Act, for purposes of providing training and information to parents of children with disabilities to help them work effectively with professionals. Your state PTIC can teach you strategies for participating in the educational decision-making process, train you to communicate with teachers and other professionals involved in your child's education, and advise you about appropriate programs, resources, and services available to your child. In some states, centers also teach parents how to train other parents in their communities as educational advocates. Appendix B provides a list of all federally funded Parent Training and Information Centers.

The authors of this book are staff members of the Parent Educational Advocacy Training Center (PEATC) in Alexandria, Virginia, a training and information center funded in part by the U. S. Department of Education. The experience of PEATC has shown just how effective parent groups in educational advocacy can become. Since 1978, PEATC has trained—directly and indirectly—thousands of parents to serve as educational advocates for their children. These parents come together in groups of fifteen to thirty for training focused upon the ideas discussed in this book. From this training course, parents acquire insights into the special education process in their local school jurisdictions, skills in educational advocacy to work within that process, and a sense of identity and solidarity with other parents of children with disabilities.

By attending the course, parents make contact with other parents whom they can call upon for insights, knowledge, and the psychological and moral support needed to sustain them on their journeys through the maze. As these parents have gained proficiency as educational advocates, they have often reached out to help other parents who have not attended an educational advocacy course. This mutual support and assistance is essential if parents are to ensure the responsiveness of the system to their children.

Although friends, other parents, and professionals can provide you with the support and know-how you need to become a better advocate, only you, as a parent, can convey your unique understanding of your child to educators and can monitor your child's educational programs. Unless you consciously and actively fulfill the role of educational advocate for your child, you will never be able to work as a partner with school people in making educational decisions. Unless parents throughout the country join together to acquire the knowledge, skills, and values of educational advocacy, the promise of the Education for All Handicapped Children Act will never be fully realized.

The choice is yours. By learning the basics of educational advocacy and speaking up for the rights of your child, you can help forge a strong alliance between parents and school professionals. By banding together and speaking up for the rights of children with disabilities everywhere, parents throughout the United States can help make the promise of a free, appropriate public education for *all* handicapped children a reality.

GLOSSARY

The glossary includes special education terms mentioned in the text as well as words parents may find used in the school setting. It also defines the handicapping conditions which qualify a child for special education services, but does not contain any other terms related to specific handicapping conditions.

Achievement Test: A test that measures a student's level of development in academic areas such as math, reading, and spelling.

Activity Center: A day program where staff members assist disabled adults with activities emphasizing community skill training (e.g., learning to use public transportation) and vocational skill development.

Adaptive Behavior: The extent to which an individual is able to adjust to and to apply new skills to new environments, tasks, objects, and people.

Adaptive Physical Education: A physical education program that has been modified to meet the specific needs of a disabled student; e.g., inclusion of activities to develop upper body strength in a student with limited arm movement.

Administrative Review: A review process whereby disagreements between parents and school systems may be resolved by a committee of school system individuals not directly involved with the case. Also called a conciliatory conference.

Advocacy: Speaking or acting on behalf of another individual or group.

Aged Out (Aging Out): Refers to students with special needs who have reached the maximum age limit mandated in their state for special education and related services.

Annual Goal: Statement describing the anticipated growth of a student's skill and knowledge written into a student's yearly Individualized Education Program.

Annual Review: A yearly review of a student's Individualized Education Program (IEP) and the development of a new IEP for the next year.

Appropriate: See FAPE.

Aptitude Test: A test that measures an individual's potential in a specific skill area, such as clerical speed, numerical ability, or abstract thinking.

Assessment: See **Evaluation.**

At-Risk: Term used to describe children who are considered likely to have difficulties in school because of home life circumstances, medical difficulties at birth, or other factors, and who may need early intervention services to prevent future difficulties.

Audiologist: A professional non-medical specialist who measures hearing levels and evaluates hearing loss.

Auditory Discrimination: The ability to identify and distinguish among different speech sounds; e.g., the difference between the sound of "a" in *say* and in *sad*.

Autism: A developmental disability usually characterized by language disorders (or no language), self-stimulating or self-injuring behaviors, and inability to interact with others.

Behavior Disordered (BD): Term used to describe individuals whose behavior is considered inappropriate, excessive, chronic, and abnormal. Educationally, BD children have difficulty learning, establishing satisfactory relationships with others, and behaving appropriately.

Blind (Blindness): Complete loss of sight. Educationally, individuals who are severely visually impaired, or have no vision and must learn to read by braille, are considered blind. See also **Legally Blind.**

Buckley Amendment: More commonly known name for the Family Educational Rights and Privacy Act of 1974. The law gives parents and students (over age 18) the right to see, correct, and control access to school records.

Career Education: A progression of activities intended to help students acquire the knowledge, skills, and attitudes that make work a meaningful part of life. Career education has four stages: 1) awareness/orientation, 2) exploration, 3) preparation, including vocational education and 4) job placement/follow-up.

Carl D. Perkins Vocational Education Act (1984): A Federal law stipulating that handicapped students be guaranteed participation in vocational programs that receive federal funding and specifying certain criteria that programs must follow.

Child Find: A state and local program mandated by P. L. 94–142 to identify all individuals with handicaps between the ages of birth and twenty-one and to direct them to appropriate educational programs.

Cognitive: A term describing mental processes such as awareness, memory, judgment, and reasoning.

Communication Disorder: A general term for any language and/or speech impairment.

Compliance File: School records containing all reports of meetings, correspondence, and other contacts between parents and school officials.

Conciliatory Conference: See **Administrative Review.**

Confidential File: A file having restricted access and containing records of a child's evaluation and other materials related to special education (medical reports, independent evaluations, reports of eligibility meetings, etc.).

Confidentiality: As used in the educational setting, confidentiality is the limiting of access to a child's school records to his/her parents and to school personnel having direct involvement with the child as covered in the Buckley Amendment.

Congenital: A term referring to a condition present or existing at birth.

Consent: Consent refers to parental permission initially needed to evaluate a child or to place a child in a special education program.

Contract Services: School systems may arrange with private service providers (private schools, institutions, therapists, etc.) to serve students with disabilities when the school system is unable to provide the needed service.

Cumulative File: A file containing report cards, standardized achievement test scores, teacher reports, and other records of a student's school progress.

Deaf (Deafness): A hearing impairment so severe that an individual cannot process sounds even with amplification such as hearing aids.

Deaf-Blind: The combination of visual and hearing impairments causing such severe communication and other developmental and educational problems that a child cannot adequately be served in a special education program solely for deaf or blind children.

Developmentally Delayed: Term used to describe an infant or child whose development is slower than normal in one or more areas of development.

Developmental Disability (DD): Any severe disability, mental and/or physical, which is present before an individual becomes eighteen years old, which substantially limits his activities, is likely to continue indefinitely, and requires life-long care, treatment, or other services. Examples of developmental disabilities include Down syndrome, autism, and cerebral palsy.

Due Process: A system of procedures ensuring an individual will be notified of, and have the opportunity to contest, decisions made about him. As pertains to special education, due process refers to the legal right to appeal any decision regarding any portion of the special education process

Due Process Hearing: A formal session conducted by an impartial hearing officer to resolve special education issues between parents and school systems.

Early Intervention: Providing services and programs to infants and toddlers (under two) with disabilities in order to minimize or eliminate the disability as they mature.

Education for All Handicapped Children Act: Often referred to as P.L. (Public Law) 94–142, this act mandates a free, appropriate public education for all children and youth with handicaps.

Education of the Handicapped Act (EHA): A collection of several federal, special education statutes, including P.L. 94–142 and P.L. 99–457, providing grants to states for initiating, expanding, and improving programs for the education of children with disabilities. Changed by P.L. 101–476 to "Individuals with Disabilities Education Act (IDEA)."

Education of the Handicapped Act Amendments of 1986: Known also as P. L. 99–457, this act authorizes an early intervention program for handicapped infants and toddlers (0-2) and their families.

Educational Advocate: An individual who speaks or acts knowledgeably for the educational needs of another.

Educational Diagnostician: A professional who is certified to conduct educational assessments and to design instructional programs for students.

Eligibility: The determination of whether or not a child qualifies to receive special education services based on meeting the established criteria for handicapping conditions.

Employability Skills: Personal habits and traits such as cleanliness, dependability, and punctuality that are necessary for successful employment; sometimes called "work adjustment skills."

Emotionally Disturbed (ED): See **Behavior Disordered.**

Expressive Language: The ability to communicate through speech, writing, or gestures.

Evaluation: The process of obtaining detailed information about a student's educational needs through a series of tests (academic, performance, psychological, etc.) and observations. May also be called ASSESSMENT.

FAPE: Free, appropriate public education—phrase from P. L. 94–142 describing the education to which handicapped children are entitled. The term "appropriate" refers to an educational program that meets the needs of a student with disabilities.

Fine Motor Skills: Body movements which use small muscles; for example: writing, eating, or tying shoes.

Goal: See **Annual Goal.**

Gross Motor Skills: Body movements which use large muscles; for example: walking, running, or throwing a ball.

Habilitation: The process of helping an individual develop specific skills and abilities (e.g., dressing, eating, maneuvering a wheelchair) in order to become as independent and productive as possible.

Handicapped Children's Protection Act: The law providing for the reimbursement of reasonable attorneys' fees to parents who win their cases in administrative proceedings under the Education for All Handicapped Children Act, P. L. 94–142.

Hard-of-Hearing: Impaired hearing which can be corrected sufficiently with a hearing aid to enable an individual to hear and process sounds. Also used to describe hearing loss occurring after an individual has developed some spoken language.

Hearing Impaired: This term includes both individuals who are deaf and who are hard-of-hearing. The difference between deafness and hard-of-hearing is defined by amount of hearing loss.

Homebound Instruction: Educational instruction given in a student's home when he is unable to attend school for medical or other reasons.

IEP: See **Individualized Education Program.**

IFSP: See **Individualized Family Service Plan.**

I.Q.: See **Intelligence Quotient.**

Impartial Hearing Officer: Individual presiding over a due process hearing, appointed by the state education agency, and not connected with the parties involved in the case in any way.

Independent Evaluation: An evaluation/assessment of a student conducted by a professional not employed by the school system.

Independent Living Skills: Basic skills needed by disabled people to function on their own, with as little help as possible. Skills include self-help (e.g., bathing, dressing), housekeeping, community living (e.g., shopping, using public transportation), etc.

Individualized Education Program (IEP): A written statement for each student in special education describing his present level of performance, annual goals including short-term objectives, specific special education and related services the student is to receive, dates for beginning and duration of service, and how the IEP will be evaluated.

Individualized Family Service Plan: A written statement for each infant or toddler receiving early intervention services that includes goals for the child, goals for the family, and a transition plan for the child into services for children over age 2.

Infant Stimulation: Refers to a program designed to provide specific activities that encourage growth in developmental areas such as movement, speech and language, etc., in infants with developmental delays.

Intelligence Quotient (I.Q.): A measurement of thinking (cognitive) ability for comparison of an individual with others in his age group.

Itinerant Teacher: A teacher who provides services to students in a variety of locations.

Job Coach: A service agency professional who works with a disabled individual at the job site, teaches the needed job skills, and provides ongoing assistance and follow-up.

Learning Disability: A disorder in one or more of the processes involved in understanding or using language, spoken or written, resulting in difficulty with listening, thinking, speaking, writing, spelling, or doing mathematical calculations. This term does not include children with learning problems related to other handicapping conditions such as mental retardation.

Learning Style: An individual's unique way of learning, for example, by reading a book, listening to a lecture, handling materials. Most people learn best through a combination of processes.

Least Restrictive Environment (LRE): Placement of a student with disabilities in a setting that allows maximum contact with non-disabled students, while appropriately meeting all of the student's special education needs.

Legally Blind: An individual is considered to be legally blind if his vision is 20/200 or less, which means being able to see at 20 feet what a person with normal vision sees at 200 feet.

LRE: See **Least Restrictive Environment.**

Mainstreaming: The concept that students with disabilities should be educated with non-disabled students to the maximum extent possible.

Mediation: A formal intervention between parents and school systems to achieve reconciliation, settlement, or compromise.

Mental Retardation: A broad term describing delayed intellectual development resulting in developmental delays in other areas like academic learning, communication, social skills, rate of maturation, and physical coordination.

Minimum Competency: In order to receive a regular high school diploma, many states require students to pass a minimum competency test, demonstrating their academic skills to be at a state-defined level of achievement.

Multidisciplinary Evaluation: The testing of a child by a group of professionals: psychologists, learning disabilities specialists, speech and language therapists, etc.

Multihandicapped: Students having a combination of impairments such as mental retardation and blindness or orthopedic impairments and deafness which cause such educational problems that they cannot be accommodated in programs for any one impairment. This term does not include deaf-blind children.

Non-Categorical: Term relating to programs based on instructional needs rather than on categories of handicapping conditions. Many states have only non-categorical programs; e.g., Maryland, Massachusetts, Minnesota, and others.

Nondiscriminatory Evaluation: An evaluation in which the materials and procedures are not racially or culturally biased. In addition, an individual's handicapping condition must be accommodated; e.g., allowing more test-taking time for an individual who writes slowly as a result of a physical disability.

Objective: An objective is a short-term step taken to reach a long-range goal. IEP objectives are the steps between a student's present level of performance and an annual goal.

Occupational Therapy: Activities focusing on fine motor skills and perceptual abilities that assist in improving physical, social, psychological, and/or intellectual development; e.g., rolling a ball, finger painting.

On-the-Job-Training (OJT): Programs incorporating the learning of job skills and behaviors while doing an actual job.

Orthopedically Impaired: A physical disability that is severe enough to affect a child's educational performance. Orthopedic impairments can be congenital, or caused by disease or injury.

Other Health Impaired: Term used to describe conditions that adversely affect a child's educational performance not covered by other handicapping condition definitions (e.g., Learning Disabilities, Mental Retardation, etc.). This term is frequently used for various medical conditions such as a heart condition, diabetes, cystic fibrosis, leukemia, etc.

P. L. 94–142: See **Education for All Handicapped Children Act.**

P. L. 99–457: See **Education of the Handicapped Amendments of 1986.**

Physical Therapy (PT): Activities or routines designed to increase movement skills.

Placement: The setting in which a child with disabilities is to be educated. Placement includes the school, the classroom, related services, and the amount of time the child will spend with non-disabled peers.

Psychiatrist: A physician (M.D.) with advanced training in psychiatry who specializes in the diagnosis and treatment of emotional disorders.

Psychological Evaluation: The portion of a child's overall evaluation/assessment for special education that tests his general intelligence, eye-hand coordination, social skills, emotional development, and thinking skills.

Psychologist: A professional with advanced training in the study of mental processes and human behavior.

Reasonable Accommodation: The modification of programs in ways that permit students with disabilities to participate in educational programs which receive federal funding. The concept also applies to the modification of job requirements for workers with disabilities.

Receptive Language: The process of receiving and understanding written or spoken language.

Reevaluation: See **Triennial Evaluation.**

Referral: A formal notification to the local school that a child is experiencing educational difficulties and may need a full evaluation for special education.

Related Services: Those services a student must receive to benefit from special education; for example, transportation, occupational therapy, speech therapy, counseling, and medical services.

Residential Placement: The placement of a student in a setting that provides educational instruction and 24-hour care.

Resource Room: The setting in a school where a student receives instruction for a portion of the school day from a special education teacher.

School-Based Screening Committee: See **Screening Committee.**

Screening Committee: A local school-based committee, whose members determine if a student should be fully evaluated for special education eligibility.

Section 504 (Rehabilitation Act of 1973): Section 504 affirms a handicapped child's right to a free, appropriate public education and stipulates that individuals may not be excluded from participating in programs and services receiving federal funds because they are disabled. It also prohibits job discrimination against people with disabilities.

Self-Contained Classroom: A classroom in which a group of students with disabilities receive their entire instructional program with little or no interaction with non-handicapped students.

Sheltered Workshop: A work setting in which persons with disabilities do contract work usually on a piece-rate basis and productivity is at least 50 percent of a nondisabled worker.

Social Worker: In an educational context, a school social worker provides a link between school personnel and the families of disabled children through activities such as individual pupil evaluation, parent interviews, and contact with community support services.

Sociocultural Report: The portion of a child's overall evaluation/assessment for special education that describes a child's background and behavior at home and at school. It is usually completed by a social worker.

Special Education File: See **Confidential File.**

Specific Learning Disability (SLD): See **Learning Disability.**

Speech Impaired: A communication disorder involving poor or abnormal production of the sounds of language.

Speech-Language Pathologist: A professional who evaluates and develops programs for individuals with speech or language problems.

Speech Therapy: Activities or routines designed to improve and increase communication skills.

Supported Employment: Competitive employment in settings with nondisabled workers for individuals with disabilities who require on-going assistance to do their jobs.

Transition: The process of moving from one situation to another. Frequently used to mean moving from preschool programs into elementary school or from school to work and the community.

Triennial Review: Every three years, a student in special education has a completely new evaluation/assessment and determination of eligibility for continued special education services.

Visual-Motor Integration: The extent to which an individual can coordinate vision with body movement or parts of the body; e.g., being able to copy words from the blackboard.

Visually Impaired: Having a mild to severe vision disorder, which adversely affects a child's educational performance.

Vocational Assessment (Evaluation): A systematic process of evaluating an individual's skills, aptitudes, and interests as they relate to job preparation and choice.

Vocational Education: Formal training designed to prepare individuals to work in a certain job or occupational area.

Vocational Rehabilitation: A comprehensive system that assists temporarily or permanently disabled individuals in the areas of assessment, counseling, training, physical rehabilitation, and job placement.

Work Adjustment Skills: See **Employability Skills.**

APPENDIX A

Federal Offices

Department of Education

Office of Special Education and
Rehabilitative Services
330 C Street, SW
Mary Switzer Building
Washington, D.C. 20202
202/732-1245

Office of Special Education Programs
330 C Street, SW
Mary Switzer Building
Washington, D.C. 20202
202/732-1007

Rehabilitative Services Administration
330 C Street, SW, Room 3028
Mary Switzer Building
Washington, D.C. 20202
202/732-1282

Office for Civil Rights
303 Independence Avenue, SW
Washington, D.C. 20201
202/245-6118

Regional Offices: Office for Civil Rights

Region I. Connecticut, Maine, Massachusetts, New Hampshire, Rhode Island, Vermont

Office for Civil Rights
Room 222, J. W. McCormack Post Office and Courthouse
Boston, MA 02109
617/835-1340

Region II. New York, New Jersey, Puerto Rico, Virgin Islands

Office for Civil Rights
Federal Building
26 Federal Plaza, 33rd Floor
New York, NY 01278
212/264-5180

Region III. Delaware, District of Columbia, Maryland, Pennsylvania, Virginia, West Virginia

Office of Civil Rights
Gateway Building, 6th Floor
3535 Market Street, P.O. Box 13716
Philadelphia, PA 19101
215/596–6772

Region IV. Alabama, Florida, Georgia, Kentucky, Mississippi, North Carolina, South Carolina, Tennessee

Office for Civil Rights
101 Marietta St., NW, 27th Floor
Atlanta, GA 30323
404/221–2954

Region V. Illinois, Indiana, Minnesota, Michigan, Ohio, Wisconsin

Office for Civil Rights
300 South Wacker Drive, 8th Floor
Chicago, IL 60606
312/886–3456

Region VI. Arkansas, Louisiana, New Mexico, Oklahoma, Texas

Office for Civil Rights
1200 Main Tower Building, Room 1935
Dallas, TX 75202
214/767–3959

Region VII. Iowa, Kansas, Missouri, Nebraska

Office for Civil Rights
10220 N. Executive Hills Blvd, 8th Floor
Kansas City, MO 64153
816/891–8026

Region VIII. Colorado, Montana, North Dakota, South Dakota, Utah, Wyoming

Office for Civil Rights
Federal Office Building, Room 1185
1961 Stout St.
Denver, CO 80294
303/844–5695

Region IX. Arizona, California, Hawaii, Nevada, Guam, American
Samoa, Trust Territory of Pacific Islands, Wake Island

Office for Civil Rights
221 Main Street, 10th Floor
San Francisco, CA 94103
415/227–8040

Region X. Alaska, Idaho, Oregon, Washington

Office for Civil Rights
2901 Third Avenue, M/S 106
Seattle, WA 98121
206/442–1635

Other Federal Offices

Administration on Developmental Disabilities
Office of Development Services
330 C Street, SW, Room 3070
Washington, D.C. 20201
202/245–2890

Architectural and Transportation Barriers Compliance Board
330 C Street, SW
Switzer Building, Room 1010
Washington, D.C. 20202
202/245–1591 Voice/TDD

Bureau of Indian Affairs
1951 Constitution Avenue, NW
Washington, D.C. 20202
202/343–5831

National Council on Disability
800 Independence Avenue, SW
Washington, D.C. 20591
202/267–3846

National Institute of Education
Brown Building
19th and M Streets, NW
Washington, D.C. 20208
202/254–5740

President's Committee on Employment of People with Disabilities
111 20th Street, NW, Suite 636
Washington, D.C. 20036
202/653–5044

President's Committee on Mental Retardation
330 Independence Avenue, SW
Washington, D.C. 20201
202/245–7634

Program Information and Coordination Staff
Clearinghouse on the Handicapped
Switzer Building, Room 3132
330 C Street, SW
Washington, D.C. 20202–2319
202/732–1723/1245/1250

APPENDIX B

State Offices

For each state, the following offices are listed:
1. Director of Special Education
2. Protection and Advocacy
3. Vocational Rehabilitation Agency
4. Parent Training and Information Project(s)*

Alabama

Director of Special Education
Student Instructional Services
State Department of Education
1020 Monticello Court
Montgomery, AL 36117–1901
205/261–5099

Program Director
Alabama Disabilities Advocacy Program
P.O. Drawer 2847
Tuscaloosa, AL 35487–2847
205/348–4928

Director
Rehabilitation & Crippled Children Service
P.O. Box 11586
Montgomery, AL 36111–0586
205/281–8780

Special Education Action Committee
P.O. Box 161274
Mobile, AL 36606
205/478–1208

Alaska

Director of Special Education
Office of Special Services
Alaska Department of Education
P.O. Box F
Juneau, AK 99811
907/465–2970

Director
Advocacy Services of Alaska
325 E. 3rd Avenue, 2nd Floor
Anchorage, AK 99501
907/273–3658

Director
Division of Vocational Rehabilitation
Pouch F, MS 0581
Juneau, AK 99811
907/465–2814

American Samoa

Director of Special Education
Special Education
Department of Education
Pago Pago, American Samoa 96799
684/633–1323

Client Assistance Program
P.O. Box 3407
Pago Pago, American Samoa 96799
4–011–684–633–2418

Arizona

Director of Special Education
Special Education Section
Department of Education
1535 W. Jefferson
Phoenix, AZ 85007–3280
602/255–3183

---

* Not every state has a Parent Training and Information Project and a few states have several.

Protection & Advocacy
Arizona Center for Law in the Public
    Interest
112 N. Central Ave., Suite 400
Phoenix, AZ 85004
602/252–4904

Administrator
Rehabilitative Services Administration
1300 W. Washington St.
Phoenix, AZ 85007
602/255–3332

Pilot Parents
2005 N. Central Avenue, #100
Phoenix, AZ 85004
602/271–4012

Arkansas

Director of Special Education
Special Education Section
Arkansas Department of Education
Education Bldg., Room 105–C
#4 Capitol Mall
Little Rock, AR 72201
501/371–2161

Executive Director
Advocacy Services, Inc.
Medical Arts Bldg., Suite 311
12th and Marshall Streets
Little Rock, AR 72202
501/371–2171

Commissioner
Arkansas Department of Human Ser-
    vices
Rehabilitation Services Division
P.O. Box 3781
Little Rock, AR 72203

Arkansas Coalition for the Handicapped
519 East Fifth Street
Little Rock, AR 72202
501/376–3420

FOCUS
2917 King Street, Suite C
Jonesboro, AR 72401
501/935–2750

California

Director of Special Education
Specialized Programs Branch
Special Education Division
P.O. Box 844272
Sacramento, CA 94244–2720
916/323–4768

Executive Director
Protection & Advocacy, Inc.
2131 Capitol Avenue, Suite 100
Sacramento, CA 95816
916/447–3327
213/481–7431
415/839–0811
800/952–5746

Director
Department of Rehabilitation
830 K St. Mall
Sacramento, CA 95814
916/445–3971

Team of Advocates for Special Kids
    (TASK)
18685 Santa Ynez
Fountain Valley, CA 92708
714/962–6332

Parents Helping Parents
535 Race Street, Suite 220
San Jose, CA 95126
408/288–5010

DREDF
2212 6th Street
Berkeley, CA 94710
415/644–2555

Disability Services Matrix
P.O. Box 6541
San Rafael, CA 94903
415/499–3877

Colorado

Director of Special Education
Special Education Services Unit
Colorado Department of Education
201 E. Colfax
Denver, CO 90203
303/866–6694

Executive Director
The Legal Center
455 Sherman Street, Suite 130
Denver, CO 80203
303/722–0300

Director
Division of Rehabilitation
Department of Social Services
1575 Sherman St., 4th Floor
Denver, CO 80203

Parent Education and Assistance for
Kids (PEAK)
6055 Lehman Drive, Suite 101
Colorado Springs, CO 80918
719/531–9400
800/621–8386, Ex. 338 (in Colorado)

Connecticut

Director of Special Education
Bureau of Special Education and Pupil
Personnel Services
P.O. Box 2219
Hartford, CT 06102–2219
203/566–3561

Executive Director
Office of Protection & Advocacy for
Handicapped & Developmentally
Disabled Persons
90 Washington St.
Hartford, CT 06106
203/566–7616/2102
800/842–7303 (in Connecticut)

Associate Commissioner
State Department of Education
Division of Vocational Rehabilitation
600 Asylum Ave.

Hartford, CT 06105
203/566–4440

Connecticut Parent Advocacy Center,
Inc.
P.O. Box 579
East Lyme, CT 06333
203/739–3089
800/445–CPAL (in Connecticut)

Delaware

Director of Special Education
Exceptional Children/Special Programs
Division
Department of Public Instruction
P.O. Box 1402
Dover, DE 19903
302/736–5471

Administrator
Disabilities Law Program
144 E. Market St.
Georgetown, DE 19947
302/856–0038

Director
Division of Vocational Rehabilitation
Department of Labor
State Office Building, 7th Floor
820 N. French St.
Wilmington, DE 19801
302/571–2850

Parent Information Center of Delaware,
Inc.
325 E. Main Street, Suite 203
Newark, NJ 19711
302/366–0152

District of Columbia

Director of Special Education
Division of Special Education and Pupil
Personnel Services
D.C. Public Schools
Webster Administration Bldg.
10th & H Streets, NW
Washington, D.C. 20001
202/724–4018

Executive Director
Information, Protection, and Advocacy
  Center for Handicapped Individuals, Inc.
300 Eye St., NE, Suite 202
Washington, D.C. 20002
202/547–8081

Administrator
D.C. Rehabilitation Services Administra-
  tion
Commission on Social Services
Department of Human Services
605 G St., NW, Room 1101
Washington, D.C. 20001
202/727–3227

Florida

Director of Special Education
Bureau of Education for Exceptional
  Studies
Florida Department of Education
Knott Building
Tallahassee, FL 32301
904/488–1570

Executive Director
Advocacy Center for Persons with Disabilities, Inc.
2661 Executive Center Circle, W
209 Clifton Bldg.
Tallahassee, FL 32301
904/488–9070
800/342–0823 Voice/TDD

Director
Division of Vocational Rehabilitation
1709–A Mahan Dr.
Tallahassee, FL 32399–0696
904/488–6210

Parent Education Network of Florida,
  Inc.
2215 East Henry Avenue
Tampa, FL 33610
813/238–6100

Georgia

Director of Special Education
Program for Exceptional Children
Georgia Department of Education
1970 Twin Towers East
205 Butler Street
Atlanta, GA 30334–1601
404/656–2425

Executive Director
Georgia Advocacy Office, Inc.
1447 Peachtree St., NE, Suite 811
Atlanta, GA 30309
404/885–1447
800/282–4538 (in Georgia)

Director
Division of Rehabilitative Services
Department of Human Services
878 Peachtree St., NE, Room 706
Atlanta, GA 30309
404/894–6670

Parents Educating Parents
Georgia ARC
1851 Ram Runway, Suite 104
College Park, GA 30337
404/761–2745

Guam

Director of Special Education
Special Education
Department of Education
P.O. Box DE
Agana, Guam 97910
671/472–8901, ex. 375

Administrator
The Advocacy Office
P.O. Box 8830
Tamuning, Guam 96911
671/646–9026/27 or 646–6204

Director
Department of Vocational Rehabilitation
414 W. Soledad Ave.

Government of Guam
Agana, Guam 97910
472–8806 (Dial 011671 first)

Hawaii

Director of Special Education
Special Needs Branch
State Department of Education
3430 Leahi Avenue
Honolulu, HI 96815
808/737–3720

Executive Director
Protection & Advocacy Agency of Hawaii
1580 Makaloa St., Suite 1060
Honolulu, HI 96814
808/949–2922

Administrator
Division of Vocational Rehabilitation &
    Services for the Blind
Department of Social Services
P.O. Box 339
Honolulu, HI 96809
808/548–4769

Idaho

Director of Special Education
Special Education
State Department of Education
650 W. State Street
Boise, ID 83720–0001
208/334–3940

Idaho's Coalition of Advocates for the
    Disabled, Inc.
1409 W. Washington
Boise, ID 83702
208/336–5353

Administrator
Division of Vocational Rehabilitation
Len B. Jordan Bldg., Room 150
650 West State
Boise, ID 83720
208/334–3390

Illinois

Director of Special Education
Illinois State Board of Education
Mail Code E–216
100 North First Street
Springfield, IL 62777–0001
217/782–6601

Director
Protection & Advocacy, Inc.
175 W. Jackson, Suite A–2103
Chicago, IL 60604
312/341–0022 Voice/TDD

Director
Department of Rehabilitation Services
    (Illinois)
623 E. Adams St.
P.O. Box 19429
Springfield, IL 62794–9429
217/785–0218

Coordinating Council for Handicapped
    Children
20 E. Jackson Blvd., Room 900
Chicago, IL 60604
312/939–3513

Designs for Change
220 South State Street, Room 1900
Chicago, IL 60604
312/922–0317

Indiana

Director of Special Education
Division of Special Education
Indiana Department of Education
229 State House
Indianapolis, IN 46204
317/629–9462

Indiana Protection & Advocacy
Service Commission for the Develop-
    mentally Disabled
850 N. Meridian St., Suite 2–C
Indianapolis, IN 46204
317/232–1150
800/622–4845 (in Indiana)

Commissioner
Indiana Department of Human Services
251 N. Illinois St.
P.O. Box 7083
Indianapolis, IN 46207–7083
317/232–7000

Task Force on Education for the Handicapped, Inc.
833 Northside Blvd.
South Bend, IN 46617
219/234–7101

Iowa

Director of Special Education
Division of Special Education
Iowa Department of Public Instruction
Grimes State Office Building
Des Moines, IA 50319–0146
515/281–3176

Director
Iowa Protection & Advocacy Services,
Inc.
3015 Merie Hay Rd., Suite 6
Des Moines, IA 50310
515/278–2502

Administrator
Division of Vocational Rehabilitation
Services
Department of Education
510 E. 12th St.
Des Moines, IA 50319
515/281–4311

Iowa Exceptional Parent Center
33 North 12th Street
P.O. Box 1151
Ft. Dodge, IA 50501
515/576–5870

Kansas

Director of Special Education
Kansas Department of Education
120 E. Tenth Street

Topeka, KS 66612
913/296–4945

Executive Director
Kansas Advocacy & Protection Services
513 Leavenworth, Suite 2
Manhattan, KS 66502
913/776–1541
800/432–8276 (in Kansas)

Commissioner of Rehabilitation Services
Department of Social & Rehabilitative
Services
Biddle Bldg., 2nd Floor
2700 W. 6th
Topeka, KS 66606
913/296–3911

Families Together, Inc.
P.O. Box 86153
Topeka, KS 66686
913/273–6343

Kentucky

Director of Special Education
Kentucky Department of Education
Office of Education for Exceptional
Children
Capitol Plaza Tower, Room 820
Frankfort, KY 40601
501/564–4970

Director
Department of Public Advocacy
Protection & Advocacy Division
1264 Louisville Rd.
Perimeter Park West
Frankfort, KY 40601
502/564–2967
800/372–2988 Voice/TDD

Assistant Superintendent of Rehabilita-
tion
Department of Education
Bureau of Rehabilitative Services
Capital Plaza Office Tower
Frankfort, KY 40601
502/564–4440

Kentucky Special Parent Involvement
Network
318 W. Kentucky Street
Louisville, KY 40203
502/587–5717 or 584–1104

Louisiana

Director of Special Education
Louisiana Department of Education
Special Education Services
P.O. Box 44064, 9th Floor
Baton Rouge, LA 70804–9064
504/342–3633

Executive Director
Advocate Center for the Elderly & Disabled
1001 Howard Ave., Suite 300–A
New Orleans, LA 70113
504/522–2337
800/662–7705 (in Louisiana)

Director
Division of Rehabilitation Services
P.O. Box 94371
Baton Rouge, LA 70804
504/342–2285

United Cerebral Palsy of Greater New
Orleans
1500 Edwards Avenue, Suite O
Harahan, LA 70123
504/733–7736

Maine

Director of Special Education
Division of Special Education
Maine Department of Educational and
Cultural Services
Station #23
Augusta, ME 04333
207/289–5953

Director
Advocates for the DD
2 Mulliken Court
P.O. Box 5341
Hallowell, ME 04347

207/289–5755
800/452–1948 (in Maine)

Director
Bureau of Rehabilitative Services
Department of Health & Welfare
32 Winthrop St.
Augusta, ME 04330
207/289–2266

Special Needs Parent Information Network (SPIN)
P.O. Box 2067
Augusta, ME 04330
207/582–2504
800/325–0220 (in Maine)

Maryland

Director of Special Education
Division of Special Education
Maryland State Department of Education
200 W. Baltimore Street
Baltimore, MD 21201–2595
301/333–2489

Director
Maryland Disability Law Center
2510 St. Paul St.
Baltimore, MD 21218
301/333–7600

Assistant State Superintendent
Division of Vocational Rehabilitation
State Department of Education
200 W. Baltimore St.
Baltimore, MD 21201
301/659–2294

See Parent Educational Advocacy Training Center under Virginia

Massachusetts

Director of Special Education
Division of Special Education
Massachusetts Department of Education
1385 Hancock Street, 3rd Floor

Quincy, MA 02169–5183
617/770–7468
Executive Director
DD Law Center of Massachusetts
11 Beacon Street, Suite 925
Boston, MA 02108
617/723–8455

Commissioner
Massachusetts Rehabilitation Commission
20 Park Plaza, 11th Floor
Boston, MA 02116
617/727–2172

Federation for Children with Special
Needs
312 Stuart Street, 2nd Floor
Boston, MA 02116
617/482–2915
800/331–0688 (in Massachusetts)

Michigan

Director of Special Education
Special Education Services
Michigan Department of Education
P.O. Box 30008
Lansing, MI 48909–7508
517/373–9433

Executive Director
Michigan Protection & Advocacy Service, Inc.
109 W. Michigan Ave., Suite 900
Lansing, MI 48933
517/487–1755

State Director
Michigan Rehabilitation Services
Michigan Department of Education
P.O. Box 30010
Lansing, MI 48909
517/373–0683

United Cerebral Palsy Assn. of
Metropolitan Detroit
Parents Training Parents Project
17000 West 8 Mile Road, Suite 380

Southfield, MI 48075
313/557–5070

Citizens Alliance to Uphold Special
Education (CAUSE)
313 South Washington Sq., Suite 040
Lansing, MI 48933
517/485–4084
800/221–9105 (in Michigan)

Minnesota

Director of Special Education
Special Education Section
Department of Education
812 Capitol Square Bldg.
550 Cedar Street
St. Paul, MN 55101–2233
612/359–3490

Managing Attorney
Legal Aid Society of Minneapolis
222 Grain Exchange Bldg.
323 Fourth Ave, S.
Minneapolis, MN 55415
612/332–7301

Assistant Commissioner
Division of Rehabilitation Services
Department of Jobs and Training
390 N. Robert St., 5th Floor
St. Paul, MN 55101
612/296–1822

PACER Center, Inc.
4826 Chicago Avenue South
Minneapolis, MN 55417
612/827–2966
800/53–PACER (in Minnesota)

Mississippi

Director of Special Education
Bureau of Special Services
State Department of Education
P.O. Box 771
Jackson, MS 39205–0771
601/359–3498

Executive Director
Mississippi Protection & Advocacy System, Inc.
4793B McWillie Dr.
Jackson, MS 39206
601/981–8207
800/772–4057 (in Mississippi)

Director
Department of Rehabilitation Services
Vocational Rehabilitation Division
932 N. State St.
P.O. Box 1698
Jackson, MS 39215–1698
601/354–6825

Association of Developmental Organizations of Mississippi
6055 Highway 18 South, Suite A
Jackson, MS 39209
601/922–3210
800/231–3721 (in Mississippi)

Missouri

Director of Special Education
Special Education
Department of Elementary and Secondary Education
P.O. Box 480
Jefferson City, MO 65102
314/751–2965

Missouri Protection & Advocacy Services
211–B Metro Drive
Jefferson City, MO 65101
314/893–3333
800/392–8667 (in Missouri)

Assistant Commissioner
State Department of Education
Division of Vocational Rehabilitation
2401 E. McCarty
Jefferson City, MO 65101
314/751–3251

Missouri Parents Act (MPACT)
P.O. Box 1141 G.S.

Springfield, MO 65808
417/882–7434 or 869–6694

Montana

Director of Special Education
Special Education
Office of Public Instruction
State Capitol, Room 106
Helena, MT 59620
406/444–4429

Executive Director
Montana Advocacy Program
1410 8th Avenue
Helena, MT 59601
406/444–3889
800/245–4743 (in Montana)

Administrator
Department of Social & Rehabilitative Services
Rehabilitative-Visual Services Division
P.O. Box 4210
Helena, MT 59604
406/444–2590

Parents, Let's Unite for Kids (PLUK)
1500 N. 30th Street
Billings, MT 59101
406/727–4590
800/222–PLUK (In Montana)

Nebraska

Director of Special Education
Special Education
Nebraska Department of Education
Box 94987
Lincoln, NE 68509–4987
402/471–2471

Executive Director
Nebraska Advocacy Services, Inc.
522 Lincoln Center Bldg.
215 Centennial Mall South
Lincoln, NE 68508
402/474–3183
800/422–6691 (in Nebraska)

Associate Commissioner & Director
Division of Rehabilitative Services
State Department of Education
301 Centennial Mall, 6th Floor
Lincoln, NE 68509
402/471–2961

Nevada

Director of Special Education
Special Education
Nevada Department of Education
Capitol Complex
400 W. King Street
Carson City, NV 89710–0004
702/885–3140

Project Director
Office of Protection & Advocacy
2105 Capurro Way, Suite B
Reno, NV 89431
702/789–0233
800/992–5715 (in Nevada)

Administrator, Rehabilitation Division
Department of Human Resources
Kinkead Bldg., 5th Floor
505 E. King St.
Carson City, NV 89710
702/885–4440

Nevada Association for the Handicapped
6200 W. Oakey Blvd.
Las Vegas, NV 89201–1142
702/870–7050

New Hampshire

Director of Special Education
Special Education Bureau
New Hampshire Department of Education
101 Pleasant Street
Concord, NH 03301–3860
603/271–3741

Executive Director
Disabilities Rights Center, Inc.
94 Washington St.

P.O. Box 19
Concord, NH 03302–0019
603/228–0432

Director
State Department of Education
Division of Vocational Rehabilitation
78 Regional Dr., Bldg. JB
Concord, NH 03301
603/271–3471

Parent Information Center
155 Manchester St.
P.O. Box 1422
Concord, NH 03302–1422
603/224–6299

New Jersey

Director of Special Education
Division of Special Education
New Jersey Department of Education
P.O. Box CN 500
225 W. State St.
Trenton, NJ 08625–0001
609/292–0147

Director
Division of Advocacy for the Develop-
    mentally Disabled
Hughes Justice Complex, CN850
Trenton, NJ 08625
609/292–9742
800/792–8600 (in New Jersey)

Director, Division of Vocational
Rehabilitation Services
Labor & Industry Bldg., CN398
John Fitch Plaza, Rm. 1005
Trenton, NJ 08625
609/292–5987

Parents and Children Together Or-
    ganized for Family Learning
    (PACTO)
66 Lakeview Drive
P.O. Box 114
Allentown, NJ 08501
201/324–2451

Statewide Parent Advocacy Network
(SPAN)
516 North Avenue East
Westfield, NJ 07090
201/654–7726

New Mexico

Director of Special Education
Special Education
State Department of Education
State Educational Building
Santa Fe, NM 87501–2786
505/827–6541

Protection & Advocacy System
2201 San Pedro, NE
Bldg. 4, Suite 140
Albuquerque, NM 87110
505/888–0111
800/432–4682 (in New Mexico)

DVR Director
Division of Vocational Rehabilitation
604 W. San Mateo
Santa Fe, NM 87503
505/827–3511

Education for Indian Children with Special Needs (EPICS)
P.O. Box 788
Bernalillo, NM 87004
505/867–3396

New York

Director of Special Education
New York State Department of Educa-
tion
Office of Education of Children with
Handicapping Conditions
Education Building Annex, Room 1073
Albany, NY 12234–0001
518/474–5548

Commissioner
New York Commission on Quality of
Care for the Mentally Disabled

99 Washington Ave., Suite 1002
Albany, NY 12210
518/473–4057

Deputy Director
Office of Vocational Rehabilitation
One Commerce Plaza, Room 1907
Albany, NY 12234
518/474–2714

Parent Network Center
1443 Main Street
Buffalo, NY 14209
716/885–1004

North Carolina

Director of Special Education
Division of Exceptional Children
North Carolina State Department of
Public Instruction
Education Bldg., Room 442
116 W. Edenton
Raleigh, NC 27603–1712
919/733–3921

Director
Governor's Advocacy Council for Persons with Disabilities
1318 Dale St., Suite 100
Raleigh, NC 27605
919/733–9250

Director
Division of Vocational Rehabilitation
Services
Department of Human Resources
State Office
P.O. Box 26053
Raleigh, NC 27611
919/733–3364

Exceptional Children's Advocacy
Council
P.O. Box 16
Davidson, NC 28036
704/892–1321

ARC, North Carolina
Family and Infant Preschool Program
Western Carolina Center
300 Enola Road
Morganton, NC 28655
704/433–2661

North Dakota

Director of Special Education
Special Education
Department of Public Instruction
State Capitol
Bismarck, ND 58505–0440
701/224–2277

Director
Protection & Advocacy Project
State Capitol Judicial Wing, 1st Floor
Bismarck, ND 58505
701/224–2972
800/472–2670 (in North Dakota)

Division Director
Division of Vocational Rehabilitation
State Capitol Bldg.
Bismarck, ND 58505
701/224–2907

Pathfinder Services of North Dakota
RRI Box 18–A
Maxbass, ND 58760
701/268–3390

Ohio

Director of Special Education
Ohio Department of Education
Division of Special Education
933 High Street
Worthington, OH 43085–4017
614/466–2650

Executive Director
Ohio Legal Rights Service
8 E. Long St., 6th Floor
Columbus, OH 43215
614/466–7264
800/282–9181 (in Ohio)

Administrator
Ohio Rehabilitation Services Commission
4656 Heaton Rd.
Columbus, OH 43229
614/438–1210

SOC Information Center
106 Wellington Place, Suite LL
Cincinnati, OH 45219
513/381–2400

Ohio Coalition for the Education of
Handicapped Children
933 High Street, Suite 106
Worthington, OH 43085
614/431–1307

Oklahoma

Director of Special Education
Special Education Section
State Department of Education
Oliver Hodge Memorial Bldg.
2500 N. Lincoln, Room 215
Oklahoma City, OK 73105–4599
405/521–3352

Director
Protection & Advocacy Agency
9726 E. 42nd Street
Osage Bldg., Suite 133
Tulsa, OK 74146
918/664–5883

Administrator of Rehabilitation Services
Department of Human Services
23rd & Lincoln, Sequoyah Bldg.
P.O. Box 25352
Oklahoma City, OK 73125
405/521–3646

PRO-Oklahoma (Parents Reaching Out
in Oklahoma)
1917 S. Harvard Avenue
Oklahoma City, OK 73128
405/681–9710
800/PL94–142 (in Oklahoma)

Oregon

Director of Special Education
Special Education and Student Services
  Division
Oregon Department of Education
700 Pringle Parkway, S.E.
Salem, OR 97310–0290
503/378–2677

Executive Director
Oregon Developmental Disabilities Advocacy Center
400 Board of Trade Bldg.
310 S.W. 4th Avenue
Portland, OR 97204
503/243–2081

Administrator
Division of Vocational Rehabilitation
Department of Human Resources
2045 Silverton Rd., NE
Salem, OR 97310
503/378–3830

Oregon Coalition for Exceptional
Children and Young Adults/COPE
Oregon COPE Project
999 Locust Street, NE, #42
Salem, OR 97303
503/373–7477

Pennsylvania

Director of Special Education
Bureau of Special Education
Pennsylvania Department of Education
333 Market Street
Harrisburg, PA 17126–0333
717/783–6913

Pennsylvania Protection & Advocacy,
  Inc.
116 Pine St.
Harrisburg, PA 17101
717/236–8110
800/692–7443 (in Pennsylvania)

Executive Director
Office of Vocational Rehabilitation

Labor & Industry Bldg.
Seventh & Forster Streets
Harrisburg, PA 17120
717/787–5244

Parents Union for Public Schools
401 North Broad Street, Room 916
Philadelphia, PA 19108
215/574–0337

Parent Education Network
240 Haymeadow Drive
York, PA 17402
717/845–9722

Puerto Rico

Director of Special Education
Special Education
Department of Education
G.P.O. Box 759
Hato Rey, PR 00919–0759
809/764–8059

Director
Planning Research and Special Projects
Ombudsman for the Disabled
Governor's Office
Chardon Ave., #916
Hato Rey, PR 00936
809/766–2333/2388

Assistant Secretary for Vocational
  Rehabilitation
Department of Social Services
P.O. Box 118
Hato Rey, PR 00919
809/725–1792

Associacion Padres Pro Bienestar/Ninos
Impedidos de Puerto Rico
P.O. Box 21301
Rio Piedras, PR 00928
809/765–0345/763–4665

Rhode Island

Director of Special Education
Special Education Program Services Unit

R.I. Department of Education
Roger Williams Bldg., Room 209
22 Hayes Street
Providence, RI 02908–5025
401/277–3505

Executive Director
Rhode Island Protection & Advocacy-
  System
55 Bradford St.
Providence, RI 02903
401/831–3150 Voice/TDD

Administrator, Vocational Rehabilitation
Division of Community Services
Department of Human Services
40 Fountain St.
Providence, RI 02903
401/421–7005 (TDD 421–7016)

South Carolina

Director of Special Education
Office of Programs for Handicapped
South Carolina Department of Education
100 Executive Center Drive, A–24
Columbia, SC 29201
803/737–8710

Executive Director
South Carolina Protection & Advocacy
  System for the Handicapped, Inc.
2360–A Two Notch Road
Columbia, SC 29204

Commissioner
South Carolina Vocational Rehabilita-
  tion Department
P.O. Box 15
W. Columbia, SC 29171–0015
803/734–4300

South Dakota

Director of Special Education
Section for Special Education
State of South Dakota Department of
  Education
Richard F. Kneip Office Bldg.
700 N. Illinois St., 3rd Floor

Pierre, SD 57501–2293
605/773–3678
Executive Director
South Dakota Advocacy Project, Inc.
221 S. Central Ave.
Pierre, SD 57501
605/224–8294
800/742–8108 (in South Dakota)

Secretary
Division of Rehabilitative Services
Department of Vocational Rehabilitation
State Office Bldg.
700 Governors Dr.
Pierre, SD 57501
605/773–3195

South Dakota Parent Connection
P.O. Box 84813
330 N. Main Avenue, Suite 301
Sioux Falls, SD 57118–4813
605/335–8844
800/422–6893 (in South Dakota)

Tennessee

Director of Special Education
Special Programs
State of Tennessee Department of
  Education
132 Cordell Hull Bldg.
Nashville, TN 37219
615/741–2851

Director
E.A.C.H., Inc.
P.O. Box 121257
Nashville, TN 37212
615/298–1080
1–800–342–1660 (in Tennessee)
Voice/TTY

Assistant Commissioner
Division of Rehabilitation Services
1808 W. End Bldg., Room 900
Nashville, TN 37203
615/741–2095

Texas

Director of Special Education
Special Education Programs
Texas Education Agency
1701 N. Congress Ave., Room 5–120
Austin, TX 78701–2486
512/463–9734

Executive Director
Advocacy, Inc.
7700 Chevy Chase Dr., Suite 300
Austin, TX 78752
512/454–4816
800/252–9108 (in Texas)

Commissioner
Texas Rehabilitation Commission
118 E. Riverside Drive
Austin, TX 78704
512/445–8100

Partnerships for Assisting Texans with
Handicaps (PATH)
6465 Calder Ave., Suite 202
Beaumont, TX 77707
409/866–4762

Utah

Director of Special Education
Utah State Office of Education
250 E. 500 South
Salt Lake City, UT 84111
801/533–5982

Executive Director
Legal Center for the Handicapped
254 W. 400 South, Suite 300
Salt Lake City, UT 84101
801/363–1347
800/662–9080 (in Utah)

Executive Director
Vocational Rehabilitation Agency
250 E. 500 South
Salt Lake City, UT 84111
801/533–5991

Utah Parent Center
4984 South 300 West
Murray, UT 84107
801/265–9883

Vermont

Director of Special Education
Division of Special and Compensatory
    Education
Vermont Department of Education
State Office Bldg.
120 State Street
Montpelier, VT 05602–3403
802/828–3141

Director
Vermont DD Protection and Advocacy,
    Inc.
6 Pine St.
Burlington, VT 05401
802/863–2881

Director
Vocational Rehabilitation Division
Osgood Bldg., Waterbury Complex
103 S. Main St.
Waterbury, VT 05676
802/241–2189

Vermont Association for Retarded
    Citizens
Information and Training Network
37 Champlain Mill
Winooski, VT 05404
802/655–4016

Virgin Islands

Director of Special Education
Department of Education
State Office of Special Education
P.O. Box 6640
Charlotte Amalie, St. Thomas
Virgin Islands 00801
809/774–4399

Director
Committee on Advocacy for the
    Developmentally Disabled, Inc.

31–A New Street, Apt. No.2
Fredericksted, St. Croix
U. S. Virgin Islands 00840
809/722–1200

Administrator
Division of Disabilities & Rehabilitation
Services
Department of Human Services
Barbel Plaza South
St. Thomas, VI 00801
809/774–0930

Virginia

Director of Special Education
Office of Special and Compensatory
Education
Virginia Department of Education
P.O. Box 6Q
Richmond, VA 23216–2060
804/225–2402

Director
Department of Rights for the Disabled
James Monroe Bldg.
101 N. 14th St., 17th Floor
Richmond, VA 23219
804/225–2042
800/552–3962 (in Virginia)

Commissioner
Department of Rehabilitation Services
Commonwealth of Virginia
P.O. Box 11045
4901 Fitzhugh Ave.
Richmond, VA 23230
804/257–0316

Parent Educational Advocacy Training
Center
228 S. Pitt St., Suite 300
Alexandria, VA 22314
703/836–2953
(Serves Virginia, Maryland, and West
Virginia)

Washington

Director of Special Education
Special Education Section
Superintendent of Public Instruction
Old Capital Bldg.
Olympia, WA 98502–0001
206/753–6733

Washington Protection & Advocacy System
1550 W. Armory Way, Suite 204
Seattle, WA 98119
206/284–1037
800/562–2702 (in Washington)

Director, Division of Vocational
Rehabilitation
State Office Bldg., No. 2
Department of Social & Health Services
P.O. Box 1788 (MS 21–C)
Olympia, WA 98504
206/753–0293

Washington PAVE
6316 South 12th South
Tacoma, WA 98645
206/565–2266 Voice/TDD
800/5–PARENT (in Washington)

West Virginia

Director of Special Education
Special Education
West Virginia Department of Education
Bldg., #6, Room B–304
Charleston, WV 25305
304/348–2696

Executive Director
West Virginia Advocates for the
Developmentally Disabled, Inc.
1200 Brooks Medical Bldg.
Quarrier St., Suite 27
Charleston, WV 25301
304/346–0847
800/642–9205 (in West Virginia)

Director
Division of Rehabilitation Services
West Virginia State Board of Rehabilitation
State Capitol Bldg.
Charleston, WV 25305

See Parent Educational Advocacy Training Center under Virginia

Wisconsin

Director of Special Education
Division of Handicapped Children and
Pupil Services
Department of Public Instruction
125 S. Webster
P.O. Box 7841
Madison, WI 53707
608/266–1649

Executive Director
Wisconsin Coalition for Advocacy, Inc.
30 W. Mifflin, Suite 508
Madison, WI 53703
608/251–9600
800/328–1110 (in Wisconsin)

Administrator
Division of Vocational Rehabilitation
Department of Health & Social Services
1 Wilson St., Room 850
P.O. Box 7852
Madison, WI 53702
608/266–5466

Parent Education Project
United Cerebral Palsy of SE Wisconsin
230 W. Wells Street
Milwaukee, WI 53203
414/272–4500

Wyoming

Director of Special Education
State Department of Education
Hathaway Bldg.
2300 Capitol Avenue
Cheyenne, WY 82002–0050
307/777–7417

Executive Director
Protection & Advocacy System, Inc.
2424 Pioneer Ave., No. 101
Cheyenne, WY 82001
307/632–3496
800/624–3496 (in Wyoming)

Administrator
Division of Vocational Rehabilitation
Department of Health & Social Services
326 Hathaway Bldg.
Cheyenne, WY 82002
307/777–7385

Indian Affairs

Director of Special Education
Bureau of Exceptional Education
Office of Indian Education Program
Bureau of Indian Affairs
18th & C Streets, NW, Room 4642
Washington, D.C. 20245
202/343–6675

APPENDIX C

National Organizations Concerned with Disabled Persons

The organizations listed in this appendix offer a range of information and services. Many regularly publish journals or newsletters of interest to parents and individuals with a particular disability. In addition, many organizations also publish a variety of materials relating to a disability or to the specific concerns of individuals, their parents, and/or professionals. Many organizations have regional or local chapters across the United States.

This list is not intended to be all-inclusive, but rather, a place to begin reaching out and gathering information. Each organization listed provides most or all of the resources mentioned above. If an organization provides a particularly unique service or resource to parents, it is noted below the entry.

Organizations Serving a Broad Population

Accent on Information (AOI)
P.O. Box 700
Bloomington, IL 61702
309/378–2961
Information on products and devices which assist physically disabled persons. Individuals can request data base search.

American Alliance for Health, Physical
    Education, Recreation and Dance
    (AAHPERD)
1900 Association Drive
Reston, VA 22091
703/476–3400

American Coalition of Citizens with Dis-
    abilities
1200 15th Street, NW, Suite 201
Washington, D.C. 20005
202/785–4265
American Federation of Teachers (AFT)

AFT Teachers' Network for Education
    of the Handicapped
555 New Jersey Avenue, NW
Washington, D.C. 20001
202/879–4460

Association for Persons with Severe
    Handicaps (TASH)
11201 Greenwood Ave., North
Seattle, WA 98133
206/361–8870

Center for Law and Education
Larsen Hall, 6th Floor
14 Appian Way
Cambridge, MA 02138
617/495–4666

Center for Special Education
    Technology
1920 Association Drive
Reston, VA 22091
703/620–3660
800/345–TECH (Limited Hours)

Children's Defense Fund
25 E St., NW
Washington, D.C. 20001
202/628-8787

The Council for Exceptional Children
(CEC)
1920 Association Drive
Reston, VA 22091
703/620-3660

Education Resources Information Center
Central ERIC
National Institute of Education
U.S. Department of Education
Washington, D.C. 20208
202/254-7934
ERIC is a nationwide network that collects educational documents and makes them available to interested persons. Currently, there are six clearinghouses that have information concerning individuals with disabilities. They are: Adult, Career and Vocational Education; Counseling and Personnel Services; Elementary and Early Childhood Education; Handicapped and Gifted Children; Reading and Communication Skills; and Tests, Measurement, and Evaluation.

Foundation for Science and the Handicapped, Inc. (FISH)
154 Juliet Court
Clarendon Hills, IL 60514
312/323-4181

HEATH Resource Center
National Clearinghouse on Postsecondary Education for Handicapped Individuals
One Dupont Circle
Suite 670
Washington, D.C. 20036-1193

202/939-9320 (Voice/TDD)
800/544-3284 (Voice/TDD)

Independent Living Research Utilization Project (ILRU),
The Institute for Rehabilitation and Research
P.O. Box 20095
Houston, TX 77225
713/797-0200
National resource center for independent living.

Mexican-American Legal Defense & Education Fund
604 Mission St., 10th Floor
San Francisco, CA 94105
415/543-5598

National Association of the Deaf Legal Defense Fund
P.O. Box 2304
800 Florida Avenue, NE
Washington, D.C. 20002
202/651-5343

National Center for a Barrier-Free Environment
Suite 1006
1140 Connecticut Ave., NW
Washington, D.C. 20036
202/466-6896

National Center for Education in Maternal and Child Health
38th and R Streets, NW
Washington, D.C. 20057
202/625-8400
Provides information on maternal and child health, including genetics.

National Committee of Citizens in Education
10840 Little Patuxent Parkway, Suite 301
Columbia, MD 21044
301/997-9300
800/NETWORK

National Health Information
Clearinghouse (NHIC) and
National Information Center for Orphan
Drugs and Rare Diseases
(NICODARD)
P.O. Box 1133
Washington, D.C. 20013–1133
703/522–2590 (in Virginia)
800/336–4797

National Information Center for
Children and Youth with Disabilities
(NICHCY)
P.O. Box 1492
Washington, D.C. 20013
703/893–6061
800/999–5599 (recorded message)

National Juvenile Law Center
St. Louis University School of Law
3701 Lindell Blvd.
St. Louis, MO 63108
314/652–5555

National Library Service for the Blind
and Physically Handicapped (NLS)
Library of Congress
1291 Taylor Street, NW
Washington, D.C. 20542
202/287–5100

National Organization for Rare Disorders (NORD)
P.O. Box 8923
New Fairfield, CT 06812
203/746–6518

National Rehabilitation Information
Center (NARIC)
8455 Colesville Road, Suite 935
Silver Spring, MD 20910–3319
301/588–9284
800/34–NARIC

Registry of Interpreters for the Deaf,
Inc. (RID)
814 Thayer Avenue
Silver Spring, MD 20910
301/588–2406 Voice/TDD

Sibling Information Network
1776 Ellington Rd.
S. Windsor, CT 06074
203/648–1205

STOMP (Specialized Training of
Military Parents)
The STOMP Project assists military
families residing in the United States or
stationed overseas.
West Coast Office:
STOMP
12208 Pacific Highway, SW
Tacoma, WA 98499
206/588–1741 (Parents may call collect)
East Coast Office:
ARC/Georgia STOMP Project
1851 Ram Runway, #104
College Park, GA 30337
404/568–0042 (Parents may call collect)

United Together (UT)
348 Haworth Hall
Lawrence, KS 66045
913/864–4950
Self-advocacy organization.

World Institute on Disability (WID)
1720 Oregon Street
Suite 4
Berkeley, CA 94703
415/486–8314

Organizations Serving a Specific Population

Allergies
Asthma & Allergy Foundation of
  America (AAFA)
1717 Massachusetts Ave., NW
Suite 305
Washington, D.C. 20036
202/265–0265

Autism
Autism Society of America
8601 Georgia Ave.
Silver Spring, MD 20901
301/565–0433

Birth Defects
March of Dimes Birth Defects Foundation (MOD)
303 S. Broadway
Tarrytown, NY 10591
914/428–7100

Blind and Visually Impaired
American Council of the Blind (ACB)
Suite 110
1010 Vermont Avenue, NW
Washington, D.C. 20005
202/393–3666
800/424–8666

American Foundation for the Blind
  (AFB)
15 West 16th Street
New York, NY 10011
212/620–2000

National Association for Visually Handicapped (NAVH)
22 W. 21st. St., Sixth Floor
New York, NY 10010
212/889–3141

National Federation of the Blind (NFB)
1800 Johnson Street
Baltimore, MD 21230
301/659–9314

Cerebral Palsy
United Cerebral Palsy Association
66 East 34th Street
New York, NY 10016
212/481–6300
800/USA–1UCP

National Easter Seal Society
2023 West Ogden Avenue
Chicago, IL 60612
312/243–8400 (234–8880 TDD)
800/221–6827 (outside Illinois)

Chronic Illness
Association for the Care of Children's
  Health (ACCH)
7910 Woodmont Ave., Ste. 300
Bethesda, MD 20814
301/654–6549

The Candlelighters Childhood Cancer
  Foundation
1901 Pennsylvania Ave., NW
Suite 1001
Washington, D.C. 20006
202/659–5136

Children's Hospice International
1101 King St., Suite 131
Alexandria, VA 22314
703/684–0330

Sick Kids (Need) Involved People, Inc.
  (SKIP)
216 Newport Drive
Severna Park, MD 21146
301/647–0164

Deaf and Hearing Impaired
Alexander Graham Bell Association for
  the Deaf
4317 Volta Place, NW
Washington, D.C. 20007
202/337–5220 Voice/TDD

American Society for Deaf Children
(ASDC)
814 Thayer Avenue
Silver Spring, MD 20910
301/585–5400

National Information Center on Deafness (NICD)
Gallaudet University
800 Florida Avenue, NE
Washington, D.C. 20002
202/651–5051 Voice
202/651–5052 TDD

Diabetes
American Diabetes Association
National Service Center
1660 Duke Street
Alexandria, VA 22314
703/549–1500 (local)
800/ADA–DISC

Juvenile Diabetes Foundation International
4423 Park Avenue, S.
New York, NY 10016
212/889–7575
800/223–1138

National Diabetes Information
Clearinghouse
Box NDIC
Bethesda, MD 20892
301/468–2162

Down Syndrome
National Down Syndrome Congress
(NDSC)
1605 Chantilly Rd.
Atlanta, GA 30324
800/232–NDSC

National Down Syndrome Society
(NDSS)
666 Broadway
New York, NY 10012

212/460–9330
800/221–4602

Epilepsy
Epilepsy Foundation of America
4351 Garden City Drive
Suite 406
Landover, MD 20785
301/459–3700
800/EFA–1000

Emotional Disorders
National Alliance for the Mentally Ill
1901 N. Ft. Myer Drive
Suite 500
Arlington, VA 22209
703/524–7600

National Mental Health Association
(NMHA)
1021 Prince Street
Alexandria, VA 22314–2971
703/684–7722

Portland State University
Research & Training Center
Regional Research Institute for Human
Services
P.O. Box 751
Portland, OR 97207–0751
503/464–4040

Head Injury
National Head Injury Foundation, Inc.
P.O. Box 567
Framingham, MA 01701
617/879–7473

Learning Disabilities
Learning Disabilities Association
4156 Library Road
Pittsburgh, PA 15234
412/341–1515
412/341–8077

National Center for Learning Disabilities
(NCLD)
381 Park Ave., South, Ste. 1420
New York, NY 10016
212/545–7510

Orton Dyslexia Society (ODS)
724 York Road
Baltimore, MD 21204
301/296–0232
800/222–3123

Mental Retardation
Association for Retarded Citizens of the
United States (ARC)
National Headquarters
2501 Avenue J
Arlington, TX 76011
817/640–0204
800/433–5255

People First International
P.O. Box 12642
Salem, OR 97309
503/378–5143

Muscular Dystrophy
Muscular Dystrophy Association (MDA)
810 Seventh Avenue
New York, NY 10019
212/586–0808

Respiratory Diseases
American Lung Association (ALA)
810 Seventh Avenue
New York, NY 10019
212/315–8700

Cystic Fibrosis Foundation
6931 Arlington Road, Suite 200
Bethesda, MD 20814

301/951–4422
800/FIGHT–CF

Speech and Language Disorders
National Association for Hearing and
Speech Action (NAHSA)
10801 Rockville Pike
Rockville, MD 20850
301/897–8682 (Voice/TDD)
800/638–8255 (Voice/TDD)

National Council on Stuttering (NCOS)
P.O. Box 8171
Grand Rapids, MI 49508
616/241–2372

National Institute of Neurological and
Communication Disorders and
Stroke
National Institutes of Health
Building 31A, Room 8A–06
Bethesda, MD 20892
301/496–5751

Spina Bifida
Spina Bifida Association of America
(SBAA)
4590 MacArthur Blvd., #250
Washington, D.C. 20007
202/944–3285

Tourette Syndrome
Tourette Syndrome Association (TSA)
42-40 Bell Blvd.
Bayside, NY 11361
718/224–2999
800/237–0717

Toll-Free Numbers
American Association on Mental
Deficiency
800/424–3688

AMC Cancer Information Center
800/525–3777

American Cleft Palate Education Foundation
800/242–5338

American Council of the Blind
800/424–8666

American Diabetes Association
800/232–3472

American Foundation for the Blind
800/232–5463

American Kidney Fund
800/638–8299

American Liver Foundation
800/223–0179

American Paralysis Association
800/225–0292

Association for Retarded Citizens of the United States (ARCUS)
800/433–5255

Association of Heart Patients
800/241–6993

Beech Nut Hotline (Information on infant–related subjects)
800/523–6633

Better Hearing Institute Helpline
800/424–8576

Cancer Information Service National Line
800/4–CANCER

Captioned Films for the Deaf
800/237–6213

Center for Special Education Technology Information Exchange
800/345–TECH

Children's Defense Fund
800/424–9602

Chrysler Corporation Assistance Line for the Disabled Driver
800/255–9877

Cooley's Anemia Foundation, Inc.
800/221–3571 (in New York: 1–800–522–7222)

Cornelia de Lange Syndrome Foundation
800/223–8355

Cystic Fibrosis Foundation
800/634–5895

Educators Publishing Service Specific Language Disabilities (Dyslexia)
800/225–5750

Epilepsy Foundation of America
800/332–1000

Epilepsy Information Line
800/426–0660

ERIC Clearinghouse on Adult Career and Vocational Education
800/848–4815

Heartline
800/241–6993

HEATH Resource Center (National Clearinghouse on Postsecondary Education for Handicapped Individuals)
800/544–3284

International Shriners Headquarters
800/237–5055

Job Accommodation Network (JAN) (Puts employers in touch with other employers who have accommodated workers with disabilities)
800/JAN–PCEH

Job Opportunities for the Blind
800/638–7516

Juvenile Diabetes Foundation International
800/223–1138

Latinos and Asians who need help obtaining services for the developmentally disabled
800/221–1975

Lung disease—information about research and treatments available
800/222–LUNG

Lupus Foundation of America
800/558–0121

Military Family Resource Center (for professionals who serve military families in the area of family advocacy)
800/336–4592

National Adoption Center
800/862–3678

National Alliance of Blind Students
800/424–8666

National Association for Hearing and Speech Action
800/638–8255

National Association for Parents of the Visually Impaired
800/562–6265

National Association for Sickle Cell Disease
800/421–8453

National Captioning Institute
800/535–WORD

National Center for Stuttering
800/221–2483

National Child Abuse Hotline
800/4–A–CHILD

National Committee for Citizens in Education
800/NETWORK

National Crisis Center for the Deaf (TDD only)
800/446–9876

National Down Syndrome Congress
800/232–6372

National Down Syndrome Society
800/221–4602

National Easter Seal Society
800/221–6827

National Head Injury Foundation
800/444–NHIF

National Health Information Clearinghouse
800/336–4794

National Hearing Aid Society
800/521–5247

National Information Center for Developmental Disabilities
800/922–9234

National Information Center for Educational Media
800/421–8711

National Information Center for Children and Youth with Handicaps
800/999–5599

National Information System for Health Related Services
800/922–9234

National Multiple Sclerosis Society
800/624–8236

National Organization on Disability
800/248–2253

National Rehabilitation Information
    Center (NARIC)
800/34–NARIC (Voice/TDD)

National Retinitis Pigmentosa Founda-
    tion
800/638–2300

National Special Needs Center
800/233–1222; 800/833–3232 (TDD only)

National Spinal Cord Injury Hotline
800/526–3456 (in Maryland: 800/638–
    1733)

National Tuberous Sclerosis Association
800/225–NTSA

Orton Dyslexia Society
800/222–3123

Poison Information
800/542–6319

Retinitis Pigmentosa Association
800/344–4877

Retinitis Pigmentosa Foundation Fight-
    ing Blindness
800/638–2300

Second Surgical Opinion
800/638–6833

Social Security Administration
800/562–6350

Spina Bifida Association of America
800/621–3141

Tripod Service for Hearing Impaired
800/352–8888

APPENDIX D
Selected Reading

This bibliography contains further reading on topics regarding special education and other educational issues; books containing general information about a variety of handicapping conditions; and bibliographies on handicapping conditions and related topics. Books about specific disabilities have been deliberately omitted. For materials on specific disabilities, contact disability organizations such as the Association for Retarded Citizens or the Tourette Syndrome Association (these organizations are listed in Appendix C), and request bibliographies from them. These organizations should be able to recommend current and comprehensive materials.

Many of the books listed here will be available in your local public library. If you would like to order a copy of any book for yourself, you can find publishers' addresses through a publication called *Books in Print*, which is updated annually and is available at any library or bookstore. *Books in Print* has a subject index that you can use to see what is currently available on any topic.

Books of General Interest

Armstrong, Thomas. *In Their Own Way: Discovering and Encouraging Your Child's Personal Learning Style*. Los Angeles: Jeremy P. Tarcher, Inc., 1987.
Based on the premise developed by Howard Gardner that people have seven different kinds of intelligence, the author explains the way children learn as a function of intellectual strengths and weaknesses. All individuals possess all seven kinds of intelligence in varying proportions. They are: linguistic, logical-mathematical, spatial, musical, bodily-kinesthetic, interpersonal, and intrapersonal. This book helps parents identify their children's learning strengths and weaknesses and provides suggestions for improving learning experiences at home and at school. This is an excellent, thought-provoking book, written simply and clearly. Good list of resources.

Batshaw, Mark L. & Yvonne M. Perret. *Children with Handicaps: A Medical Primer*. 2nd edition. Baltimore: Paul H. Brookes, 1986.
Heredity, birth defects, prematurity, and various disabilities are discussed. Also covers child development. Rather textbook-like in tone. Good introductory material. Has glossary, table of syndromes, resources for handicapped children, and a list of university-affiliated programs.

Baum, Dale D., ed. *The Human Side of Exceptionality.* Baltimore: University Park
    Press, 1982.
Arranged in sections by disability, each section contains several accounts of the
successes and difficulties in dealing with that particular disability. Written by
parents and individuals with a disability. Each section has a general introduction,
and each account is followed by questions for discussion.

Dickens, Monica. *Miracles of Courage: How Families Meet the Challenge of a Child's
    Critical Illness.* New York: Dodd, Mead, 1985.
Case histories—how families find strength, "rise to the occasion." Illustrated by
actual events.

The Exceptional Parent. Published eight times a year. Yearly subscription rates: $16
    for individuals, $24 for organizations, libraries, schools, and agencies. Addi-
    tional postage for foreign countries, add $3.
This magazine is an excellent source of information for parents of exceptional
children. Featured articles are always on current topics. Each issue has a special
focus and there are regular features that appear monthly and annually. For an
ongoing source of all kinds of information, this magazine is the single most helpful
publication on this list.

Featherstone, Helen. *A Difference in the Family: Life with a Disabled Child.* New York:
    Basic Books, 1982.
The definitive book about how it really feels to raise a child with a severe
disability. The author, both a parent and a teacher, speaks with such sensitivity
that parents can identify with her and professionals can appreciate the struggles
and delights parents face when living with a child who is different.

Goldfarb, Lori A., Mary Jane Brotherson, Jean Ann Summers & Ann P. Turnbull.
    Meeting the Challenge of Disability or Chronic Illness—A Family Guide. Baltimore:
    Paul H. Brookes, 1986.
A self-study guide for families, divided into two main sections: "Taking Stock"
and "Problem Solving." The first section discusses how families cope with
difficult situations; the second section helps families structure problem solving.
Each chapter has suggested exercises. These exercises are also found at the end
of the book with enough space to write directly on the page. Excellent references
and resources.

Mulick, James A. & Siegfried M. Pueschel, eds. *Parent Professional Partnerships in
    Developmental Disability Services.* Cambridge, MA: Academic Guild Publish-
    ers, 1983.
This book is for parents interested in working together with professionals:
educators, therapists, doctors and others. "The main themes are sharing of
information and informed decision-making." The main topics covered are: Coun-

seling Perspectives, Services and Service Providers, The Family and the Community and Societal Perspectives.

Perske, Robert. *Circles of Friends: People with Disabilities and Their Friends Enrich the Lives of One Another.* Nashville, TN: Abingdon Press, 1988.
Illustrated by Martha Perske, this book describes "true stories of friendships." Based on a belief that all people should be members of the community, *Circles of Friends* alternates between accounts of friendships and points to consider. Friendship settings range from housing cooperatives to schools to neighborhoods.

Perske, Robert. *Hope for the Families: New Directions for Parents of Persons with Retardation or Other Disorders.* Nashville, TN: Abingdon Press, 1981.
Sensitively written and illustrated, this book assists parents in beginning to explore their feelings about having a child with special needs. Each chapter ends with a section titled "Consider These Options," encouraging the reader to view concerns from different perspectives. Excellent book.

Powell, Thomas H. & Peggy Ahrenhold Ogle. *Brothers and Sisters: A Special Part of Exceptional Families.* Baltimore: Paul H. Brookes, 1985.
Divided into two main sections: I) Families and siblings: explores relationships in families, "special" brothers and sisters, special concerns and unique needs; and II) Strategies to help siblings: the need for information, counseling, group interaction, siblings as teachers, siblings at school, siblings as adults. Information and Service sources for siblings and parents (organizations). Readings, references.

Simons, Robin. *After the Tears: Parents Talk about Raising a Child with a Disability.* San Diego: Harcourt Brace Jovanovich, 1987.
An emotional handbook for parents that explores the range of feelings parents have about parenting a child with disabilities. Parents' comments about their personal situations are scattered throughout and add depth to the text. Practical self-help suggestions are included along with chapters on grandparents' and siblings' concerns, dealing with professionals, and educational issues. Practical and sensitive, there is a lot packed into this slim book.

Thompson, Charlotte E. *Raising a Handicapped Child: A Helpful Guide for Parents of the Physically Disabled.* New York: William Morrow, 1986.
This is a very practical book, sensitive to the emotional difficulties families experience when learning a child has a disability. There are many suggestions for parents from learning to take time out for themselves, to handling siblings, to finding professional help for a child, to learning to cope with a progressive disease and/or the eventual death of a child. Several appendices describe professionals parents may meet, define handicaps, list agencies that provide information, suggest places to "have fun," and list books for additional reading.

Wiener, Florence. *No Apologies: A Guide to Living with a Disability, Written by the Real Authorities—People with Disabilities, Their Families and Friends*. New York: St. Martin's Press, 1986.
Rich with individual examples and insights, this book does what the title implies. It focuses on various aspects of living and how people with disabilities manage their lives. Topics covered include education, independent living, working, and organizing. Many resources are listed throughout and it is generously illustrated with photographs.

Early Childhood/Early Intervention

Bluma, S., M. Shearer, A. Frohman & J. Hilliard. *A Parents' Guide to Early Education* (A special edition of the *Portage Guide to Early Education*). Portage, WI: Cooperative Educational Service Agency, 1976.
This is a workbook for parents, divided into two main sections: a checklist of developmental skills and a "card" section of activities for parents and their children. The checklist and activities are for children from birth to age 6. The developmental skills covered are arranged in the order and at the appropriate age for a child of normal development. Brief instructions at the beginning assist parents in utilizing the contents in a systematic way.

Pueschel, Siegfried M., James C. Bernier & Leslie E. Weidenman. *The Special Child: A Source Book for Parents of Children with Developmental Disabilities*. Baltimore: Paul Brookes, 1988.
Written for parents, *The Special Child* contains a great deal of medical information, including descriptions of various disabilities, procedures and treatments, tests, and adaptive equipment. At the same time, an overview of parents' feelings and concerns and the need for parent-professional partnerships are presented. A description of early intervention programs and an introduction to special education and legal issues are also covered. An excellent source of basic information, presented clearly and succinctly. List of organizations and further reading.

Smolak, Linda. *Infancy*. Englewood Cliffs, NJ: Prentice-Hall, 1986.
In this scholarly book on normal infancy and its influence on children's later development, the author explores various areas of infant development including attachment, motor development, cognitive development, language, and social development. A chapter on at-risk infants is included. While some of the material is more theoretical than practical, boxed examples sprinkled throughout help explain and illustrate the text. Includes an extensive reference section.

Tingey-Michaelis, Carol. *Handicapped Infants and Children: A Handbook for Parents and Professionals*. Baltimore: University Park Press, 1983.
Knowing how to care for a handicapped infant or toddler at home can seem overwhelming at times. This book is designed to give basic instructions in child

care areas like bathing, feeding, sleeping, toilet training, and movement skills. While the simplistic and occasionally didactic tone of the author may make some readers uncomfortable, the information is valuable, and the author's concern for families is self-evident.

Weiner, Roberta & Jane Koppelman. *From Birth to 5: Serving the Youngest Handicapped Children.* Alexandria, VA: Capitol Publications, 1987.
Although written for professionals in a variety of education-related fields, this book provides an overview of the challenge of developing early intervention programs. Using case studies and a review of programs currently in place, the authors present a thoughtful picture of the complexity of serving young children. The book is rounded out by several appendices, including the entire text of P.L. 99–457, and a state resource directory.

Winton, Pamela J., Ann P. Turnbull & Jan Blacher. *Selecting a Preschool: A Guide for Parents of Handicapped Children.* Baltimore: University Park Press, 1984.
Parents have a wealth of knowledge about their child and their family that can help them make important decisions about preschool programs. *Selecting a Preschool* assists parents in considering their child's needs and matching them with the appropriate preschool program. Additional chapters discuss preparing a child for preschool and assessing how well the program is working. An extensive resources section lists organizations and books and other media on a range of topics.

Young Children. Published six times a year. Professional journal of the National Association for the Education of Young Children. Non-member subscriptions, $25/year.
Although intended for professionals working with young children without disabilities, the writing is not overly scholarly and many issues discussed are appropriate for children with disabilities. New books for adults and children are reviewed regularly.

Special Education and Legal Rights

Goldman, Charles D. *Disability Rights Guide: Practical Solutions to Problems Affecting People with Disabilities.* Lincoln, NE: Media Publishing, 1987.
This book is intended for people with disabilities and those who work with them. Chapters cover a variety of issues confronting people with disabilities, such as attitudinal barriers, employment, architectural barriers, education, and transportation. The laws governing these areas are explained and discussed in clear language. A glossary of terms and a list of state contacts are included.

Henderson, Anne T., Carl L. Marburger & Theodora Ooms. *Beyond the Bake Sale: An Educator's Guide to Working with Parents.* Columbia, MD: The National Committee for Citizens in Education, 1986.

The authors address ways of developing positive home/school relations. They demonstrate that parents can and do make a big difference in promoting the positive characteristics of effective schools. Parents are challenged to be involved in what happens to their children in school and school staff is challenged to nurture positive relationships with parents.

How to Get Services by Being Assertive. Chicago: Coordinating Council for Handicapped Children, 1980.

Intended to be a training manual to teach parents assertiveness skills, this book is written with a very positive attitude. Practical exercises strengthen parents' skills at organizing their information and conveying their point of view to school people. Through use of question/answer, practice responses, and personal testimonials, the book presents parents with assertive techniques that will help in situations from parent-teacher conferences to meetings with school administrators.

How to Organize an Effective Parent/Advocacy Group and Move Bureaucracies. Chicago: Coordinating Council for Handicapped Children, 1980.

Step-by-step workbook to develop a parent advocacy group and use the group to address various issues in the community (parents' rights, school programs, lobbying for change, etc.). Personal accounts illustrate the text. Includes discussion of funding issues. Excellent advice, inexpensive book.

Krupp, Judy-Arin & Robert Parker. *When Parents Face the Schools.* Manchester, CT: Adult Development and Learning, 1984.

The authors firmly believe in parent-professional cooperation, although the title might imply an adversarial stance. The skills and techniques presented enable parents to understand and communicate better with teachers and other school personnel. Stress is always placed on how the student can be helped by both parents and school people. While written for parents of students in regular education, the techniques can be well used by parents of any student. Excellent glossary of educational terms.

Lillie, David L. & Patricia A. Place. *Partners: A Guide to Working with Schools for Parents of Children with Special Instructional Needs.* Glenview, IL: Scott, Foresman, 1982.

Intended as a self-study workbook, the authors provide step-by-step information and exercises that build confidence and skill in parents to enhance more effective partnerships with school professionals. Resources, glossary.

Mopsik, Stanley, & Judith A. Agard, eds. *An Education Handbook for Parents of Handicapped Children.* Cambridge, MA: Brookline Books, 1985.

Series of chapters written by different authors on educational topics like legislation, litigation, parents' rights, parent-school partnerships, the IEP, instructional and related services, etc. Written for parents; clear; uses some question-and-answer format. Includes a chapter on program advocacy.

Pizzo, Peggy. *Parent to Parent: Working Together for Ourselves and Our Children.* Boston: Beacon Press, 1983.
Parents have learned to look to other parents for answers to problems encountered when they have a child with special needs. Parents can help other parents through support groups and advocacy groups working toward legislative changes. Very practical book, list of parent and advocacy organizations, bibliography.

Schimmel, David and Louis Fischer. *Parents, Schools and the Law.* Columbia, MD: The National Committee for Citizens in Education, 1987.
Using a question/answer format throughout, everything parents might want to know about their own and their children's legal rights in regard to education is covered. Chapters include discipline and due process, freedom of religion, racial and sexual discrimination, school records, accountability, and the curriculum. This book is written in a straightforward, jargon-free manner and includes two sample Supreme Court cases.

Shrybman, James A. *Due Process in Special Education.* Rockville, MD: Aspen Publications, 1982.
Careful outline of the process of special education, parents' rights and roles, procedures of the due process hearing, effective presentations at a hearing, hearing decisions. Very clear, detailed, logical presentation. Probably the best book available on due process at this time.

Turnbull, Ann P. & H. Rutherford Turnbull III. *Families, Professionals, and Exceptionality: A Special Partnership.* Columbus, OH: Merrill Publishing, 1986.
Families, people with disabilities, and professionals can work together more effectively. This book begins with an exploration of family life and how individual family members interact. Communication between families and professionals is discussed, along with strategies for improvement. The special education system is explained thoroughly, with suggestions for improved parent-professional relationships. List of parent information centers, references. Excellent book.

Turnbull, H. Rutherford, III. *Free Appropriate Public Education: The Law and Children with Disabilities.* Denver: Love Publishing, 1986.
A clear, precise account of the development of The Education for All Handicapped Children Act, the six major principles of the law, enforcing the law, and the law and the American value system. Precedent-setting Supreme Court cases, Education for All Handicapped Children Act, definitions, glossary.

Wodrich, David L. *Children's Psychological Testing: A Guide for Nonpsychologists.* Baltimore: Paul H. Brookes, 1984.
Although written for professionals involved with children in a variety of ways (social workers, pediatricians, attorneys, educators, speech pathologists, etc.), the information is presented clearly with samples of some tests and sample case histories. Frequently used tests are explained in detail; an appendix briefly describes others. References.

Your Child's School Records: Questions and Answers about a Set of Rights for Parents & Students. Washington, DC: Children's Defense Fund, 1986.
This small booklet, written in question-and-answer format, covers all aspects of school records and parents' and students' rights to them.

Transition, Future Planning & Community Life

Appolloni, Tony & Thomas P. Cooke. *A New Look at Guardianship: Protective Services That Support Personalized Living.* Baltimore: Paul H. Brookes, 1984.
Both individual guardianship and group guardianship programs are explored. Some chapters include sample forms. Bibliography at end of each chapter. Goes beyond traditional alternatives for guardians (friends, relatives, lawyers).

Brolin, Donn E. *Vocational Preparation of Persons with Handicaps.* 2nd edition. Columbus, OH: Charles E. Merrill, 1982.
An introductory textbook to vocational services for persons in late elementary years to late adulthood. Vocational evaluation and career development are covered, as well as background information on vocational services. Several program models are discussed. References.

Holdren, Don P. *Financial Planning for the Handicapped.* Springfield, IL: Charles C. Thomas, 1985.
Precise description of financial planning considerations for persons with physical and/or mental handicaps. Includes introduction to finance, investments, health and disability insurance, life insurance, taxes, social security, retirement income, fundamentals of estate planning, wills, and trusts.

How to Provide for Their Future: Suggestions for Parents Concerned with Providing Lifetime Protection for a Child with Mental Retardation. Arlington, TX: Association for Retarded Citizens, 1984.
Sensible information that can get a parent started planning for the future. Topics include: guardianship, wills, trusts, and general estate planning, insurance benefits, government benefits (social security, Medicaid, etc.). Excellent list of government publications (most free) and further essential readings.

Paul, James L., ed. *The Exceptional Child: A Guidebook for Churches and Community Agencies.* Syracuse, NY: Syracuse University Press, 1983.
Community groups and organizations often lack basic information about the special needs of exceptional children and their families. This guidebook offers practical advice for the non-specialist to improve the experiences of families with exceptional members in the community.

Russell, L. Mark. *Alternatives: A Family Guide to Legal and Financial Planning for the Disabled.* Evanston, IL: First Publications, 1983.
Clearly written discussion of wills, guardianship, trusts, government benefits, taxes, insurance, and financial planning. Many legal terms defined and explained. List of organizations, glossary, and bibliography.

Salisbury, Christine L. & James Intagliata. *Respite Care: Support for Persons with Developmental Disabilities and Their Families.* Baltimore, MD: Paul H. Brookes, 1986.
"Having access to respite services is finally being recognized as a critical factor in parents' ability to keep their child with a handicap at home and integrated into the community." Provides practical information aimed at finding ways to support families needing respite care.

Scheiber, Barbara & Jeanne Talpers. *Unlocking Potential: College and Other Choices for Learning Disabled People: A Step-by-Step Guide.* Bethesda, MD: Adler & Adler, 1987; distributed by Woodbine House.
A wealth of information for the learning disabled student to help him explore options for postsecondary education. Not intended to be a directory of programs, but rather a guidebook to assist a student in making choices, finding ways to be accommodated in a higher learning institution, developing good study skills, and finding counseling help. List of helpful organizations.

Summers, Jean Ann. *The Right to Grow Up: An Introduction to Adults with Developmental Disabilities.* Baltimore, MD: Paul H. Brookes, 1986.
Sensitive appraisal of the changing emotional and physical needs of maturing young adults. Many developmentally disabled young adults experience the desire for sexual expression, for self-determination, for peer companionship, for vocational activity, or for spiritual support. In addition to recognizing these needs, this book examines services that are, or should be, available to adults with developmental disabilities.

Turnbull, H. Rutherford, III, Ann P. Turnbull, J. G. Bronicki, Jean Ann Summers & Constance Roeder-Gordon. *Disability and the Family: A Guide to Decisions for Adulthood.* Baltimore: Paul H. Brookes, 1989.
Parents can find their own answers to questions about the future needs of their sons and daughters with disabilities using the guidelines and exercises in this

book. The authors have based their approach to adulthood decision-making on six specific premises, the first being that individuals with disabilities have the right to freedom of choice about every aspect of their lives. Topics addressed in the book include decision-making; financial planning; planning for community life; and advocacy. Basic information, planning forms, varied approaches to problem-solving and real-life situations highlight this readable, practical guide for parents. The appendices contain a glossary, a list of resources, sample documents, and recommended reading.

Bibliographies

Azarnoff, Pat. *Health, Illness and Disability: A Guide to Books for Children and Young Adults.* New York: Bowker, 1983.
A wealth of books for children and young adults are contained in this guide. Each entry has a recommended grade range and a short annotation. Indexed by subject and title, publishers' addresses included.

Griffin, Barbara K. *Special Needs Bibliography: Current Books for/about Children and Young Adults Regarding Social Concerns, Emotional Concerns, the Exceptional Child.* DeWitt, NY: The Griffin, 1984, 1986 update.
Arranged by subject in a loose-leaf notebook for easy up-dating, this bibliography contains a range of books for young children up to adults. Each entry has suggested grade levels and well-written annotations.

Moore, Cory. *A Reader's Guide for Parents of Children with Mental, Physical, or Emotional Disabilities.* Revised edition. Rockville, MD: Woodbine House, 1990.
Arranged by subject, this guide contains not only books for parents, but organizations that serve different disability groups. Each subject is further divided into sections, including Your Child at Home, Your Child Grows Up, Personal Accounts, The Early Years, School Years, and When Children Become Adults. One section includes books for children.

INDEX

Integration, xi, 105
Intelligence quotient. *See* IQ
Intensive developmental centers, 144
IQ, 50
Jargon, educational, 196
Job coach, 144
Job training, transitional, 145
Key people, 8
Key people chart, 10–13, 205
Labels, inaccurate, 186
Language skills. *See* Communication
Lawyer. *See* Attorney
Lay advocate, 176, 177, 184–85
Learning style, 23–24, 26
Learning style questionnaire, 29–31
Least restrictive environment (LRE),
    xi, 103, 105–06, 108
    definition of, 105
M-Team. *See* Eligibility committee
Mainstreaming. *See* Integration
Mediation. *See* Administrative review
Medical services, 111
Mentally retarded, definition of, 84
Monitoring. *See also* Reviews
    evaluation process, 56
IEP, 190
    techniques for parents, 191–93
Motor skills. *See* Movement
Movement, 15, 25, 48
Multidisciplinary team, 7, 47, 50
Notebooks, exchanging, 192
Objectives
    appropriate, 99
    definition of, 98
    setting, 97–102
    well–written, 115–16
Observation, behavioral, 154
Observations of child
    analyzing, 24–27
    deciding on focus for, 17–18
    guidelines for planning, 19–20
    importance of, 16
    in classroom, 192, 194–96
    interpreting, 18
    keeping record of, 32–34
    organizing, 21–22
    strategies for, 17–19
    time of, 18
Occupational therapy, 111

Organizations, disability, 245–50
    toll–free numbers for, 250–53
Parent action–steps for evaluation
    chart, 57, 59–60
Parent counseling, 111
Parent Educational Advocacy Training
    Center (PEATC), 209
Parent-professional partnership, 153,
    205
Parent resource centers, 205–06
Parent Training and Information Cen-
    ter (PTIC), 208–09
Parent training and information
    projects, 228–43
Parents' observation record, 32–34
Perception. *See* Senses/perception
Perkins Act, 139
Carl D. Perkins Vocational Education
    Act, *See* Perkins Act
Permission forms, 44–46
Personal profile, 146–53
Physical therapy, 111
P.L. 94–142, vii, viii, 168
    ages covered by, ix, 169
    and free, appropriate education, x,
        104–05, 108, 169
    and IEP, x, 169
    and least restrictive environment, xi,
        103, 105–06, 108, 169
    and resolution of conflicts, xi, 171
    disabilities covered by, viii
    evaluation requirements of, 49–51,
        170, 171
    requirements for parent
        participation, xii, 170
    testing requirements of, 170–71
P.L. 98–154. *See* Perkins Act
P.L. 98–199, 208–09
P.L. 99–372, 176, 185
P.L. 99–457, x, 40, 169
Placements, 94, 103–10
    criteria for making, 103
    during a due process hearing, 184
    evaluation guidelines for, 133–36
    examples of, 109–10
    refusing, 170
    visiting, 132–36
Placement Advisory Committee
    (PAC). *See* Eligibility committee